## THE REVELS PLAYS

*Former general editors*
David Bevington
F. David Hoeniger
E. A. J. Honigmann
Clifford Leech
J. R. Mulryne
Eugene M. Waith
Martin White

*General editors*
Karen Britland, Richard Dutton, Alison Findlay,
Rory Loughnane, Helen Ostovich and Barbara Ravelhofer

# THE FALSE ONE

Manchester University Press

# THE REVELS PLAYS

ANON  *Thomas of Woodstock
or King Richard the Second, Part One*

BARRY  *The Family of Love*

BEAUMONT  *The Knight of the Burning Pestle*

BEAUMONT AND FLETCHER  *A King and No King
The Maid's Tragedy   Philaster, or Love Lies a-Bleeding*

CHAPMAN  *All Fools
Bussy d'Ambois   An Humorous Day's Mirth*

CHAPMAN, JONSON, MARSTON  *Eastward Ho*

DEKKER  *The Shoemaker's Holiday   Old Fortunatus*

FLETCHER AND MASSINGER  *Love's Cure, or The Martial Maid*

FORD  *Love's Sacrifice   The Lady's Trial*

HEYWOOD  *The First and Second Parts of King Edward IV*

JONSON  *The Alchemist   The Devil Is an Ass
Epicene, or The Silent Woman   Every Man In His Humour
Every Man Out of His Humour   The Magnetic Lady
The New Inn   Poetaster   Sejanus: His Fall
The Staple of News   Volpone*

LYLY  *Campaspe* and *Sappho and Phao   Endymion
Galatea* and *Midas   Love's Metamorphosis
Mother Bombie   The Woman in the Moon*

MARLOWE  *Doctor Faustus   Edward the Second
The Jew of Malta   Tamburlaine the Great   The Massacre at Paris*

MARSTON  *Antonio and Mellida
Antonio's Revenge   The Malcontent*

MASSINGER  *The Roman Actor*

MIDDLETON  *A Game at Chess   Michaelmas Term
A Trick to Catch the Old One*

MIDDLETON AND DEKKER  *The Roaring Girl*

MUNDAY AND OTHERS  *Sir Thomas More*

PEELE  *The Troublesome Reign of John, King of England
David and Bathsheba*

SHIRLEY  *Hyde Park*

WEBSTER  *The Duchess of Malfi*

THE REVELS PLAYS

# THE FALSE ONE

## JOHN FLETCHER AND PHILIP MASSINGER

edited by Domenico Lovascio

MANCHESTER
UNIVERSITY PRESS

Introduction, critical apparatus, etc.
© Domenico Lovascio 2022

The right of Domenico Lovascio to be identified as the editor of this work has been asserted by them in accordance with the Copyright, Designs and Patents Act 1988.

This edition published by Manchester University Press
Oxford Road, Manchester M13 9PL

www.manchesteruniversitypress.co.uk

British Library Cataloguing-in-Publication Data
A catalogue record for this book is available from the British Library

ISBN  978 1 5261 5163 6  hardback
ISBN  978 1 5261 8422 1  paperback

First published 2022
Paperback published 2025

The publisher has no responsibility for the persistence or accuracy of URLs for any external or third-party internet websites referred to in this book, and does not guarantee that any content on such websites is, or will remain, accurate or appropriate.

EU authorised representative for GPSR:
Easy Access System Europe – Mustamäe tee 50, 10621 Tallinn, Estonia,
gpsr.requests@easproject.com

Typeset
by New Best-set Typesetters Ltd

*For Giulia, Cesare, and Juno*

# Contents

| | |
|---|---|
| ILLUSTRATIONS | viii |
| GENERAL EDITORS' PREFACE | ix |
| ACKNOWLEDGEMENTS | xii |
| ABBREVIATIONS AND REFERENCES | xv |
| INTRODUCTION | 1 |
|    Dating and authorship | 1 |
|    A Blackfriars play? | 3 |
|    Staging Rome: Republic and Empire | 11 |
|    Sources | 16 |
|    The title | 37 |
|    Critical reception | 39 |
|    Stage history | 48 |
|    The text | 51 |
| *THE FALSE ONE* | 61 |
| APPENDICES | |
|    1. Latin transcription of passages from Lucan's *Pharsalia* cited in the Commentary | 197 |
|    2. 'Look out, bright eyes, and bless the air' | 202 |
| INDEX | 205 |

# Illustrations

1 Portrait of John Fletcher, from life, about 1620, oil on oak panel, unknown artist (© National Portrait Gallery, London)   4
2 The Egyptians defeated by the Romans at the end of the play, in *The Works of Mr. Francis Beaumont and Mr. John Fletcher*, 7 vols (London: Tonson, 1711), 3.1149 (ULB Bonn, Fb 407). Reproduced by permission of Universitäts und Landesbibliothek Bonn   19
3 Pothinus shows the head of Pompey to Caesar, in *The Dramatic Works of Beaumont and Fletcher*, edited by George Colman the elder, 10 vols (London: Evans and Elmsley, 1778), 4.75 (Württembergische Landesbibliothek Stuttgart, Book number Fr.D.oct.61). Reproduced by permission of Württembergische Landesbibliothek Stuttgart   22
4 Opening text of *The False One*, in *Comedies and Tragedies Written by Francis Beaumont and John Fletcher Gentlemen* (London, 1647), sig. Qq. Source: Pennsylvania State University Library, Digital Collections, https://digital.libraries.psu.edu/digital/collection/emblem/id/4553/rec/4 (Public Domain Mark 1.0)   52

# General Editors' Preface

Clifford Leech conceived of the Revels Plays as a series in the mid-1950s, modelling the project on the New Arden Shakespeare. The aim, as he wrote in 1958, was 'to apply to Shakespeare's predecessors, contemporaries, and successors the methods that are now used in Shakespeare's editing'. The plays chosen were to include well-known works from the early Tudor period to about 1700, as well as others less familiar but of literary and theatrical merit. 'The plays included', Leech wrote, 'should be such as to deserve and indeed demand performance'. We owe it to Clifford Leech that the idea became reality. He set the high standards of the series, ensuring that editors of individual volumes produced work of lasting merit, equally useful for teachers and students, theatre directors and actors. Clifford Leech remained General Editor until 1971, and was succeeded by F. David Hoeniger, who retired in 1985.

Ever since then, the Revels Plays have been under the direction of four or five general editors: initially David Bevington, E. A. J. Honigmann, J. R. Mulryne, and E. M. Waith. E. A. J. Honigmann retired in 2000 and was succeeded by Richard Dutton. E. M. Waith retired in 2003 and was succeeded by Alison Findlay and Helen Ostovich. J. R. Mulryne retired in 2010, David Bevington passed away in 2019, and Martin White retired in the same year. They were succeeded by Karen Britland, Rory Loughnane, and Barbara Ravelhofer. Published originally by Methuen, the series is now published by the Manchester University Press, embodying essentially the same format, scholarly character, and high editorial standards of the series as first conceived. The series now concentrates on plays from the period 1558–1642. Some slight changes have been made: for example, starting in 1996 each index lists proper names and topics in the introduction and commentary, whereas earlier indexes focused only on words and phrases for which the commentary provided a gloss. Notes to the introduction are now placed together at the end, not at the foot, of the page. Collation and commentary notes continue, however, to appear on the relevant pages.

The introduction to each Revels play undertakes to offer, among other matters, a critical appraisal of the play's significant themes and images, its poetic and verbal fascinations, its historical context, its characteristics as a piece for the theatre, and its uses of the stage for which it was designed. Stage history is an important part of the story. In addition, the introduction presents as lucidly as possible the criteria for choice of copy-text and the editorial methods employed in presenting the play to a modern reader. The introduction also considers the play's date and, where relevant, its sources, together with its place in the work of the author and in the theatre of its time. If the play is by an author not previously represented in the series, a brief biography is provided.

The text of each Revels play, in accordance with established practice in the series, is edited afresh from the original text of best authority (in a few instances, texts), in modern spelling and punctuation and with speech headings that are consistent throughout. Elisions in the original are also silently regularised, except where metre would be affected by the change. Emendations, as distinguished from modernized spellings and punctuation, are introduced only in instances where error is patent or at least very probable, and where the corrected reading is persuasive. Act divisions are given only if they appear in the original, or if the structure of the play clearly points to them. Those act and scene divisions not in the original are provided in small type. Square brackets are also used for any other additions to, or changes in, the stage directions of the original.

Rather than provide a comprehensive and historical variorum collation, Revels Plays editions focus on those variants which require the critical attention of serious textual students. All departures of substance from the copy-text are listed, including any significant relineation and those changes in punctuation which involve to any degree a decision between alternative interpretations. The collation notes do not include such accidentals as turned letters or changes in the font. Additions to stage directions are not noted in the collations, since those additions are already made clear by the use of brackets. On the other hand, press corrections in the copy-text are duly collated, as based on a careful consultation of as many copies of the original edition or editions as are needed to ensure that the printing history of those originals is accurately reported. Of later emendations of the text by subsequent editors, only those are reported which still deserve attention as alternative readings.

One of the hallmarks of the Revels Plays is the thoroughness of their annotations. Besides explaining the meanings of difficult words and passages, the annotations provide commentary on customs or usage, on the text, on stage business – indeed, on anything that can be pertinent and helpful. On occasion, when long notes are required and are too lengthy to fit comfortably at the foot of the page below the text, they are printed at the end of the complete text.

Appendices are used to present any commendatory poems on the dramatist and play in question, documents about the play's reception and contemporary history, classical sources, casting analyses, music, and any other relevant material.

Each volume contains an index to the commentary, in which particular attention is drawn to meanings for words not listed in the OED, and (starting in 1996, as indicated above) an indexing of proper names and topics in the introduction and commentary.

Our hope is that plays edited in this fashion will promote further scholarly and theatrical investigation of one of the richest periods in theatrical history.

KAREN BRITLAND
RICHARD DUTTON
ALISON FINDLAY
RORY LOUGHNANE
HELEN OSTOVICH
BARBARA RAVELHOFER

# Acknowledgements

I have toyed with the idea of editing John Fletcher and Philip Massinger's *The False One* for about a decade. I had been baffled, after reading this brilliant play while working on my PhD thesis in 2010, that there was no standalone edition of it. At the time, however, I did not have the necessary skills or resources to undertake the task myself. Yet that desire never abandoned me in the following years. I finally mustered the courage to submit a proposal to edit *The False One* for the Revels Plays series to Commissioning Editor Matthew Frost and to General Editors Richard Dutton, Alison Findlay, and Helen Ostovich in 2019. They enthusiastically and quickly accepted – honestly, to my surprise. I thank all of them wholeheartedly, and I hope that this edition does justice to this undeservedly neglected play.

My work on *The False One* has been made possible largely thanks to funding made available from the Italian Ministry of Education, University and Research (MIUR), which supported the project 'Classical Receptions in Early Modern English Drama' as a Research Project of National Interest (PRIN2017XAA3ZF). This edition is part of that broader research. The Principal Investigator was Silvia Bigliazzi (University of Verona), while the three local units were coordinated by Carlo Maria Bajetta (University of Aosta), Alessandro Grilli (University of Pisa), and me at the University of Genoa. I am grateful to all the participants in the project for many fruitful discussions and stimulating exchanges.

I extend particular thanks to Lia Wallace and Sarah Enloe at the American Shakespeare Center. Lia showed extraordinary generosity in sharing with me all the material in her possession related to the staged reading that she directed at the Blackfriars Playhouse in Staunton, VA, on 4 October 2015, including footage of the entire performance, which was extremely helpful as I edited the play. Sarah provided the press release for the same staged reading. I am also grateful to Will Tosh and Victoria Lane at Shakespeare's Globe in London for helping me acquire additional information regarding the 'Read Not Dead' performance of the play directed by Jason Morell on 19 March 2017.

## ACKNOWLEDGEMENTS

David McInnis provided encouragement and advice as I was putting my proposal together. Alan Dessen, Lisa Hopkins, Roslyn Knutson, David McInnis, Lucy Munro, Matthew Steggle, and Leslie Thomson provided help with heads as props. Martin Wiggins kindly shared with me the full recording of the Zoom reading of the play that took place on 11 December 2020 as part of the 'Reading Early Plays' project he is currently leading. José A. Pérez Díez made invaluable suggestions regarding the list of roles and the use of parentheses and dashes. Jennifer Moss Waghorn kindly checked my transcription of the musical setting in Appendix 2 and shared some thoughts on John Wilson. I extend my gratitude to all of them.

I am grateful to a number of friends and colleagues who have commented on parts of the edition or have provided useful information, namely Lisa Hopkins, Cristiano Ragni, and Emanuel Stelzer. Special thanks go to Michela Compagnoni, who nobly read the entire typescript before submission to the publisher. Luca Baratta, Fabio Ciambella, and Emanuel Stelzer supplied material I could not have accessed without their help. Maddalena Repetto helped me check my text against F1 before submission and providentially spotted three typos. Special thanks go to Andrew Kirk for his meticulous copy-editing and to Lianne Slavin for steering the publication process so competently and efficiently. All these people have made this a much better book than it would have been otherwise, and if any errors remain, they are entirely my responsibility.

The colleagues working in English at the Department of Modern Languages and Cultures at Genoa have been a delight to work with: Laura Colombino, Stefania Michelucci, Paola Nardi, Luisa Villa, Annalisa Baicchi, Marco Bagli, Cristiano Broccias, Ilaria Rizzato, Laura Santini, and Elisabetta Zurru.

I owe deep gratitude to the staff of my department library. In particular, Simone Tallone has been helpful, diligent, and resourceful, while Franco Reuspi has once again proved to be the most efficient librarian in the world by responding promptly to my book orders and my requests for interlibrary loan materials. This book would simply not exist without them.

Martina Steden-Papke at the Universitäts- und Landesbibliothek Bonn and Luitgard Nuß at the Württembergische Landesbibliothek Stuttgart were vitally helpful in providing images very quickly during the COVID pandemic. Thanks also go to the Bodleian Library for providing a reproduction of the musical setting of the song 'Look out, bright eyes, and bless the air'.

The Introduction incorporates material from 'The Anonymous *Caesar's Revenge* and John Fletcher and Philip Massinger's *The False One*', *Notes and Queries*, 62.2 (2015), 242–5, and 'She-Tragedy: Lust, Luxury and Empire in John Fletcher and Philip Massinger's *The False One*', in *The Genres of Renaissance Tragedy*, edited by Daniel Cadman, Andrew Duxfield, and Lisa Hopkins (Manchester University Press, 2019), 166–83. I am thankful to all the relevant editors and publishers who have granted permission to reproduce previously published material.

I have been extremely lucky to have Richard Dutton as my General Editor. He has been splendidly generous and supportive, and he patiently bore with the naïve questions that often came from such an inexperienced editor as I was when I started work on this edition, invariably replying with sound advice and encouraging words. He has taught me more than he will ever imagine, and his infallible eye has saved me from embarrassing mistakes more times than I would like to admit.

As always, my most heartfelt thanks go to my wonderful family: Giulia, our son Cesare, and our dog Juno.

Domenico Lovascio<br>
Genoa, 23 April 2021

# Abbreviations and References

EDITIONS AND TEXTUAL REFERENCES

1711     *The False One*, in vol. 3 of *The Works of Mr Francis Beaumont and Mr John Fletcher*, 7 vols (London: Tonson, 1711)

Colman     *The False One*, in vol. 4 of *The Dramatic Works of Beaumont and Fletcher, Collated with All the Former Editions, and Corrected, with Notes, Critical and Explanatory, by Various Commentators; and Adorned with Fifty-four Original Engravings in Ten Volumes*, ed. George Colman the elder, 10 vols (London: Evans and Elmsley, 1778)

Dyce     *The False One*, in vol. 9 of *The Works of Beaumont and Fletcher; The Text Formed from a New Collation of the Early Editions, with Notes and a Biographical Memoir*, ed. Alexander Dyce, 11 vols (London: Moxon, 1844)

F1     *The False One*, in *Comedies and Tragedies Written by Francis Beaumont and John Fletcher Gentlemen. Never Printed Before, and Now Published by the Authors' Original Copies* (London, 1647)

F2     *The False One*, in *Fifty Comedies and Tragedies. Written by Francis Beaumont and John Fletcher, Gentlemen, All in One Volume. Published by the Authors' Original Copies, the Songs to Each Play Being Added* (London, 1679)

Heath     Manuscript commentary by Benjamin Heath on the plays in the Beaumont and Fletcher Folios, mentioned in Dyce

Luce     *The False One*, ed. Morton Luce, in vol. 4 of *The Works of Francis Beaumont and John Fletcher: Variorum Edition*, ed. A. H. Bullen (London: Bell and Sons, 1912)

Mason     John Monck Mason, *Comments on the Plays of Beaumont and Fletcher, with an Appendix Containing Some Further Observations on Shakespeare* (London: Harding, 1798)

Seward     *The False One*, in vol. 4 of *The Works of Mr Francis Beaumont, and Mr John Fletcher*, ed. by Messrs Theobald,

|  | *Seward and Sympson*, 10 vols (London: Tonson and Draper, 1750) |
|---|---|
| Sympson | John Sympson's conjectures, mentioned in Seward |
| Theobald | Lewis Theobald's conjectures, mentioned in Seward |
| Turner | *The False One*, ed. Robert Kean Turner, in vol. 8 of *The Dramatic Works in the Beaumont and Fletcher Canon*, ed. Fredson Bowers, 10 vols (Cambridge University Press, 1992) |
| Weber | *The False One*, in vol. 5 of *The Works of Beaumont and Fletcher, in Fourteen Volumes, with an Introduction and Explanatory Notes*, ed. Henry Weber, 14 vols (Edinburgh: Ballantyne, 1812) |

### FLETCHER'S WORKS

Quotations from other works in the Fletcher canon are taken from *The Dramatic Works in the Beaumont and Fletcher Canon*, gen. ed. Fredson Bowers, 10 vols (Cambridge University Press, 1966–96), with the exception of Martin Wiggins's edition of *Valentinian*, in *Four Jacobean Sex Tragedies* (Oxford University Press, 1998), the New Mermaid edition of *The Tamer Tamed* by Lucy Munro (London: Methuen, 2010), and the Revels Plays edition of *Love's Cure, or The Martial Maid* by José A. Pérez Díez (Manchester University Press, 2022). Titles of Fletcher's works are abbreviated as follows:

| Bond | *Bonduca* |
|---|---|
| Corinth | *The Queen of Corinth* |
| Cure | *Love's Cure* |
| CustCount | *The Custom of the Country* |
| Lawyer | *The Little French Lawyer* |
| Loyal | *The Loyal Subject* |
| Monsieur | *Monsieur Thomas* |
| NW | *The Night-Walkers* |
| Tamer | *The Woman's Prize, or The Tamer Tamed* |
| Val | *Valentinian* |
| Woman | *A Very Woman* |
| Wife | *A Wife for a Month* |

### MASSINGER'S WORKS

Quotations from Massinger's other works are taken from *The Plays and Poems of Philip Massinger*, ed. Philip Edwards and Colin Gibson,

ABBREVIATIONS AND REFERENCES                xvii

5 vols (Oxford: Clarendon Press, 1976), with the exception of the Revels Plays edition of *The Roman Actor* by Martin White (Manchester University Press, 2007). Quotations from Dekker and Massinger's *The Virgin Martyr* are from *The Dramatic Works of Thomas Dekker*, ed. Fredson Bowers, 4 vols (Cambridge University Press, 1953–61), 3.365–480. Titles of Massinger's works are abbreviated as follows:

| | |
|---|---|
| *Bondman* | *The Bondman* |
| *Duke* | *The Duke of Milan* |
| *MH* | *The Maid of Honour* |
| *Parl* | *Parliament of Love* |
| *Pict* | *The Picture* |
| *RA* | *The Roman Actor* |
| *UnnComb* | *The Unnatural Combat* |
| *VM* | *The Virgin Martyr* |

SHAKESPEARE'S WORKS

Titles of Shakespeare's works are abbreviated as follows:

| | |
|---|---|
| *3H6* | *Henry VI Part 3*, ed. Eric Rasmussen and John D. Cox (London: Thomson Learning for Arden Shakespeare, 2001) |
| *A&C* | *Antony and Cleopatra*, ed. David Bevington (Cambridge University Press, upd. edn, 2005) |
| *JC* | *Julius Caesar*, ed. David Daniell (Walton-on-Thames: Nelson for Arden Shakespeare, 1998) |
| *KL* | *King Lear*, ed. R. A. Foakes (Walton-on-Thames: Nelson for Arden Shakespeare, 1997) |
| *LLL* | *Love's Labours Lost*, ed. H. R. Woudhuysen (Walton-on-Thames: Nelson for Arden Shakespeare, 1998) |
| *Mac* | *Macbeth*, ed. Sandra Clark and Pamela Mason (London: Bloomsbury Arden Shakespeare, 2015) |
| *MAdo* | *Much Ado about Nothing*, ed. Claire McEachern (London: Bloomsbury Arden Shakespeare, rev. edn, 2016) |
| *Per* | *Pericles*, ed. Suzanne Gossett (London: Thomson Learning for Arden Shakespeare, 2004) |
| *Temp* | *The Tempest*, ed. Virginia Mason Vaughan and Alden T. Vaughan (London: Bloomsbury Arden Shakespeare, rev. edn, 2011) |

ABBREVIATIONS AND REFERENCES

JONSON'S WORKS

Quotations from Jonson's works are taken from *The Cambridge Edition of the Works of Ben Jonson* (*CWBJ*), gen. ed. David Bevington, Martin Butler, and Ian Donaldson, 7 vols (Cambridge University Press, 2012). Titles of Jonson's works are abbreviated as follows:

| | |
|---|---|
| Beauty | *The Masque of Beauty* |
| Blackness | *The Masque of Blackness* |
| Epigr | *Epigrams* |
| Sej | *Sejanus* |
| Volp | *Volpone* |

OTHER REFERENCES

| | |
|---|---|
| Aesop | Aesop, *The Complete Fables*, trans. Olivia and Robert Temple (London: Penguin, 1998) |
| Alexander, *Julius Caesar* | William Alexander, *The Tragedy of Julius Caesar*, in *The Poetical Works of Sir William Alexander*, ed. L. E. Kastner and H. B. Charlton, 2 vols (Manchester University Press, 1921) |
| Appian | Appian, *An Ancient History and Exquisite Chronicle of the Romans' Wars*, trans. W[illiam] B[arker] (London, 1578) |
| Appleton | William W. Appleton, *Beaumont and Fletcher: A Critical Study* (London: Allen and Unwin, 1956) |
| Armitage | David Armitage, 'Literature and Empire', in *The Oxford History of the British Empire: The Origins of Empire*, ed. William Roger Louis, Alaine M. Low, and Nicholas P. Canny (Oxford University Press, 1998), 99–123 |
| Ayres | Harry Morgan Ayres, 'Shakespeare's *Julius Caesar* in the Light of Some Other Versions', *PMLA*, 25 (1910), 183–227 |
| Bald | R. C. Bald, *Bibliographical Studies in the Beaumont & Fletcher Folio of 1647* (Oxford University Press for The Bibliographical Society, 1938 for 1937) |
| Baldwin | Thomas Whitfield Baldwin, *The Organization and Personnel of the Shakespearean Company* (Princeton University Press, 1927) |

| | |
|---|---|
| Bawcutt | N. W. Bawcutt, *The Control and Censorship of Caroline Drama: The Records of Sir Henry Herbert, Master of the Revels, 1623–73* (Oxford: Clarendon Press, 1996) |
| Bowden | William R. Bowden, *The English Dramatic Lyric, 1603–42: A Study in Stuart Dramatic Technique* (New Haven, CT: Yale University Press, 1951) |
| Breitenberg | Mark Breitenberg, *Anxious Masculinity in Early Modern England* (Cambridge University Press, 1996) |
| Browne | Thomas Browne, *Pseudodoxia Epidemica, or Enquiries into Very Many Received Tenets and Commonly Presumed Truths* (London, 1646) |
| Burstein | Stanley Mayer Burstein, *The Reign of Cleopatra* (Westport, CT: Greenwood Press, 2007) |
| Bushnell, 'Tyranny' | Rebecca W. Bushnell, 'Tyranny and Effeminacy in Early Modern England', in *Reconsidering the Renaissance*, ed. Mario A. Di Cesare (Binghamton, NY: Medieval and Renaissance Texts and Studies, 1992), 339–54 |
| Bushnell, *Tyrants* | Rebecca W. Bushnell, *Tragedies of Tyrants: Political Thought and Theater in the English Renaissance* (Ithaca, NY: Cornell University Press, 1990) |
| Caesar | Gaius Julius Caesar, *Civil War*, ed. and trans. Cynthia Damon (Cambridge, MA: Harvard University Press, 2016) |
| *Caesar's Revenge* | Anonymous, *The Tragedy of Caesar's Revenge*, ed. F. S. Boas (Oxford: Malone Society, 1911) |
| Canfora | Luciano Canfora, *Julius Caesar: The Life and Times of the People's Dictator*, trans. Marian Hill and Kevin Windle (Berkeley, CA: University of California Press, 2007) |
| Cantor | Paul A. Cantor, *Shakespeare's Rome: Republic and Empire* (Ithaca, NY: Cornell University Press, 1976) |
| Cary, *Mariam* | Elizabeth Cary, *The Tragedy of Mariam*, ed. Ramona Wray (London: Methuen for Arden Shakespeare, 2012) |
| Cassius Dio | Cassius Dio, *Roman History*, ed. and trans. Earnest Cary (London: Heinemann, 1914–27) |

| | |
|---|---|
| Chapman, Caesar and Pompey | George Chapman, *Caesar and Pompey: A Roman Tragedy*, in *The Plays and Poems of George Chapman: The Tragedies*, ed. Thomas Marc Parrott (London: Routledge, 1910) |
| Cicero | Cicero, *On Duties*, ed. and trans. Walter Miller (London: Heinemann, 1913) |
| Clark | Ira Clark, *The Moral Art of Philip Massinger* (Lewisburg, PA: Bucknell University Press, 1993) |
| Curran | John E. Curran, Jr, 'Fletcher, Massinger, and Roman Imperial Character', *Comparative Drama*, 43 (2009), 317–54 |
| Cutts | John P. Cutts, *La musique de scène de la troupe de Shakespeare. The King's Men sous le règne de Jacques Ier* (Paris: Centre National de la Recherche Scientifique, 1959) |
| Dessen and Thomson | Alan C. Dessen and Leslie Thomson, *A Dictionary of Stage Directions in English Drama, 1580–1642* (Cambridge University Press, 1999) |
| Dimitrova | Miryana Dimitrova, 'Labienus and Sceva: Two Classical Supporting Characters and Their Early Modern Dramatic Life in Fletcher and Massinger's *The False One*', *Early Theatre*, 18 (2015), 101–14 |
| Donaldson | Ian Donaldson, *Ben Jonson: A Life* (Oxford University Press, 2011) |
| Dustagheer | Sarah Dustagheer, *Shakespeare's Two Playhouses: Repertory and Theatre Space at the Globe and the Blackfriars, 1599–1613* (Cambridge University Press, 2017) |
| Dutton, Mastering | Richard Dutton, *Mastering the Revels: The Regulation and Censorship of English Renaissance Drama* (Basingstoke: Macmillan, 1991) |
| Dyce, 'Account' | Alexander Dyce, 'Some Account of the Lives and Writings of Beaumont and Fletcher', in *The Works of Beaumont and Fletcher*, 11 vols (London: Moxon, 1844), 1.v–lxxxvii |
| Farmer and Henley | J. S. Farmer and W. E. Henley, *Slang and Its Analogues*, 7 vols (London: Routledge and Kegan Paul, 1890–1904) |

| | ABBREVIATIONS AND REFERENCES xxi |
|---|---|
| Finkelpearl | Philip J. Finkelpearl, *Court and Country Politics in the Plays of Beaumont and Fletcher* (Princeton University Press, 1990) |
| Fitzmaurice | Andrew Fitzmaurice, *Humanism and America: An Intellectual History of English Colonisation, 1500–1625* (Cambridge University Press, 2003) |
| Florus | *The Roman Histories of Lucius Julius Florus from the Foundation of Rome till Caesar Augustus for above DCC Years, and from Thence to Trajan near CC Years, Divided by Flor[us] into IV Ages*, trans. Edmund Bolton (London, 1619). The Latin text is quoted from Lucius Anneus Florus, *Epitome of Roman History*, trans. E. S. Forster (London: Heinemann, 1929) |
| Foucault | Michel Foucault, *The History of Sexuality*, trans. Robert Hurley, 3 vols (New York: Vintage, 1978–86) |
| Gayley | Charles Mills Gayley, *Beaumont, the Dramatist: A Portrait: With Some Account of His Circle, Elizabethan and Jacobean, and of His Association with John Fletcher* (New York: Century, 1914) |
| Gentillet | Innocent Gentillet, *A Discourse upon the Means of Well Governing and Maintaining in Good Peace a Kingdom or Other Principality*, trans. Simon Patrick (London, 1602) |
| Graves | R. B. Graves, *Lighting the Shakespearean Stage, 1567–1642* (Carbondale, IL: Southern Illinois University Press, 1999) |
| Gray | Robert Gray, *A Good Speed to Virginia* (London, 1609) |
| Griffin | Julia Griffin, 'Shakespeare's *Julius Caesar* and the Dramatic Tradition', in *A Companion to Julius Caesar*, ed. Miriam Tamara Griffin (Hoboken, NJ: Wiley, 2009), 371–98 |
| Grillo | Luca Grillo, *The Art of Caesar's* Bellum Civile: *Literature, Ideology, and Community* (Cambridge University Press, 2012) |
| Gurr and Ichikawa | Andrew Gurr and Mariko Ichikawa, *Staging in Shakespeare's Theatres* (Oxford University Press, 2000) |

| | |
|---|---|
| Hall | Kim F. Hall, *Things of Darkness: Economies of Race and Gender in Early Modern England* (Ithaca, NY: Cornell University Press, 1995) |
| Hatchuel | Sarah Hatchuel, *Shakespeare and the Cleopatra/Caesar Intertext: Sequel, Conflation, Remake* (Madison, WI: Fairleigh Dickinson University Press, 2011) |
| Hazlitt | William Hazlitt, *Lectures on the Dramatic Literature of the Age of Elizabeth* (New York: Wiley, 1849) |
| Henderson and McManus | Katherine Usher Henderson and Barbara F. McManus, *Contexts and Texts of the Controversy about Women in England, 1540–1640* (Urbana, IL: University of Illinois Press, 1985) |
| Hensman | Bertha Hensman, *The Shares of Fletcher, Field and Massinger in Twelve Plays of the Beaumont and Fletcher Canon*, 2 vols (Salzburg: Institut für Englische Sprache und Literatur, 1974) |
| Hila | Marina Hila, 'Dishonourable Peace: Fletcher and Massinger's *The False One* and Jacobean Foreign Policy', *Cahiers Élisabéthains*, 72 (2007), 21–30 |
| Hirrel | Michael J. Hirrell, 'Alcazar, The Lord Admiral's, and Aspects of Performance', *Review of English Studies*, 66 (2015), 40–59 |
| Holmberg | Eva Johanna Holmberg, *Jews in the Early Modern English Imagination: A Scattered Nation* (Farnham: Ashgate, 2011) |
| Honigmann | E. A. J. Honigmann, 'Re-Enter the Stage Direction: Shakespeare and Some Contemporaries', *Shakespeare Survey*, 29 (1976), 117–25 |
| Hopkins | Lisa Hopkins, 'Beautiful Polecats: The Living and the Dead in *Julius Caesar*', *Shakespeare Survey*, 72 (2019), 160–70 |
| Howard-Hill, Crane | T. H. Howard-Hill, *Ralph Crane and Some Shakespeare First Folio Comedies* (Charlottesville, VA: University Press of Virginia, 1972) |
| Howard-Hill, 'Crane' | T. H. Howard-Hill, 'Shakespeare's Earliest Editor, Ralph Crane', *Shakespeare Survey*, 44 (1991), 113–29 |
| Howard-Hill, 'Introduction' | T. H. Howard-Hill, 'Introduction' to *Sir John Van Olden Barnavelt* by John Fletcher and Philip Massinger (London: Malone Society, 1979), i–xiv |

| | |
|---|---|
| Hoy, 'Massinger' | Cyrus Hoy, 'Massinger as Collaborator: The Plays with Fletcher and Others', in *Philip Massinger: A Critical Reassessment*, ed. Douglas Howard (Cambridge University Press, 1985), 51–82 |
| Hoy, 'Shares' | Cyrus Hoy, 'The Shares of Fletcher and His Collaborators in the Beaumont and Fletcher Canon (II)', *Studies in Bibliography*, 9 (1957), 143–62 |
| Iyengar | Sujata Iyengar, *Shades of Difference: Mythologies of Skin Color in Early Modern England* (Philadelphia, PA: University of Pennsylvania Press, 2004) |
| *JC*, ed. Jowett | William Shakespeare, *Julius Caesar*, ed. John Jowett, in *The Oxford Shakespeare: The Complete Works*, ed. Stanley Wells and Gary Taylor (Oxford University Press, 2nd edn, 1986), 627–54 |
| *JC*, ed. Neville | William Shakespeare, *Julius Caesar*, ed. Sarah Neville, in *The New Oxford Shakespeare: The Complete Works: Modern Critical Edition*, ed. Gary Taylor, John Jowett, Terri Bourus, and Gabriel Egan (Oxford University Press, 2016), 1607–75 |
| Jenner | Simon Jenner, 'Review of *The False One*', *FringeReview*, 20 March 2017, http://fringereview.co.uk/review/fringereview-uk/2017/the-false-one/ (accessed 1 October 2020) |
| Jensen, 'Florus' | Freyja Cox Jensen, 'Reading Florus in Early Modern England', *Renaissance Studies*, 23 (2009), 659–77 |
| Jensen, *Reading* | Freyja Cox Jensen, *Reading the Roman Republic in Early Modern England* (Leiden: Brill, 2012) |
| Jowitt | Claire Jowitt, '*The Island Princess* and Race', in *Early Modern English Drama: A Critical Companion*, ed. Garrett A. Sullivan, Patrick Cheney, and Andrew Hadfield (Oxford University Press, 2005), 287–97 |
| Karim-Cooper | Farah Karim-Cooper, *Cosmetics in Shakespearean and Renaissance Drama* (Edinburgh University Press, 2006) |
| Kewes | Paulina Kewes, 'Julius Caesar in Jacobean England', *Seventeenth Century*, 17 (2002), 155–86 |

| | |
|---|---|
| Kyd, *Cornelia* | Thomas Kyd, *Cornelia*, ed. Marie-Alice Belle and Line Cottegnies, in *Robert Garnier in Elizabethan England: Mary Sidney Herbert's* Antonius: *Thomas Kyd's* Cornelia (Cambridge: Modern Humanities Research Association, 2017) |
| Lewis | Edward Danby Lewis, 'John Fletcher: His Distinctive Structural and Stylistic Contribution to English Drama' (unpublished PhD thesis, Yale University, 1941) |
| Loomba | Ania Loomba, *Shakespeare, Race, and Colonialism* (Oxford University Press, 2002) |
| Lovano | Michael Lovano, *All Things Julius Caesar: An Encyclopedia of Caesar's World and Legacy* (Santa Barbara, CA: ABC-CLIO, 2015) |
| Lovascio, 'Caesar' | Domenico Lovascio, 'Re-Writing Julius Caesar as a National Villain in Early Modern English Drama', *English Literary Renaissance*, 47 (2017), 218–50 |
| Lovascio, 'Caesar's "just cause"' | Domenico Lovascio, 'Julius Caesar's "just cause" in John Fletcher and Philip Massinger's *The False One*', *Notes and Queries*, 62 (2015), 245–7 |
| Lovascio, Fletcher's Rome | Domenico Lovascio, *John Fletcher's Rome: Questioning the Classics* (Manchester University Press, 2022) |
| Lovascio, 'She-Tragedy' | Domenico Lovascio, 'She-Tragedy: Lust, Luxury and Empire in John Fletcher and Philip Massinger's *The False One*', in *The Genres of Renaissance Tragedy*, ed. Daniel Cadman, Andrew Duxfield, and Lisa Hopkins (Manchester University Press, 2019), 166–83 |
| LPD | *Lost Plays Database*, ed. Roslyn L. Knutson, David McInnis, Matthew Steggle, and Misha Teramura (Washington, DC: Folger Shakespeare Library, 2009–) |
| Lucan | Lucan, *The Civil War: Books I–X (Pharsalia)*, trans. J. D. Duff (London: Heinemann, 1962). The Latin text is quoted from *M. Annaei Lucani Pharsalia sive De Bello Civili Caesar et Pompeii Libri X*, ed. Thomas Farnaby (London, 1618) |
| MacDonald | Joyce Green MacDonald, *Women and Race in Early Modern Texts* (Cambridge University Press, 2002) |

| | |
|---|---|
| Marlowe, *Dr Faustus* | Christopher Marlowe, *Doctor Faustus: A- and B-texts (1604, 1616)*, ed. David Bevington and Eric Rasmussen (Manchester University Press, 1993) |
| Maxwell | Baldwin Maxwell, *Studies in Beaumont, Fletcher, and Massinger* (Chapel Hill, NC: University of North Carolina Press, 1939) |
| McDermott | James McDermott, 'Farnaby, Thomas (1574/5–1647)', *Oxford Dictionary of National Biography* (Oxford University Press, 2004), https://doi.org/10.1093/ref:odnb/9173 (accessed 9 November 2020) |
| McKeithan | Daniel Morley McKeithan, *The Debt to Shakespeare in the Beaumont-and-Fletcher Plays* (Austin, TX: privately printed, 1938) |
| Munro | Lucy Munro, *Shakespeare in the Theatre: The King's Men* (London: Bloomsbury Arden Shakespeare, 2020) |
| Neill | Michael Neill, 'Introduction' to *Anthony and Cleopatra* by William Shakespeare (Oxford University Press, 1994), 1–130 |
| Nicoll | Allardyce Nicoll, *A History of English Drama 1660–1900: Volume I: Restoration Drama 1660–1700* (Cambridge University Press, 1923) |
| Oliphant | E. H. C. Oliphant, *The Plays of Beaumont and Fletcher: An Attempt to Determine Their Respective Shares and the Shares of Others* (New Haven: CT, Yale University Press, 1927) |
| Owens | Margaret E. Owens, *Stages of Dismemberment: The Fragmented Body in Late Medieval and Early Modern Drama* (Newark, DE: University of Delaware Press, 2005) |
| Paleit | Edward Paleit, *War, Liberty, and Caesar: Responses to Lucan's Bellum Ciuile, ca. 1580–1650* (Oxford University Press, 2013) |
| Plutarch, 'Antony' | Plutarch, 'The Life of Marcus Antonius', in *The Lives of the Noble Grecians and Romans Compared Together*, trans. Thomas North (London, 1579) |
| Plutarch, 'Caesar' | Plutarch, 'The Life of Julius Caesar', in *The Lives of the Noble Grecians and Romans Compared Together*, trans. Thomas North (London, 1579) |
| Plutarch, 'Pompey' | Plutarch, 'The Life of Pompey', in *The Lives of the Noble Grecians and Romans Compared Together*, trans. Thomas North (London, 1579) |

| | |
|---|---|
| Poitevin | Kimberly Woosley Poitevin, '"Counterfeit Colour": Making Up Race in Elizabeth Cary's *The Tragedy of Mariam*', *Tulsa Studies in Women's Literature*, 24 (2005), 13–34 |
| Roche | Lucan, *De Bello Ciuili: Book VII*, ed. Paul Roche (Cambridge University Press, 2019) |
| Ronan, *'Antike Roman'* | Clifford J. Ronan, *'Antike Roman': Power Symbology and the Roman Play in Early Modern England: 1585–1635* (Athens, GA: University of Georgia Press, 1995) |
| Ronan, 'Caesar On and Off' | Clifford J. Ronan, 'Caesar On and Off the Renaissance English Stage', in *Julius Caesar: New Critical Essays*, ed. Horst Zander (London: Routledge, 2005), 71–89 |
| Ronan, 'Roman Thoughts' | Clifford J. Ronan, '*Caesar's Revenge* and the Roman Thoughts in *Antony and Cleopatra*', *Shakespeare Studies*, 19 (1987), 171–82 |
| Seneca, *Phaedra* | Seneca, *Phaedra*, in *Seneca's Tragedies*, ed. and trans. Frank Justus Miller, 2 vols (London: Heinemann, 1917) |
| Seward, 'Preface' | Thomas Seward, 'Preface' to *The Works of Mr Francis Beaumont, and Mr John Fletcher*, 10 vols (London: Tonson and Draper, 1750), 1.v–lxxvi |
| Shepard | Alexandra Shepard, *Meanings of Manhood in Early Modern England* (Oxford University Press, 2003) |
| Soellner | Rolf Soellner, 'Chapman's *Caesar and Pompey* and the Fortunes of Prince Henry', *Medieval and Renaissance Drama in England*, 2 (1985), 135–51 |
| Spear | Gary Spear, 'Shakespeare's "Manly" Parts: Masculinity and Effeminacy in *Troilus and Cressida*', *Shakespeare Quarterly*, 44 (1993), 409–22 |
| Spink | Ian Spink, 'Wilson, John (1595–1674)', *Oxford Dictionary of National Biography* (Oxford University Press, 2004), https://doi.org/10.1093/ref:odnb/29662 (accessed 7 December 2020) |
| Stern | Tiffany Stern, *Documents of Performance in Early Modern England* (Cambridge University Press, 2009) |

| | |
|---|---|
| Suetonius | *The History of Twelve Caesars Emperors of Rome*, trans. Philemon Holland (London, 1606). The Latin text is quoted from Suetonius, *The Lives of the Caesars*, trans. J. C. Rolfe (London: Heinemann, 1913–14) |
| Tacitus | *The Annals of Cornelius Tacitus. The Description of Germany*, trans. Richard Greenway (London, 1598). The Latin text is quoted from Tacitus, *The Histories. The Annals*, trans. C. H. Moore and J. Jackson, 4 vols (London: Heinemann, 1925–37) |
| Tappan | Elizabeth Tappan, 'Julius Caesar's Luck', *Classical Journal*, 27 (1931), 3–14 |
| Tarlinskaja | Marina Tarlinskaja, *Shakespeare and the Versification of English Drama, 1561–1642* (Farnham: Ashgate, 2014) |
| Turner, 'Folio' | Robert Kean Turner, 'The Folio of 1647', in *The Dramatic Works in the Beaumont and Fletcher Canon*, ed. Fredson Bowers, 10 vols (Cambridge University Press, 1966–96), 1.xxvii–xxxv |
| Turner, 'Introduction' | Robert Kean Turner, '*The False One*: Textual Introduction', in *The Dramatic Works in the Beaumont and Fletcher Canon*, ed. Fredson Bowers, 10 vols (Cambridge University Press, 1966–96), 8.115–21 |
| Turner, 'Printers' | Robert Kean Turner, 'The Printers and the Beaumont and Fletcher Folio of 1647, Section 2', *Studies in Bibliography*, 20 (1967), 35–59 |
| Ulrich | Otto Ulrich, *Die pseudohistorischen Dramen Beaumonts und Fletchers:* Thierry and Theodoret, Valentinian, The Prophetess *und* The False One *und ihre Quellen* (Straßburg: Neuesten Nachrichten, 1913) |
| Vaught | Jennifer C. Vaught, *Masculinity and Emotion in Early Modern English Literature* (Aldershot: Ashgate, 2008) |
| Waith, 'Death of Pompey' | Eugene M. Waith, 'The Death of Pompey: English Style, French Style', in *Shakespeare and Dramatic Tradition*, ed. William R. Elton and William B. Long (Newark, DE: University of Delaware Press, 1989), 276–85 |

| | |
|---|---|
| Waith, *Ideas* | Eugene M. Waith, *Ideas of Greatness: Heroic Drama in England* (London: Routledge and Kegan Paul, 1971) |
| Waith, *Pattern* | Eugene M. Waith, *The Pattern of Tragicomedy in Beaumont and Fletcher* (New Haven, CT: Yale University Press, 1952) |
| Walkington | Thomas Walkington, *The Optic Glass of Humours* (London, 1607) |
| Ward | A. W. Ward, *A History of English Dramatic Literature to the Death of Queen Anne: Volume II* (London: Macmillan, 1875) |
| Weber, 'Introduction' | Henry Weber, 'Introduction' to *The False One*, in *The Works of Beaumont and Fletcher*, 14 vols (Edinburgh: Ballantyne, 1812), 5.3–5 |
| Webster, *Duchess* | John Webster, *The Duchess of Malfi*, ed. Leah S. Marcus (London: Methuen for Arden Shakespeare, 2009) |
| Weir | Robert Weir, 'How Ben Jonson Read his Lucan and his Seneca' (2017, unpublished paper), 1–8 |
| Whitaker | Alexander Whitaker, *Good News from Virginia* (London, 1613) |
| White, 'Light' | Martin White, '"When torchlight made an artificial noon": Light and Darkness in the Indoor Jacobean Theatre', in *Moving Shakespeare Indoors: Performance and Repertoire in the Jacobean Playhouse*, ed. Andrew Gurr and Farah Karim-Cooper (Cambridge University Press, 2014), 115–36 |
| White, 'Unpicking' | Martin White, '"By indirections find directions out": Unpicking Early Modern Stage Directions', in *Stage Directions and Shakespearean Theatre*, ed. Sarah Dustagheer and Gillian Woods (London: Bloomsbury Arden Shakespeare, 2018), 191–211 |
| Wiggins, *Catalogue* | Martin Wiggins, in association with Catherine Richardson, *British Drama, 1533–1642: A Catalogue*, 9 vols (Oxford University Press, 2012–18) |
| Wiggins, *Journeymen* | Martin Wiggins, *Journeymen in Murder: The Assassin in English Renaissance Drama* (Oxford: Clarendon Press, 1990) |
| Williams | Gordon Williams, *A Dictionary of Sexual Language and Imagery in Shakespearean and Stuart Literature*, 3 vols (London: Athlone Press, 1994) |

| | |
|---|---|
| Woolf | Daniel R. Woolf, *The Idea of History in Early Stuart England: Erudition, Ideology, and 'The Light of Truth' from the Accession of James I to the Civil War* (University of Toronto Press, 1990) |
| Wray | Ramona Wray, 'Introduction' to *The Tragedy of Mariam* by Elizabeth Cary (London: Bloomsbury Arden Shakespeare, 2012), 1–69 |

Quotations from all early modern English texts are modernized in spelling and punctuation or are taken from modernized editions. The date limits for all the plays mentioned in this book are those provided by Wiggins, *Catalogue*.

# Introduction

## DATING AND AUTHORSHIP

In the absence of direct evidence, the lower and upper limits for the composition of *The False One* can only be inferred from circumstantial evidence. F2 lists 'The principal actors' of the play: John Lowin, John Underwood, Robert Benfield, Richard Sharpe, Joseph Taylor, Nicholas Tooley, John Rice, and George Birch. This list is generally taken to identify the men and youths who acted the main roles in the play's first performance (albeit with no indication as to who played which character). If that is the case, *The False One* must have been staged for the first time between 1619 and 1623, because Taylor did not join the company until about April 1619 – probably as a replacement for Richard Burbage, who had died in March 1619 – and Tooley died in June 1623. In addition, since no licence for the play is to be found among the extant transcripts of the office-book of Sir Henry Herbert, Master of the Revels (including those of his predecessor, Sir John Astley) – in which most of the plays belonging to the final years of Fletcher's career are included – the upper limit may be reasonably backdated to April 1622.[1]

Within the resulting time frame (April 1619–April 1622), other contextual considerations lead one to single out 1620 as the most probable year for the play's first production – though not, as is sometimes suggested, because that is the year in which a play titled 'The False Friend' was staged.[2] The two titles are in fact unlikely to refer to the same play, given that in *The False One* Septimius does not betray any friends – despite 1 Soldier's couplet right before Septimius' offstage execution: 'Thou dost deserve a worser end, and may / All such conclude so, that their friends betray' (5.3.70–1). As it happens, Septimius first murders his former general, Pompey the Great, and later tries to double-cross Pothinus, who is definitely not his friend.

Martin Wiggins argues that 'Massinger's collaboration with other dramatists in 1619–23, and Fletcher's securely datable work in the same years, leave relatively few slots in which to place the period's undated Massinger–Fletcher collaborations, and 1620 remains the best fit for' *The False One*.[3] Wiggins also observes that the priest

I

Acoreus' line 'The desolations that this great eclipse works' (2.1.61), in which the eclipse stands as a metaphor for Pompey's decline, might be viewed as a pointed allusion to that same year, which witnessed as many as four solar eclipses – even though it is true that references to eclipses are not infrequent in the Fletcher canon.[4]

The 1620 dating also seems to be corroborated by a number of allusions in other plays by the Fletcher–Massinger duo belonging to that same period. In *Sir John Van Olden Barnavelt* (August 1619), the reference to Pompey's beheading by the executioner from Utrecht – 'Look here puppies: / Here's the sword that cut off Pompey's head' (5.2.20–1) – would seem to signal that the two playwrights were already thinking towards their next theatrical undertaking, as *The False One* makes much of Pompey's decapitation, especially in the first two acts (see STAGING ROME, below). In *The Little French Lawyer* (1619–23, probably 1620), the Gentleman mentions Caesar (4.4.62), and La-Writ quotes directly from William Shakespeare's *Julius Caesar* – 'Et tu Brute' (4.6.165) – while Lopez in *Women Pleased* (1619–23, probably 1620) alludes to 'Cleopatra's banquet' (1.2.10). Though the exact chronological order of these plays is admittedly impossible to ascertain, such a rich cluster of allusions does at least appear to indicate a definite proximity among them all, which again makes for 1620 as the most likely year of composition for *The False One*.

This date also chimes with Fletcher and Massinger's likely recourse to Thomas Farnaby's edition of Lucan's *Pharsalia* (1618) and Edmund Bolton's translation of Florus' *Epitome of Roman History* (entered in the Stationers' Register on 19 October 1619 and published soon thereafter) as sources for the play (see SOURCES, below), given that a distinctive trait of Fletcher's playwriting seems to have been the use of recently published books as source material.[5]

Moreover, there is a passage in Thomas Dekker and Massinger's *The Virgin Martyr* (licensed in October 1620) that would seem further to confirm the 1620 dating. In Act 5, scene 2 (unanimously assigned to Massinger), the Emperor Diocletian's daughter Artemia mentions 'great Julius' Caesar (5.2.23), 'Whom war could never tame' (25), as one of the most illustrious victims of love in history in order to warn her future husband Maximinus, Diocletian's co-emperor, against the power of love and the danger represented by 'His bow and arrows' (23). Even though Caesar was 'struck deep in years' (29) when he went to Egypt – and was accordingly supposed to have forgotten 'the lusts of youth' (30) – Artemia continues, at the very moment at which he met 'fair Cleopatra, / A suppliant too, the magic of her eye, / Even in his pride of conquest, took him captive' (31–3).

These lines may be extremely significant because they appear to reference rather accurately what occurs during the first encounter between 'fair Cleopatra' (1.1.26) and 'great Caesar' (2.1.183) in *The False One*, Act 2, scene 3, when Cleopatra kneels in front of Caesar to ask him to 'right [her] as a queen' (2.3.206). Caesar is instantly enraptured by such a 'heavenly vision' (78), calls Cleopatra 'queen of beauty' (139) and declares that, if he did not help her, 'The god of love would clap his angry wings / And from his singing bow let fly those arrows / Headed with burning griefs and pining sorrows' (165–7). After the success of her scheme, Cleopatra comments aside that 'He is my conquest now, and so I'll work him / The conqueror of the world will I lead captive' (170–1). Besides openly recalling *The False One* in terms of stage business, the passage in *The Virgin Martyr* also seems to be reminiscent of Fletcher and Massinger's play in respect of phrasing ('bow', 'arrows', 'fair Cleopatra', 'conquest', 'captive'), which may suggest that Fletcher and Massinger's play had been staged not very long before Dekker and Massinger's, the memory of the earlier play thus being still very much alive in Massinger's mind.[6]

Acts 1 and 5 of *The False One* are usually attributed to Massinger; Acts 2–4 to Fletcher. This is the same arrangement as the one to which the two playwrights resorted in *The Elder Brother* (1615–25). Massinger's contribution to *The False One* was first conjectured by Henry Weber and later confirmed by Cyrus Hoy on such grounds as the presence/absence of Fletcher's typical pronominal *ye*, the use of 'hath' (Massinger) vs 'has' (Fletcher), the preference for either 'them' (Massinger) or ''em' (Fletcher), as well as Fletcher's characteristic recourse to such contractions as 'i'th'', 'o'th'', 'h'as', ''s' (for his), and 'let's'.[7] At all events, despite the stylistic differences between the parts attributed to each playwright, the impression in *The False One* is that one needs to understand this division as based on shares of work rather than on lines of the plot or on sources, such an arrangement indicating a full understanding of the entire play by each writer.

### A BLACKFRIARS PLAY?

Odd as it may sound given the seventeenth-century stage popularity of the plays in the Fletcher canon, no performance records survive

Figure 1 Portrait of John Fletcher, from life, about 1620, oil on oak panel, unknown artist

for *The False One*. F2's list of 'The principal actors' provides no information concerning when and where the play was first acted. A royal warrant dated 12 January 1669 in the Lord Chamberlain's papers lists *The False One* among 108 plays that 'were formerly acted at the Blackfriars' and allotted to Thomas Killigrew for performance by the King's Men at the Theatre Royal, subsequently known as Drury Lane.[8] No other document exists regarding early performances of *The False One*.

As a play in the repertory of the King's Men after 1608 and before 1642, *The False One* was susceptible to being staged both outdoors and indoors. As Sarah Dustagheer argues, dramatic texts written for the company after 1608 can be said to have been 'marked by a performance duality' combining 'practices from both playhouses to produce performances with valuable and distinct spatial resonances at the Globe and Blackfriars, respectively'.[9] Yet, aside from the information in the 1669 note mentioned above and apart from the fact that by 1620 the Blackfriars was clearly the more lucrative venue (so that it would have been more likely for new plays to be aimed at that playhouse rather than the Globe), some features of *The False One* would seem to suggest that Fletcher and Massinger might have conceived the play with the Blackfriars *primarily* in mind.

At first blush, this might seem counter-intuitive against a stereotyped notion of early modern English Roman plays as specimens of theatrical entertainment typically seeking to offer playgoers spectacle on a grand scale, with a full apparatus of large armies, noisy onstage fights, long trains of people following the main characters, and loud sound effects. To be sure, *The False One* features very little of all that. Even though the Prologue clearly positions the play in the repertory of the King's Men as a response and a prequel to Shakespeare's *Julius Caesar* and *Antony and Cleopatra* (see SOURCES, below), *The False One* actually offers a very different kind of spectacle. For one thing, the scope of the play is much narrower: the scene remains in Alexandria throughout, mostly inside the royal palace, to the point that the atmosphere can at times be even felt as claustrophobia-inducing. This would have been especially appropriate at the Blackfriars, where the relatively small stage was encumbered by boxes on either side and frequently hosted (beside the players) the wealthiest members of the audience, who paid an additional fee to sit on stools there. Moreover, the final battle is announced, described, and reported in detail but has very little bearing upon stage business, and there appears to be no resort at all to loud sounds – with the exception of one call of 'trumpets' (2.1.87) – in contrast with the standard practice at the Globe.

Fletcher and Massinger seem to have emphasized in their play elements of performance that can be more readily connected with the Blackfriars, the most important being the 'masque' – as Achillas calls it (4.1.44), with a blatantly anachronistic allusion to the excesses of the Jacobean court – in Act 3, scene 4. The fact that *The False One* contains a masque makes it more likely that the play was devised for indoor performance, given that, after the King's Men started performing at the Blackfriars, masques became particularly prominent in their repertory.[10] In addition, the masque organized by Ptolemy amounts to a private performance for an elite audience made up of Caesar, Cleopatra, and the Roman officers, and should be accordingly viewed as 'a very particular type of exclusive performance that audiences continued to experience on the Blackfriars stage', as Dustagheer remarks.[11] The presence and the implicit destination of the masque, however, are not sufficient on their own to argue that *The False One* was written chiefly for the Blackfriars. In this sense, what seems further to corroborate this hypothesis are the content of the masque, the props employed, and Caesar's reaction to the display of wealth.

The preceding scene creates anticipation for the masque in the audience when Ptolemy boasts to Acoreus, Pothinus, and Achillas that the riches he will show will 'take [Caesar's] *eyes*' (3.3.6, my emphasis), thereby making him forget Cleopatra. Ptolemy has decided that he 'will *dazzle* Caesar with excess of glory' (24, my emphasis), despite Acoreus' recommendation to the contrary: 'Feed not an *eye* that conquers' (17, my emphasis). This scene openly foregrounds the importance of sight in what is about to happen, and the use of the verb 'to dazzle' in particular deserves close scrutiny, having been fruitfully examined by Dustagheer in the context of *The Duchess of Malfi*.[12] Webster's choice of that verb projects enhanced meaning when it is uttered during an indoor, candlelit performance such as the one that inaugurated the Sam Wanamaker Playhouse in 2014. The light of the candles made Ferdinand's eyes literally *dazzle*, thereby fully revealing the extent to which 'the visual aesthetic of candlelight appears woven into the emotion and imagination of [the] text'.[13]

Insights from twenty-first-century revivals to illuminate potential seventeenth-century performance must be used with caution, given the significant temporal and phenomenological gap between early modern playgoing and contemporary revivals of those plays in reconstructed architectural spaces. For one thing, we cannot be sure that Blackfriars performances ever happened in almost complete darkness, given that, as Robert Graves argues in his pioneering study of lighting on early modern stages, 'such evidence as we have indicates the auditoriums were well provided with windows, admitting substantial amounts of sunshine', and there exists 'no specific evidence of windows being closed at the professional indoor theatres'.[14]

More recently, however, Martin White has brought forward a reconsideration of aspects of Graves's work, thereby showing that the operation of the lighting in an indoor playhouse would have been more flexible and more productive of scenic effects than Graves suggests. While Graves sensibly warns that 'we must not think of the stage as a modern showcase where the audience's attention was drawn toward beautiful pictures behind a proscenium frame', White has demonstrated that a well-devised and creative deployment of artificial lighting during indoor performances may have had a significant impact on emphasizing certain elements of staging that would not have emerged as effectively in outdoor playhouses.[15]

In addition, both Dustagheer and White have especially called attention to the fact that in the Jacobean and Caroline periods, both company and wealthy audience would flaunt jewellery and clothing under the candlelight, unlike what occurred at the Globe, 'where jewellery and elaborate clothing depended on catching the irregular sunlight to shimmer', and where 'small props like jewellery also had less visual impact because they appeared on a much larger stage', thereby making the visual display of clothing and jewellery less conspicuous in the repertory of the Globe.[16]

In this sense, if used skilfully, the light of candles at the Blackfriars might have rendered the display of gold and glistening wealth that is central to the masque in *The False One* all the more *dazzling* for both Caesar and the audience, thereby enhancing the effect of the scene and making wealth appear as a much more credible distraction from Cleopatra's beauty. The treasure would have glittered on the stage for the entire duration of the masque, thus making – as Ptolemy had anticipated earlier – 'in that *lustre* / Rome ... appear, in all her famous conquests / And all her riches, of no note unto it' (3.3.8–10, my emphasis). In addition, Caesar's words at the end of the scene – 'The wonder of this wealth so troubles me / I am not well. Goodnight' (3.4.100–1) – would have certainly had much more resonance. A Blackfriars staging might have also rendered Cleopatra's resentment even more evident in her attempt to belittle the masque by lamenting to Arsinoe that Caesar has preferred '*The lustre of a little art ... / And the poor glow-worm light of some faint jewels / Before the life of love and soul of beauty*' (4.2.17–19, my emphasis), since the audience would have known that the light reflected by the treasure had not been faint at all, even if the windows had not been deliberately covered by the company.

On a deeper level of interpretation, the superficial allure of riches and their position in a nexus of materiality, decadence, and corruption as crucial issues tackled in *The False One* (see CRITICAL RECEPTION, below) thematically chime with the 'particularly intense interrogation of the nature of material display, and the vanity and superficiality associated with it', that can be identified as a defining trait of the Blackfriars repertory.[17] As an important part of this materialistic vision for the stage, characters in Blackfriars plays allude to fashion, parade richly decorated clothing, and flaunt jewellery more often than they do in plays primarily devised for the Globe.[18] In this sense, the Blackfriars lighting might have more evidently emphasized Septimius' changes of clothing, which stand for his superficial transformations in terms of attitude and repentance. The light of the candles might have made his rich apparel in Act 3, scene 2, appear even more shining, thus creating a sharp contrast with his all-black attire in Act 4, scene 3.

Another element that might further weigh in on indicating that *The False One* was (principally) a Blackfriars play is the fact that Cleopatra appears not to be black. Joyce Green MacDonald is probably correct in arguing that *The False One* 'skirts the questions of ... racial difference', but Fletcher and Massinger nonetheless include some pointed references to Cleopatra's skin colour.[19] Achillas refers to 'the fair Cleopatra' and then explains that this is 'An attribute not frequent in this climate' (1.1.26–7). Unless the playwrights wanted an Egyptian to imply that female beauty was altogether infrequent in Egypt – which sounds unlikely – one probably needs to interpret Achillas' words as employing an opposition between 'fair' and 'black' that is far from unusual in early modern texts. Scholars have come to different views on the complex relationship between fairness, beauty, and whiteness. Kim F. Hall points out that '"black" in Renaissance discourses is opposed not to "white" but to "beauty" or "fairness"'; Ania Loomba remarks that 'blackness was ... powerfully equated with ugliness and fairness with beauty'; Eva Johanna Holmberg observes that 'In early modern England black skin was the opposite of "fair", white or beautiful.'[20] The most fraught aspect of this discussion is to what extent it may be possible to conflate the notions of whiteness and fairness (and, hence, beauty).

Farah Karim-Cooper argues that 'the terms "fair" and "white" are not always to be taken as interchangeable', inasmuch as 'Paleness or whiteness is one thing as complexions go; however, fairness is quite another. It conveys a lustre that is comparable to silver; ... to be "fair" is to be white and glistening, and to be thus is to be beautiful.'[21] Such a glistening effect, adds Karim-Cooper, could also be obtained through cosmetics. In this respect, Elizabeth Cary's *The Tragedy of Mariam* (1602–09) comes across as a particularly fruitful text to consider. As Ramona Wray argues, 'women are distinguished by, and registered through, a language of physical attractiveness' throughout the play, and physical comparison between them is one of the play's *Leitmotive*.[22] Interestingly, particular emphasis is placed 'on Mariam and Cleopatra as rival players', with the Egyptian queen functioning 'as a foil, one that draws attention to Mariam's manifestation of higher attributes'.[23] Cary's Cleopatra is significantly racialized as black, while 'Mariam is invariably described in terms of lightness and whiteness'.[24] In a play in which beauty is largely conflated with fairness/whiteness, it is therefore especially relevant to realize, as Kimberly Woosley Poitevin points out, that 'the ability of a "black" woman to paint herself fair and the possibility that a naturally "fair" woman may be accused of painting suggest that race and female "virtue" are not essential characteristics but rather performed behaviors'.[25] *The False One*, however, never suggests that Cleopatra's fairness might be artificial – an accusation that is levelled, for example, at Quisara in *The Island Princess*.[26]

At all events, Fletcher and Massinger have Achillas make clear a few lines into the play that this Cleopatra does not have 'a tawny front' (*A&C* 1.1.6) and is not 'with Phoebus' amorous pinches black' (*A&C* 1.5.29) in order to distinguish their Cleopatra from Shakespeare's. Later on, Apollodorus also mentions 'her fair hand' (1.2.10), and Cleopatra herself comments on her first kiss with Caesar by telling him 'You make me blush, sir, / And in that blush interpret me' (2.3.207–8), which again implies that she is not black, given that in the early modern era European writers frequently argued that black people were unable to blush.[27] Finally, Cleopatra disparagingly explains to Apollodorus that 'Caesar is amorous / And taken more with the title of a queen / Than feature or proportion' (1.2.91–3), so much so that he *even* 'loved Eunoë, / A moor' (93–4), which confirms that Cleopatra is not black as well as manifestly racializing the play's idea of female beauty.

Yet Fletcher and Massinger's choice might have even more interestingly depended on the particular playhouse they had mentally chosen for their play. As Lucy Munro points out, 'Recent performances at the Sam Wanamaker Playhouse … suggest that the material conditions of indoor playing and … the use of candlelight pose problems for actors of colour.'[28] In particular, a performance workshop led by Karim-Cooper and Erika Lin (as part of a Shakespeare's Globe festival on 'Shakespeare and Race') concluded 'that a combination of candlelight and dark surrounds makes the features of darker-skinned actors difficult to see, even for spectators sitting near the stage', a problem that might have been aggravated in the Jacobean era given that the skin of actors playing characters of colour would not have been naturally dark but 'dull and artificial'.[29]

As accomplished theatre practitioners, Fletcher and Massinger would have been fully aware of the problem and might have decided against having a black Cleopatra at least partly on the grounds that the light of candles in an indoor playhouse would have had an unsatisfactory effect on artificially blackened skin, insofar as Cleopatra's facial expressions would have been less easily intelligible as a result, thus compromising her connection with playgoers – especially so, for instance, in Act 2, scene 3, when Cleopatra remains silent on stage for as many as fifty-six lines, and the expressions on her face would have therefore been all the more important for an effective performance. In addition, the 'arousing glister of the fair face' (as Karim-Cooper aptly styles it) and the blushes of the boy playing a non-black Cleopatra would have carried much more credibility for the audience as a rival to the dazzling spectacle of the wealth of Egypt offered by Ptolemy that momentarily eclipses Cleopatra in Caesar's eyes.[30] A contrast between the sparkling gold of the Egyptian treasure and the dull, artificial black of a hypothetical Cleopatra of colour would have been excessive and inadequate for the intended effect of the masque.

Although much of the evidence produced is either conjectural or speculative in nature, it cumulatively suggests the likelihood that *The False One* would have leveraged the specific power of the Blackfriars more effectively than that of the Globe – though it would have been easy, for example, to add a battle scene or put more emphasis on different elements of staging for a Globe performance, as one needs to remember that the King's Men continued regularly to transfer plays from one venue to another. That being said, if *The False One* was indeed first performed at the Blackfriars and if the passage about Caesar and Cleopatra in *The Virgin Martyr* discussed above (see DATING AND AUTHORSHIP) does allude to *The False One*, then the window for the first performance of Fletcher and Massinger's play can be narrowed down to the first quarter of 1620.

### STAGING ROME: REPUBLIC AND EMPIRE

*The False One* was not Fletcher's first foray into the dramatization of Roman history. While references to and hints at ancient Rome span Fletcher's entire career, his Roman plays – if we rely on Wiggins's 'best guesses' on their dating – are distributed over a time frame of less than a decade (1614–22): he first wrote *Valentinian* (1610–14, probably 1614) and *Bonduca* (1613–14, probably 1614), and then went back to the matter of Rome in the early 1620s for *The False One* and *The Prophetess* (1622), both co-written with Massinger, who also collaborated with Dekker on *The Virgin Martyr* not long after working with Fletcher on *The False One* (see DATING AND AUTHORSHIP, above). These three plays were Massinger's first collaborative attempts at staging the Roman past; later, he would go on single-handedly to write *The Roman Actor* (1626), *Believe As You List* (1631), and *The Emperor of the East* (1631).[31]

Fletcher's engagement with Roman history seems therefore to have blossomed at the outset of 'the relatively amorphous five-year period (1614–19)' that Wiggins identifies in the playwright's career after he stopped collaborating with Francis Beaumont and Shakespeare.[32] Curiously, none of the plays that Fletcher wrote with Beaumont was set in ancient Rome, nor did the duo produce any kind of history plays in collaboration. All the dramatic writings dealing with historical matters to which Fletcher contributed are either solo works or collaborations with Shakespeare or Massinger: *All Is True, or King Henry VIII* (1611–13, with Shakespeare), *Thierry, King of France, and His Brother Theodoret* (1613–21, with Massinger and an unidentified collaborator), *Rollo, or The Bloody Brother* (1617–20, with an unidentified collaborator), and the aforementioned *Sir John Van Olden Barnavelt*. A few years after the termination of the partnership with Beaumont, Fletcher would find in

Massinger, with the latter's enthusiasm for history and classical antiquity, the perfect coadjutor for the crafting of two more Roman plays, namely *The False One* and *The Prophetess*. Massinger would also bring sixteenth-century Italian history on stage in *The Duke of Milan* (1621–22), though in that case without any pretence to historical accuracy.

None of the Roman plays written by Fletcher and Massinger either together or alone deviate from the dominant Jacobean trend of privileging the dramatization of events belonging to the age of the Roman Empire (27 BCE–476 CE) rather than the Republic (509–27 BCE). In chronological order, they stage Boadicea's revolt and suicide under Nero (61 CE) in *Bonduca*, Domitian's tyranny and relationship with Domitia Longina (71–96 CE) in *The Roman Actor*, Diocletian's rise to the imperial throne and ensuing abandonment of power (284–305 CE) in *The Prophetess*, Dorothea of Caesarea's martyrdom (311 CE) in *The Virgin Martyr*, Theodosius II's marriage with Aelia Eudocia (421–43 CE) in *The Emperor of the East*, and Valentinian III's rape of Lucina and death (455 CE) in *Valentinian*. Since Massinger's *The Bondman* (1623), which is set in the period of the Roman Republic, is in fact about Carthage rather than Rome, *Believe As You List* is the only real exception. Here, Massinger found himself forced to cobble up an imaginative 22-years-later follow-up to the defeat of the King of the Seleucid Empire Antiochus III the Great by the Romans at the Battle of Thermopylae (191 BCE). He had to do so to replace the excessively sensitive topical references that emerged from the original draft of the play-text to the disappearance of King Sebastian of Portugal – who was presumed killed in action in the Battle of Alcàcer Quibir in 1578 but was also said by many to have survived and to have spent the ensuing decades wandering the Mediterranean. These allusions prompted the refusal of the Master of the Revels, Sir Henry Herbert, to license the play. Because Sebastian's absence had paved the way for Spain's annexation of Portugal shortly thereafter, the censor considered the play to be potentially insulting to a Spain with which England had recently signed a peace treaty. Yet, when Massinger resubmitted the play with its setting changed to the ancient Mediterranean and the Portuguese character Sebastian renamed Antiochus, *Believe as You List* was cleared for staging.

In strictly chronological terms, *The False One* deals with the final stage of the Roman Republic (48–47 BCE); in fact, it treats Julius Caesar as an emperor in substance (though not in form): the list of 'The persons represented in the play' in F2 describes him as 'Emperor of Rome'. As a matter of fact, the Renaissance had inherited the medieval misconception that Caesar had been the first Roman emperor, a historical inaccuracy perhaps stemming from a mistranslation of the Latin noun *imperator* ('commander').

The first two acts of *The False One* deal at length with the decapitation of Pompey. Displaying a severed head on stage in late medieval and early modern English drama, argues Margaret E. Owens, 'serves as a striking, unmistakable icon signifying not only the defeat and demise of the victim but, more crucially, the transfer of political power that is often consolidated through this act of violence'.[33] When Septimius brings Pompey's head on stage at the outset of Act 2, it is clear that it symbolizes the death of the Republic and the birth of the Empire. Fletcher and Massinger seem to share Shakespeare's view as illustrated by Paul A. Cantor, who argues that, 'for Shakespeare, Roman as a term of distinction means primarily Republican Roman, and ... with the death of the Republic, true Romanness in Shakespeare's view begins to die also'.[34] As a matter of fact, whenever a positive reference to Rome emerges in Fletcher's and Massinger's plays, it is to the republican period.[35]

In one of the passages that the Master of the Revels, Sir George Buc, marked for deletion in the manuscript of *Sir John Van Olden Barnavelt*, the eponymous protagonist draws an analogy between the Dutch present and the Roman past that would appear to exemplify the view expressed in Fletcher's and Massinger's oeuvre of the momentous institutional shift that was the transition from Republic to Empire and its wide-ranging consequences for Rome:

> Octavius, when he did affect the empire
> And strove to tread upon the neck of Rome
> And all her ancient freedoms, took that course
> That now is practised on you, for, the Catoes
> And all free spirits slain or else proscribed
> That durst have stirred against him, he then seized
> The absolute rule of all. (4.5.190–6)

Fletcher and Massinger resort here to the names of Octavius and Cato as paradigmatic of the well-known political values embodied by the two different forms of government, empire and republic respectively. True *Romanitas*, it would seem, cannot survive under imperial, absolutist rule. The ancient values can be manifested only in the freedom guaranteed by the republic rather than under the control of (mostly evil, as Fletcher's and Massinger's Roman plays suggest) princes. In the opening scene of *The False One*, the Pompeian general Labienus describes Caesar's soldiers at Pharsalus 'as if they had been / So many Caesars and like him ambitious / To tread upon the liberty of Rome' (1.1.208–10), and gives a very specific interpretation of Caesar's decision to attack the senators while forbidding his troops 'To waste their force upon the common soldier' (228):

> Full well he knows that in their blood he was
> To pass to empire and that through their bowels
> He must invade the laws of Rome and give
> A period to the liberty of the world.
> Then fell the Lepidi and the bold Corvini,
> The famed Torquati, Scipios and Marcelli —
> Names, next to Pompey's, most renowned on earth. (231–7)

This speech is closely based on a passage of Lucan's *Pharsalia*, the main source for the play (see SOURCES, below), upon which it draws for the grieved expression of sorrow for the loss of *libertas* that characterized 'the Roman republic, conceived of as a framework of laws and freedom overturned by Caesar's pursuit of *imperium*', as Edward Paleit remarks.[36] In his report, Labienus very clearly identifies Caesar as the man who consciously started Rome's transition to the imperial era and put a full stop to the freedom of the western world, while at the same time destroying a host of noble and virtuous Roman *gentes*, whom Labienus duly lists in his dispiriting war bulletin. The latter actually expands on Lucan by adding the Marcelli, probably owing to Gaius Claudius Marcellus having been consul in 49 BCE when Caesar crossed the Rubicon, as well as being one of the strongest advocates of the Senate taking extreme measures against the general. The Egyptians then discuss at length what to do with Pompey, which strongly suggests that here and in Act 2, scene 1, the head of Pompey is the correlative of the Republic.

This symbolic superimposition of the two acquires even darker implications when the head of Pompey is grotesquely seized in turn by Septimius, Achillas, and Pothinus (the most negative personalities on the Egyptian side), who all hope to be able to use it as a way to enter Caesar's graces. Although their attempt to please Caesar fails miserably, the sight of the severed head of Pompey being carelessly tossed around in the Egyptian court provides a trenchant image of the ultimate fate of the Republic. It is also grimly ironic that in exulting for having managed to behead Pompey, the renegade Roman Septimius employs several rhetorical devices typical of Roman oratory:

> 'Tis here! 'Tis done! Behold, you fearful viewers!
> Shake, and behold the model of the world here,
> The pride and strength! Look, look again: 'tis finished!
> That that whole armies, nay, whole nations,
> Many and mighty kings have been struck blind at
> And fled before, winged with their fears and terrors;
> That steeled war waited on and fortune courted;
> That high-plumed honour built up for her own;
> Behold that mightiness, behold that fierceness,
> Behold that child of war with all his glories
> By this poor hand made breathless! (2.1.1–11)

This is not simply Fletcher's way of dressing Septimius' 'foolish boasts in a kind of pseudoelevated style', as Eugene M. Waith argues.[37] In fact, it is a bleak debasement of Roman rhetoric. The speech opens with a *tricolon crescens* of exclamations on line 1 ("'Tis here! 'Tis done! Behold, you fearful viewers!') and closes with another *tricolon crescens* of imperatives that takes up lines 9–11 ('Behold that mightiness, behold that fierceness, / Behold that child of war with all his glories / By this poor hand made breathless!'), further emphasized by the anaphora of 'behold'. These *tricola* frame the central section of the speech (lines 4–8), which is also based on anaphora ('That ... That ... That...'). Albeit not as rhetorically elaborate and effective as, say, Marullus' speech to the commoners in the opening scene of Shakespeare's *Julius Caesar*, Septimius' speech too employs tropes and techniques characteristic of Roman rhetoric, but it does so perversely, with a view to celebrating not only the orator's own baseness and villainy but, even more discouragingly, the death of Pompey, the last armed champion of the Republic, whose idealization obtains further resonance by his never entering the stage, other than as a decapitated head occupying what Owens describes as 'a disturbingly liminal state somewhere between subject and object status'.[38]

As implied a few lines above, Fletcher and Massinger's stance in *The False One* on the consequences of the transition of Rome from Republic to Empire largely depends on their choice of Lucan as a source, although this does not necessarily mean that the playwrights were somehow advocating a republican alternative to the Jacobean monarchical system (see CRITICAL RECEPTION, below).

SOURCES

*Lucan*

*The False One* is the first work in the history of literature to have been *entirely* based on Caesar's adventures in Egypt and his infamous affair with Cleopatra. Thomas Seward was the first to acknowledge that the play is mainly based on Lucan's epic poem *Pharsalia* (first century CE), Books 6–10.[39] Fletcher and Massinger supplemented Lucan's account – which opens with Caesar's passage across the Rubicon and ends abruptly a little earlier than the famous swimming episode dramatized towards the end of the play (5.4.154–67) – with information drawn from Plutarch's 'Life of Caesar' (and possibly his 'Life of Pompey') in Sir Thomas North's English translation, although it seems impossible to ascertain which edition they consulted. It could have been any of the early ones published in 1579, 1595, 1603, and 1612. The playwrights' most important borrowing from Plutarch is the famous account of Cleopatra's stratagem of having herself smuggled into Caesar's presence wrapped in a rolled mattress or bed-sack (i.e., a type of sack in which slaves kept the bedclothes when not in use) carried by Apollodorus the Sicilian. As will be detailed below, Fletcher and Massinger also seem to have drawn significantly on Florus' *Epitome of Roman History* (second century CE, possibly in Bolton's 1619 translation, as mentioned above); besides, they took a couple of secondary elements from Suetonius' *Lives of the Caesars* (second century CE), either in Latin or in the 1606 English translation by Philemon Holland. A couple of passages also display echoes from Ben Jonson and Tacitus. The details of Fletcher and Massinger's use of sources are given in the Commentary.

In the case of *Pharsalia*, it seems likely that Fletcher and Massinger had at hand Farnaby's 1618 edition, which featured extensive line-by-line commentary in Latin. Paleit has pointed out that it appears clear from a couple of lines in the play – 'through their bowels / He must invade the laws of Rome' (1.1.232–3) – that Fletcher and Massinger were consulting an edition of Lucan featuring the emendation *viscera legum* (i.e., the bowels of the laws) at 7.579 rather than the more frequent *viscera rerum* (i.e., the bowels of things) or the less common *viscera regum* (i.e., the bowels of the monarchs). True,

Fletcher and Massinger could have found the emendation *viscera legum* either in Hugo Grotius' 1614 edition or in Farnaby's, yet it seems more likely, on balance, that they would have used Farnaby's edition for at least three reasons: first, it was the most recent one, which would have appealed to Fletcher's penchant for mining freshly published books for dramatic material; second, it would have been more readily available to them because it had been published in London, whereas Grotius' had been printed in Antwerp; third, Farnaby was a close friend of Jonson's and had given him a copy of his edition of Lucan that is still extant.[40]

Interestingly, as Robert Weir has discovered by examining this copy, 'Across the centre of the title page and straddling the printer's emblem – but also overlying a note by Jonson of Farnaby's gift – is an inscription mentioning that Thomas May got the book from Massinger's personal effects in 1641.'[41] Weir accordingly conjectures that 'Massinger may have bought this volume from Jonson to ease his finances at some point before the fire of 1623' and observes that '[t]he highlighting of Pothinus's advice to Ptolemy in book 8 ... plausibly corresponds to Jonson's poem "A Speech out of Lucan"'.[42] Yet it appears impossible for Jonson to have consulted Farnaby's edition for the writing of 'A Speech out of Lucan', because, as Colin Burrow persuasively argues, the available evidence indicates that Jonson 'worked from a text deriving from Bersman's [1589] edition ... rather than from Grotius's ... or Farnaby's .... This ... suggests that the translation was completed before 1614; a date *c.* 1602–4, when Jonson was working on his similarly literal translation of Horace's *Ars Poetica* is highly probable.'[43]

Was this, then, the copy that Massinger had in front of him while writing *The False One*? Given that Jonson is very unlikely to have used Farnaby's edition for 'A Speech out of Lucan', he may have relinquished his own copy to Massinger prior to 1620, that is, relatively soon after Farnaby had given it to him (but possibly after checking again his own translation against the relevant passage in Book 8). Besides, Jonson had a habit of selling his books whenever he ran short of money, and some of them were sold on to friends.[44] Yet, based on Weir's findings, the book does not seem to feature annotations in the sections on which Fletcher and Massinger drew for their play. Unfortunately, the book itself is stored in a bank vault in the US, which has made it impossible for me to check it in person.

As has been repeatedly pointed out in scholarship, Fletcher and Massinger approached Lucan differently as regards the ways in which each of them carried his Latin into English. As Paulina Kewes remarks, the sections commonly attributed to Massinger (especially Act 1) include 'several set pieces translated verbatim from Lucan's Books VII and VIII that would have been instantly recognizable to anyone with a grammar school education'.[45] These passages exhibit what appears to be a conscious, 'Jonson-like' attempt to reproduce the syntactic structures of Latin as a way to recreate an 'authentic' Roman atmosphere capable of arousing a vivid sense of the immediacy of the Roman past in the audience's imagination. At times, Massinger follows Lucan's Latin so closely that clearly, as Hensman argues, 'he must have worked either with his copy of Lucan open before him, or at least, with notes, excerpts, and/or detailed copies of the main speeches at hand'.[46] The same cannot be said of Fletcher, who reworked what he found in Lucan much more freely, with no concern for the potential recreation of any syntactic movements found in Lucan's Latin. The dialogue itself in the middle acts of the play is seldom modelled tightly after lines from *Pharsalia*. Fletcher's transformative approach to Lucan is on fullest display in the 'masque' of Act 3, scene 4, which is a radical reimagining of Acoreus' description of the sources of the Nile to Caesar in Book 10 of *Pharsalia*.

Fletcher and Massinger's main task with Lucan during the creation of the plot of *The False One* was a process of dramatic compression and simplification. While history recounts that Caesar spent several months in Egypt, the action of *The False One* only occupies a period of a few days. As regards the Alexandrian War, the sources report that, following Caesar's decision to give the kingdom of Egypt jointly to Ptolemy XIII and Cleopatra and that of Cyprus to Arsinoe and her other brother Ptolemy XIV (who is absent from the play), Arsinoe escaped the palace, took command of the Egyptian army, proclaimed herself Queen of Egypt, had Achillas executed, and then besieged the Romans in the palace of Alexandria. Pothinus had already been executed on Caesar's order. Fletcher and Massinger simplify history by having the Romans side with Cleopatra, Ptolemy, and Arsinoe against the Egyptian party led by Achillas and Pothinus until the end of the hostilities. They also present a very submissive Arsinoe, who is never depicted as an active player in the Egyptian political arena. Moreover, Fletcher and Massinger have Caesar himself lead the Roman squad that executes both Pothinus and Achillas at the end of the play, so that their heads can be displayed in the final tableau as deserved punishment for the heinous murder of Pompey that they arranged (see Figure 2).

Figure 2 The Egyptians defeated by the Romans at the end of the play

In other respects, Fletcher and Massinger needed to expand on what they found in their sources, especially in their presentation of the Roman turncoat Septimius and the Roman centurion Scaeva. Lucius Septimius becomes the eponymous villain of the piece (see THE TITLE, below), even though the ancient accounts only report that he had once served Pompey and that, having been left in Alexandria, he had then taken part in the assassination of Pompey and had been punished by Caesar. Nor is his character much developed in either the anonymous *Tragedy of Caesar's Revenge* (published 1606), in which he is called Sempronius (from Appian's *Civil Wars*), or George Chapman's *Caesar and Pompey* (published 1631, though probably written around 1606). Fletcher and Massinger's expansions and alterations all seem intended to portray Septimius as a quintessentially unscrupulous, ungrateful, and false villain, led by purely materialistic motivations, worshipping gold as his only god in a play in which, as Waith remarks, 'contempt of riches is the surest indication of nobility'.[47] Above everything else, in identifying Septimius as the sole murderer of Pompey, the two playwrights seem to have followed Florus rather than Lucan or Plutarch – who both placed Achillas together with Septimius at the crime scene (Plutarch also mentions the centurion Salvius) – with a view to making their villain appear as wicked as possible.

The character of Scaeva also proves to be almost completely the playwrights' own invention. Historically, Marcus Cassius Scaeva was one of Caesar's bravest centurions, who managed to resist the assault of Pompey's legions at the Battle of Dyrrachium though vastly outnumbered, as reported by Caesar in his own *Commentarii de bello civili* (as well as by Lucan and Plutarch). Scaeva's *virtus* and penchant for fighting is indeed alluded to in the play – especially in his impulsive verbal aggressiveness against all things Egyptian – though he is predominantly characterized as a humorously blunt, impetuously loyal, gruffly misogynistic, and pungently ironic counterpoint to Caesar's erotic folly. In serving as the voice of reason for Caesar with such slyness of thought and outspoken sagacity, Fletcher and Massinger's Scaeva emerges as one of the most memorable characters in the play, somewhat redolent of (or even 'a great improvement on') Shakespeare's more celebrated Enobarbus.[48]

The depiction of Caesar and Cleopatra deserves a lengthier discussion and a little detour that by necessity brings up other historical sources too, because the playwrights significantly depart from Lucan, who unequivocally demonizes the lovers throughout his poem. Lucan portrays Caesar as a tyrannical enemy of his own country and Cleopatra as a royal harlot. Although these aspects are not entirely absent from *The False One*, Fletcher and Massinger eschew Lucan's completely negative portrayal of the couple by depicting them with greater nuance as flawed individuals who turn out to be at least partly capable of transcending their own limits and improving as the play progresses.[49]

Even though at the outset of the play the other characters tend to describe Caesar in terms akin to Lucan's poem as an unstoppable, blood-lusting, 'all-conquering' (1.2.70) destroyer of the Roman Republic, it becomes clear from Act 2 onwards that *The False One*'s Caesar is not a one-dimensional villain. For one thing, as Paleit points out, 'Whereas Lucan's protagonist is boastfully regret-free, *The False One*'s Caesar is remorsefully conscious of his criminality.'[50] This is evidenced by Caesar's poignant and heartfelt monologue of Act 2, scene 3, in which he laments the carnage and destruction perpetrated during the conflict against Pompey. It is also particularly significant that Fletcher and Massinger overturn Lucan's account of Caesar's reaction at the sight of Pompey's severed head in *Pharsalia*, 9.1035–108 (see Figure 3). While Lucan describes Caesar's grief and indignation as simulated, *The False One* suggests that Caesar's feelings are sincere. In fact, as John E. Curran, Jr, remarks, 'Lucan's indignation at the effeminate Egyptians and their boy king, as horridly inadequate to doom such a hero as they are to memorialize him, is transferred to Caesar's own mouth.'[51] The only character who sounds sceptical regarding the sincerity of Caesar's tears over Pompey's head is Scaeva, who manages to instil in the audience some doubts about the genuineness of Caesar's sorrow by observing that 'great men may dissemble' (2.1.161). However, this possibility is not endorsed anywhere else in the play, and the other Roman officers who witness the scene, Antony and Dolabella, show no hesitation in taking Caesar's reaction to be sincere. True, the Machiavellian Pothinus claims to be certain that Caesar 'is pleased, and, for all his sorrows, / Which are put on for forms and mere dissemblings, / I am confident he's glad' (2.1.236–8), but his stance is far too partial to be seriously considered. Caesar's passionate tribute over Pompey's head and his wish to commemorate his rival's remains with a solemn funeral ceremony also contribute to making him appear more honourable than his Lucanic counterpart.

That being said, Caesar is still portrayed as a controversial leader, insofar as he turns out to be excessively susceptible to the allure of

Figure 3 Pothinus shows the head of Pompey to Caesar

fleshly pleasures. This weakness makes him undergo a process of emasculation at the hands of Cleopatra, who is here at once the origin and the object of dangerous desire. She is also a cunning schemer, in line with previous depictions of her, at least in the first part of the play. The aside with which she concludes Act 1, scene 2, perfectly epitomizes her opportunistic determination: 'Though I purchase / His grace with loss of my virginity, / It skills not if it bring home majesty' (1.2.104–6). Cleopatra's still-preserved virginity is an unusual albeit historically credible trait, in that her husband-brother Ptolemy was only thirteen when Caesar arrived in Egypt, yet early in the play she hardly figures as an *exemplum* of dignified maidenly virtue, an impression confirmed by the ruse that she devises in order to gain secret access to Caesar's presence. Here, a slight divergence from Plutarch's account is crucial in establishing Cleopatra's agency from the beginning, while at the same time undermining her respectability. Plutarch narrates that Caesar secretly sent for Cleopatra to come to him; in the play, which in this respect partly follows Lucan (10.56–8), it is on her own initiative that she orders her servant Apollodorus to bring her to the unknowing Caesar. As soon as she springs out of the '*packet*' (2.3.61.1SD), Caesar starts to describe her in courtly Petrarchan fashion (102–5). The folly and inappropriateness of such language, which sounds 'mangily, / Poorly and scurvily' in a Roman general's mouth, is immediately censured by the disgusted Scaeva, who does not hesitate to make fun of Caesar's dreamlike amorous rantings, all the more ridiculous because of his age (105–11): Caesar was 52 (and Cleopatra only 21) at the time, and therefore already in 'old age' by Renaissance standards.[52] While Caesar is convinced that Cleopatra is 'a thing divine' (98), Scaeva keeps labelling her as an 'apparition' (79), a 'spirit' (80), a 'tempting devil' (82), a 'damned woman' (90), 'sent to dispossess you of your honour, / A sponge, a sponge to wipe away your victories' (86–7). The image of the sponge is metaphorically deployed with regard to the weakening consequences of immoderate sexual activity and reveals Scaeva's awareness of the danger that Cleopatra's allure embodies for Caesar's martial spirit.

Cleopatra appeals to Caesar's generosity as much as to his masculinity, just as a damsel in distress would conventionally address a noble – and nearly divine, given her choice of words ('sacred', 'holy altar') – knight in a medieval romance (143–55): she begs him to help 'one distressed that flies unto thy justice, / One that lays sacred hold on thy protection / As on a holy altar to preserve me' (136–8).

Complying with the conventions of courtly romance, Caesar explains that a request made by 'A suitor of your sort and blessèd sweetness / That hath adventured thus to see great Caesar / Must never be denied' (160–4) and promises that he will make her the Queen of Egypt again (165–9). In an aside, the ultimate source of which is Lucan (10.65) but which also seems influenced by the portrayal of Caesar as a slave to love offered in Petrarch's *Triumphi*, Cleopatra instantly rejoices at the success of her plan: 'He is my conquest now, and so I'll work him / The conqueror of the world will I lead captive' (2.3.170–1). Caesar may well regard Cleopatra as a goddess, but she looks all too human in the pursuit of her strategy – 'a woman who means business', as Waith would have it.[53]

It does not take long for news of the dangerous liaison to reach the Roman soldiers, who start criticizing and deriding Caesar for forgetting 'his wisdom, / His age and honour' (3.2.10–1) and for being too busy employing his strategic skills not in war but for sex. As Scaeva explains – in a sequence of *doubles entendres* that leave no room for imagination and that frame 'Cleopatra as a besieged city and her suitor more as a rapist/conqueror than a lover', as suggested by Sarah Hatchuel – Caesar's mind is no longer turned to military conflicts, concerned as he is with studying 'her fortifications and her breaches, / And how he may advance his ram to batter / The bulwark of her chastity' (3.2.4–6).[54] The time and energies devoted to sex have dulled Caesar's martial zeal, thereby fulfilling Scaeva's sponge metaphor/prophecy. Rather unsurprisingly in the context of the misogynistic frame of mind that dominated the early modern age, even though Caesar has his own share of responsibility, the blame falls mostly on Cleopatra, a 'tempter' (2.3.182), a 'wanton bane of war, thou gilded lethargy, / In whose embraces ease, the rust of arms, / And pleasure, that makes soldiers poor, inhabits' (186–8). Caesar's feminizing process, however, is not limited to the loss of his self-governance and the softening of his military vigour. Perhaps even more debasingly, he now spends his days writing sonnets, fiddling, and singing.

By offering such a depiction of Caesar, *The False One* dramatizes a set of early modern anxieties regarding the peril of feminization as embodied by erotic relationships infused with excessive passion for all men, but especially for rulers and men of war, insofar as such relationships were perceived as likely to 'disrupt the very ground-work of cultural conceptions that define[d] the essence of masculinity in strict self-discipline and psychic disavowals', as Gary Spear points out.[55] Intemperance and lack of self-governance were considered signs of effeminacy according to a frame of mind borrowed from ancient Greece; a man not sufficiently in control of his pleasures was regarded as feminine, because he was under the power of his own and others' appetites.[56] In *The False One*, these traits are significantly associated with the man often regarded as the mightiest general in history, a choice that intensifies the sense of danger that female sexuality allegedly represented for the military *ethos*, in that it hindered great enterprises and put the greater good at risk for the sake of individual pleasure.[57]

As for the characterization of Cleopatra, it was customary in early modern England to portray women 'as possessed of a powerful, potentially disruptive sexuality', the embodiment of 'the principle of the lower and ferocious power of desire usurping the sovereignty of reason', in Rebecca W. Bushnell's felicitous phrasing.[58] The popular stereotype of the sexually insatiable seductress was pervasive at all levels of literature.[59] The man seduced by a lustful woman placed in jeopardy the well-being of his mind, body, and soul: as a matter of fact, in early modern English the word '*effeminate* could also be used as a verb, meaning to weaken, to corrupt, to cause to degenerate'.[60] In this sense, *The False One* can at least partly be construed as a cautionary tale against intemperance, the consequence of which is a disregard for military activities and matters of state on Caesar's part, which proves to be particularly dangerous for Rome. 'Early modern readers', as Freyja Cox Jensen explains, 'connected the personal failings of the protagonists with their inability to rule well; the question of what made a good prince was inextricably bound up with a ruler's personal virtue', given that 'private sins in rulers were thought to have a detrimental effect upon the entire state they ruled'.[61] This was not a new theme for Fletcher, as numerous examples of tyrants feminized by an excessive indulgence in sensual pleasures and an insane submission to their own urges populate his plays – for example, *The Maid's Tragedy* (1610–11, with Beaumont), *Valentinian*, *A King and No King* (1611, with Beaumont), and *A Wife for a Month* (1624). A few years later, Massinger himself would offer a disturbing portrayal of the tyrant Domitian, crazed by lust and bursting into violence, in *The Roman Actor*.

None of this would suggest that in the second half of the play, after the pivotal 'masque' of Act 3, scene 4, in which Caesar's attraction for Cleopatra is momentarily outshone by his greed for the

Egyptian riches that Ptolemy shows him, Cleopatra could become a positive force for Caesar's redemption. It is to regain her love and admiration that Caesar makes an unexpected and all-important decision: surrounded by the Egyptians, he heroically decides to 'run the hazard: fire the palace / And the rich magazines that neighbour it, / In which the wealth of Egypt is contained' (5.2.78–80), thereby seeking to create a diversion while he tries to open a breach 'to / [His] conquering legions' (84–5). The Savonarola-like act of setting the palace afire with all its riches carries crucial symbolic value, the significance of which is further underlined by a deviation from the historical accounts, none of which report that Caesar had the palace itself burned to the ground, as will be detailed below. This is Fletcher and Massinger's invention and seeks to symbolize Caesar's rejection of material riches and personal profit, and his decision to pursue honour and glory in their stead.[62] It is a veritable bonfire of the vanities that might have even perversely reminded the audience of the destruction of the sumptuous sceneries at the end of Jacobean court masques, given that it is Ptolemy's 'masque' that ultimately prompts Caesar's act.[63]

The complete recovery of Caesar's former masculinity and nobility bears down on the Egyptians like a bolt from the blue. In Achillas' account of the decisive battle, Caesar's martial zeal is hailed as even superior to that of Mars: he is once again a god of war in his destructive splendour, as vividly epitomized by his swim towards Pharos (5.4.157–62). The anecdote is found with slight variations in Plutarch, Suetonius, and Cassius Dio.[64] They all relate that Caesar swam while keeping a parchment roll out of the water so that it would not get wet, but no one mentions a sword. The image of Caesar keeping the roll above the waves while hitting them with his sword – likened to Neptune's trident to underscore the 'divine' connotations of Caesar's power – testifies to the completion of his regeneration; it sharply contrasts with the depiction offered in Shakespeare's *Julius Caesar*, in which the titular character is even said to have had to be saved from drowning by Cassius (*JC* 1.2.102–17).

That credit for Caesar's redemption should go primarily to Cleopatra might appear unreasonable in light of her negative characterization in the first part of the play. Nevertheless, the concluding scenes foreground a very different side of her personality, eventually proving that she is, in Waith's words, 'obviously made of sterner stuff than Shakespeare's heroine, who, for all her courage and all her appreciation of Antony's heroism, is slippery and "riggish"'.[65]

Confronted with the danger embodied by the siege of the palace, Cleopatra turns out to be able to 'stand unmoved' (5.4.15), 'And with a masculine constancy deride / Fortune's worst malice' (18–19), thus displaying dignity, courage, and nobility in the face of potentially imminent death (22–34) and rising as a positive example that infuses courage in her frightened sister Arsinoe (34–7). Cleopatra is stoically willing to die nobly rather than live in shame (139) and has nerve enough disdainfully to address the armed Pothinus: 'I am the mistress of my fate, / ... to confirm it, / I spit at thee and scorn thee ... / I was born to command, and I will die so' (130–2, 134). The queen has such strength of mind that she does not even surrender to tears upon seeing her brother Ptolemy's corpse, shockingly 'trod to death' (168), because only 'common women do so' (137). All in all, Cleopatra's superb exhibition of dignity and fortitude in the play's concluding segment does appear to offset 'her earlier willingness to sleep with [Caesar] in return for political support', as Julia Griffin argues.[66]

In departing significantly from Lucan, the play ultimately seems to suggest that love, when joined with proportion, can be reconciled with martial virtue, because Caesar demonstrates in the end that he can be a soldier, a general, and a man while loving Cleopatra. The reconciliation between Venus and Mars can also be linked to a specific literary vogue of the period, the salient traits of which Jennifer C. Vaught has outlined, observing how English writers tended to combine the emphasis placed in Aristotle's *Nicomachean Ethics* on the possibility of moderating rather than eliminating potentially destructive emotions with the criticism levelled at stoicism in Augustine's *City of God*.[67] Fletcher and Massinger seem to imply not only that a balance can be struck between martial *ethos* and an amorous disposition but also that love can even turn into a positive force and inspire heroic enterprises when joined with measure and temperance, in a sort of Ciceronean moderated indulgence.[68] In fact, as Curran interestingly points out, 'That P[oth]inus is a eunuch means much in the play, for through him sexlessness is connected with Machiavellian maneuvering; the suggestion is that strict self-control and immunity to eros are the province of a false one.'[69]

Nevertheless, one might argue that Caesar's healing seems worryingly incomplete, inasmuch as he needs to destroy those riches in order not to be tempted by them. Moreover, Caesar's last words carry disturbingly tyrannical overtones, which may foreshadow his imminent downgrading of the Senate to a mere office rubber-stamping his decrees, as well as clearly positioning Egypt as client state.⁷⁰ As he proudly tells Cleopatra, 'we'll for Rome, where Caesar / Will show he can give kingdoms, for the Senate, / Thy brother dead, shall willingly decree / The crown of Egypt, that was his, to thee' (5.4.205–8). Here, Fletcher and Massinger seem to hint at a sinister line by Shakespeare's Caesar – 'What is now amiss / That Caesar and *his* Senate must redress?' (*JC* 3.1.31–2, my italics) – in which Caesar shows that he regards the Senate as his property. It is a notion consistent with the words Fletcher and Massinger's Caesar pronounces before setting the palace on fire, claiming that fortune would never allow the man 'she hath led triumphant / Through the whole western world, and *Rome acknowledged / Her sovereign lord*, to end ingloriously / A life admired by all' (5.2.73–6, my emphasis).

A few shadows keep hovering over Cleopatra too. Her conclusive remark reminds the audience of her original motivations: 'He is all honour, / *Nor do I now repent me of my favours*, / Nor can I think nature e'er made a woman / That in her prime deserved him' (5.4.192–5, my emphasis).⁷¹ The primary goal of such an observation, however, appears to be to underline that at the end of this path Caesar, consciously re-masculated, is again worthy of her love (203–4), rather than simply to designate their affair as a straightforward sexual transaction between virginity and crown, as Ira Clark contends. Yet it is undeniable that Cleopatra ultimately obtains what she wanted all along, 'The crown of Egypt' (208).⁷²

## *Florus*

The mention of Florus' *Epitome of Roman History* among the sources of *The False One* requires detailed explanation, as his name does not usually appear in connection with the play despite Otto Ulrich's early twentieth-century intuition, which he, however, did not fully develop.⁷³ Fletcher and Massinger's use of Florus appears evident in a number of passages, and some lexical analogies would even seem to indicate, as mentioned above, that the playwrights used Bolton's translation.

First, as already remarked, like Florus, Fletcher and Massinger identify the renegade Septimius as the sole murderer of Pompey.⁷⁴ Second, in *The False One* Labienus mentions that, after being defeated at Pharsalus, Pompey 'came to Lesbos / And with Cornelia, his wife, and *sons* / He touched upon [Egypt's] shore' (1.1.250–2, my emphasis). Again, the only source to mention both the sons of Pompey (Gnaeus Pompey, also known as Pompey the Younger, and

Sextus Pompey) in this context is Florus' *Epitome*, which highlights the misfortune that 'under the eyes of his wife and children [Pompey] should conclude his days'.[75]

Third, Acoreus brands Septimius as a 'fugitive / From Pompey's army' (1.1.152-3), which may recall Florus' description of him as 'Septimius, [Pompey's] fugitive' in Bolton's translation.[76] Similarly, when Caesar bewails that he, 'That would not brook great Pompey his superior' (5.2.52), now has to tolerate being insulted by the eunuch Pothinus, his deployment of the verb 'to brook' may again signal the playwrights' recourse to Bolton's translation: 'Pompey now was jealous of Caesar's greatness, and Caesar badly endured Pompey's supereminence. The one brooked no equal, the other no superior.'[77] True, this could also come from Lucan (1.125-6) – which would make Fletcher and Massinger's and Bolton's use of the same verb 'brook' a coincidence – but if that were the case, it would be the only borrowing from Book 1 of *Pharsalia* in the entire play, which makes Bolton's Florus more likely as the source of the passage.

Finally, as regards Caesar's aforementioned decision to 'run the hazard: fire the palace / And the rich magazines that neighbour it, / In which the wealth of Egypt is contained' (5.2.78-80), while no source says that Caesar set the palace on fire, Florus' account is nevertheless closer to what occurs in the play, because Florus is the only authority that at least mentions the neighbouring buildings:

> he [i.e., Caesar], being forthwith beset in the palace royal by the same instruments who murdered Pompey, with wondrous valour and a slender company did bear the brunt of a mighty army. For, by firing the next tenements and the arsenal, he dislodged the enemy, who plied him from thence with shot.[78]

Whether Fletcher and Massinger drew upon the *Epitome* in Latin or in English, the fact that they resorted to Florus in the first place ought not to be perceived as particularly unusual. As Jensen argues, 'Florus was a key text in the early modern grammar schools and universities of England'; besides, it was 'the most readily available synopsis of republican history', as Daniel R. Woolf points out.[79]

*Shakespeare*

Many of the plays in the Fletcher canon stand in more or less explicit conversation with those of Shakespeare. As a matter of fact, a few are *defined* against Shakespeare's, as is the case, for example, of *The Woman's Prize, or The Tamer Tamed* (1607–11), the success of which must have at least partly depended on the audience's knowledge of *The Taming of the Shrew*. As I argue elsewhere, Fletcher's diachronic collaboration with Shakespeare emerges as especially important in the Roman plays of the Fletcher canon, insofar as Shakespeare's Roman world apparently becomes for Fletcher and Massinger an integral part of the storehouse of Roman stories, contexts, characters, incidents, and attitudes upon which they could draw in crafting a Roman play for the London commercial stage.[80] Put differently, the Roman plays in the Fletcher canon frequently depict events and personalities of Roman history as filtered through Shakespeare's lens.

Fletcher often puts Shakespeare's Roman plays on the same level as the accounts of the classical historians, to the point of interweaving Shakespeare's dramatic retellings of Roman history with the actual historical accounts in order to infuse his characters with a heightened awareness of themselves and their historical context, as well as spurring reflections in the audience regarding the validity of Roman *exempla*. Far from merely producing a pattern of sophisticated allusions to their predecessor's writings or simply parodying successful plays in the company's repertory, the Shakespearean reminiscences are so woven into the Fletcherian texts as to make those stories part of the characters' memories and have them decisively influence their thoughts, decisions, and actions by bestowing on them a kind of prescience of future events and an increased awareness of both the inward and the outward worlds.

*The False One* is linked both to *Julius Caesar* and (much more closely) *Antony and Cleopatra*. While Fletcher's conversation with Shakespeare's Roman plays spans his entire career, it strikingly intensifies in the 1619–23 period, which seems to show a near obsession with those two plays, ranging from verbal echoes to the re-enactment of theatrical situations.[81] The numerous allusions to *Julius Caesar* and *Antony and Cleopatra* in this period of Fletcher's career might indicate that the two plays had been recently revived on stage – though we have no direct evidence to confirm it. However, as I suggest elsewhere, Fletcher seems to have been especially attracted at this time to previously unpublished plays by Shakespeare (including *The Tempest* and *Coriolanus*), which might have had something to do with the planning and the gathering of texts for the 1623 Folio of *Mr William Shakespeare's Comedies, Histories, & Tragedies* that occurred in the same time span.[82]

The Prologue to *The False One* – which, as Baldwin Maxwell points out, is 'certain [to have been] originally penned for the first production' – expresses the keen awareness that a new play focusing on Caesar and Cleopatra in 1620 would inevitably be expected to reckon with Shakespeare's Roman plays:

> New titles warrant not a play for new,
> The subject being old, and 'tis as true
> Fresh and neat matter may with ease be framed
> Out of their stories that have oft been named
> With glory on the stage. What borrows he
> From him that wrote old Priam's tragedy
> That writes his love to Hecuba? Sure, to tell
> Of Caesar's amorous heats and how he fell
> In the Capitol can never be the same
> To the judicious, nor will such blame
> Those that penned this for barrenness when they find
> Young Cleopatra here and her great mind
> Expressed to the height, with us a maid and free,
> And how he rated her virginity.
> We treat not of what boldness she did die,
> Nor of her fatal love to Antony.
> What we present and offer to your view,
> Upon their faiths, the stage yet never knew.
>  Let reason then first to your wills give laws
>  And after judge of them and of their cause. (Prol. 1–20)[83]

In advertising *The False One* as a sort of prequel to *Julius Caesar* and *Antony and Cleopatra*, the Prologue primarily tries to foreground the novelty and originality of Fletcher and Massinger's play so as to distinguish their theatrical offering from Shakespeare's and thus avoid their being taxed with 'barrenness': *The False One* stages Caesar in love with a young, virginal Cleopatra, something 'the stage yet never knew'.[84] As remarked above, Fletcher and Massinger's Cleopatra also differs from Shakespeare's in that she appears not to be black.

Yet the Prologue's dwelling at length on Fletcher and Massinger's decision not to depict 'how [Caesar] fell / In the Capitol' or 'of what boldness [Cleopatra] did die, / Nor of her fatal love to Antony' spells out their simultaneous desire to build an explicit connection between their play and Shakespeare's. While forewarning playgoers regarding 'what they will not see', the Prologue acknowledges – as Hatchuel argues – that such famous episodes as Caesar's assassination or Cleopatra's suicide 'have already been shown and dramatized in other works', thereby establishing 'a kind of "continuity in dissociation" between the events in *The False One* and those in *Julius Caesar* and *Antony and Cleopatra*'.[85]

This continuity is upheld by many verbal echoes and by the play's alluding to the famously changing moods of Shakespeare's Cleopatra, which Scaeva effectively foregrounds in one of his descriptions of the queen: 'She will be sick, well, sullen, / Merry, coy, overjoyed and seem to die, / All in one half hour, to make an ass of him' (3.2.36–8).[86] In order for their play to fit in a sort of partially shared universe with Shakespeare's tragedies, Fletcher and Massinger have Scaeva offer a condensation of Cleopatra's volatility as staged in *Antony and Cleopatra*; in addition, as illustrated above, they provide in Act 2, scene 3, a full dramatization of the mattress episode reported by Plutarch, thereby developing the passing allusion to it in *Antony and Cleopatra*:

> *Pompey.* ... I have heard Apollodorus carried —
> *Enobarbus.* No more of that. He did so.
> *Pompey.*                                  What, I pray you?
> *Enobarbus.* A certain queen to Caesar in a mattress. (*A&C* 2.6.70–2)

Fletcher and Massinger make this a pivotal scene in the economy of the play, the moment at which Caesar is enthralled by Cleopatra and which determines his successive path of temptation, fall, and regeneration. Fletcher and Massinger's decision to bring this spectacular episode on stage displays their desire to establish a connection with Shakespeare while at the same time setting their own work in programmatic contrast with the majoritarian theatrical tradition by opposing a dazzling birth-like debut for Cleopatra to her far more frequently staged glorious death.

Reflecting on the play's conclusion, Hatchuel notes that, by 'end[ing] after Caesar has overcome all obstacles and escaped death', *The False One* 'comes to compete with Shakespeare's *Julius Caesar*, in which everything leads to, and then departs from, Caesar's demise. Cleopatra's enemies, P[oth]inus and Achillas, plot to rid themselves of Caesar and attack the royal palace, but Julius remains unscathed.'[87] Caesar's ability to thwart a plot against his life would seem to show that he has learned the lesson taught by Shakespeare's *Julius Caesar*, which conversely revolves around the fall of an (almost) completely clueless Caesar in the Senate at the hands of his (alleged) friends. An analogous pattern can be observed in *The False One*'s Caesar's successful break from his overindulgence with Cleopatra and ultimate recovery of his role as military and political leader: in never even thinking of asking Cleopatra to join him on the battlefield, in managing 'These strong Egyptian fetters [to] break' (*A&C* 1.1.112), and in defeating the enemy, this Caesar seems oddly to have learned from the mistakes of Shakespeare's Antony, which he is careful to avoid, thereby finding a comfortable middle ground between the passionate heat of love and the cool rationality required of politics.

Cleopatra too seems at some junctures to be acting in relation to an earlier dramatic instantiation of her own story by having knowledge of what will happen to her in the future when she comments that 'Had I been old / Or blasted in my bud, [Caesar] might have showed / Some shadow of dislike' (4.2.14–16). With these words, she appears eerily to anticipate Antony's insulting her several years later 'as a morsel, cold upon / Dead Caesar's trencher; nay, you were a fragment / Of Cneius Pompey's' (*A&C* 3.1.119–21) – the image of the blasted bud possibly echoing the idea of Cleopatra as a chewed, unappealing leftover of Roman generals. Along the same lines, when Cleopatra, enraged at Caesar because he has ignored her during the masque (distracted as he was by the display of the wealth of Egypt), tells Caesar that she finds 'my soft embraces / And those sweet kisses you called Elysium, / As letters writ in sand, no more remembered' (4.2.118–20), her questioning of Caesar's effusions of love recalls how Shakespeare's Cleopatra expresses doubts about the sincerity of Antony's hyperbolic claims that 'Eternity was in our lips and eyes, / Bliss in our brows' bent; none our parts so poor / But was a race of heaven' (*A&C* 1.3.35–7).

*The Anonymous* Tragedy of Caesar and Pompey, *or* Caesar's Revenge

*The False One* also displays a number of remarkable similarities with the anonymous *Tragedy of Caesar and Pompey, or Caesar's Revenge* (publ. 1606). They seem to suggest that Fletcher and Massinger might have drawn upon it in crafting their own play, despite their assertion in the Prologue that 'What we present and offer to your view / … the stage yet never knew' (Prol. 17–18) – a claim that can be considered true only if restricted to the commercial stage, since the title page of the 1607 edition of *Caesar's Revenge* claims that the play was performed by the students of Trinity College, Oxford.

The first analogy between the two plays is that they happen to be the only two early modern English plays to portray Caesar's affair with Cleopatra.[88] One of the major themes in both plays is Caesar's loss of masculinity, which results from his inability to restrain himself from overindulging in the sensual pleasures offered by Cleopatra. In both plays, Caesar picks up 'unmanly' activities, such as plaiting garlands of flowers for Cleopatra in *Caesar's Revenge* (2.3.898–906), or sonneteering, singing, and fiddling in *The False One* (3.2.25–31). To be sure, these affinities cannot be taken as sufficient proof of Fletcher and Massinger's knowledge of the anonymous tragedy; in fact, they might simply be the independent results of the playwrights' shared interest in the same historical personalities and in issues central to early modern sociocultural debates.

That being said, there are nonetheless a few more specific analogies between the two plays, which would seem to provide more solid evidence for Fletcher and Massinger's acquaintance with *Caesar's Revenge*. First, there are some intriguing verbal parallels. Scaeva's use of the phrase 'imperious looks' (2.3.193) in *The False One* metonymically to describe the power of Cleopatra's seductive wiles might draw on the use of the exact same phrase by Caesar and Antony in two passages of *Caesar's Revenge* (1.4.571, 3.2.1299). Two more turns of phrase are very similar but not identical, namely the Genius's address to Antony, 'Thou woman's soldier, fit for night's assaults' (3.3.1313) in *Caesar's Revenge*, compared to Scaeva's description of Caesar as 'Grown now a woman's warrior' (3.2.3) and engaged in 'women's wars' (2.3.126) in *The False One*.

Second, both plays share features of the heroic romance. In this respect, the most notable analogies are Caesar's and Antony's use of Petrarchan courtly language to address Cleopatra and express their feelings, and the emphasis on Caesar's inability to refuse to aid the damsel in distress who is pleading for his help when they first meet, even though the words Caesar uses in the two plays are not the same (*Caesar's Revenge*, 1.4.482–9; *The False One*, 2.3.155–69).

It might be objected, however, that the verbal parallels are an inevitable consequence of the similar stance assumed by the different writers towards their material and that the romance-like features shared by the plays simply stem from the fact that the poets were influenced by the same literary tradition. Yet three further analogies would appear to weigh in favour of the existence of a direct relationship between the two plays, in that they entail some major alterations of the historical record.

First, both plays feature a scene displaying Caesar's expression of remorse and grief over the destruction and the deaths of fellow citizens brought about by the civil war after his victory at Pharsalus (*Caesar's Revenge*, 1.1.221–31, 255–67, 288–306; *The False One*, 2.3.29–59). The words used in the two pieces bear no particular verbal affinity – except for the deployment of the noun phrase 'tender breast' in *Caesar's Revenge* (1.2.226) and 'tender womb' in *The False One* (2.3.38) to describe Rome as a nursing mother – but Caesar's repentance over the civil conflict is an episode that is nowhere to be found in the historical sources.[89] This means either that the anonymous author and the Fletcher and Massinger duo had the same idea independently – possible, but unlikely – or that the latter drew on the former.

Second, in both plays Caesar is in Egypt with Antony and Dolabella. Yet historically Dolabella's relationship with Antony was not friendly but fraught with tension; more importantly, Dolabella did not follow Caesar to Alexandria. Again, it is striking that two different plays share such a specific deviation from the historical records.

Third, in both plays Antony meets Cleopatra for the first time while in Egypt with Caesar – which is historically untrue – and in both cases he seems to fall in love with her. His attraction to her in *The False One* is only incipient and certainly less blatant than in *Caesar's Revenge*; besides, as Hatchuel observes, in contrast with *Caesar's Revenge*, '*The False One* does not stage a meeting that involves both Caesar and Mark Antony. Nevertheless, the process of mimetic desire is dramatized when Antony, during a discussion with Dolabella and Sc[a]eva, defends Caesar for doting on Cleopatra with such intensity' that 'Antony's future devotion for Cleopatra is anticipated in his admiration for the Egyptian queen and his ardent defence of Caesar', and Cleopatra's charm is further emphasized.[90]

These last three similarities between the two plays seem to me rather difficult to explain away as the work of mere chance: they are three specific deviations from the historical accounts that appear in two plays that also have different main sources as the foundations of their plots, namely Appian's *Civil Wars* for *Caesar's Revenge* and Lucan's *Pharsalia* for *The False One*. As early as 1910, Harry

Morgan Ayres hinted at a few – unspecified – 'slight resemblances' between the two plays but dismissed them as 'almost undoubtedly fortuitous'.[91] In light of the parallels illustrated above, *pace* Ayres, it is at least plausible that Fletcher and Massinger sifted through *Caesar's Revenge* and mined it for ideas to deploy in their own take on the Caesar–Cleopatra liaison.

*Innocent Gentillet*

It was Bertha Hensman who first proposed as a source for *The False One* Innocent Gentillet's *Discours sur les moyens de bien gouverner (Anti-Machiavel) et maintenir en bonne paix un royaume ou autre principauté, divisé en trois parties, a savoir, du Conseil, de la Religion & de la Police que doit tenir un Prince. Contre Nicolas Machiavel* (1576), translated by Simon Patrick as *A Discourse upon the Means of Well Governing and Maintaining in Good Peace a Kingdom or Other Principality* (1602, repr. 1608). Hensman claimed that Massinger had certainly consulted Gentillet because 'at the beginning of Act I, he gives, in relationship to Cleopatra, a synopsis of the Salic Laws of which a succinct summary is given in the introduction to' Gentillet's work; in addition, Hensman argued that Gentillet was 'Massinger's chief supplementary source ... also for the Ptolemy–Pothinus plot in Act V'.[92] Scholars seem to have accepted Hensman's suggestion unquestioningly, the only one to express reservations being Robert K. Turner, who observes that 'Gentillet's story of Egyptian scheming and the plot details of the play are not very close'.[93]

A fresh examination of the passage of Gentillet's book singled out by Hensman as a source for the play confirms Turner's view that the two share very few similarities. Moreover, the first segment of the conversation between Acoreus and Achillas that opens the play (1.1.1–34) does not provide any description of the Salic Law but rather illustrates Ptolemy and Pothinus' breach of the Egyptian custom of *not* preventing female heirs from ascending the throne, which is in fact the opposite of the Salic Law, according to which women *were excluded* from inheriting thrones. Yet it is true that none of the ancient authorities report that it was Pothinus and Achillas together who presented Caesar with Pompey's head upon his arrival, whereas Gentillet's account reads: 'Caesar soon after arrived in Egypt, unto whom Pothinus and Achillas presented the head of Pompey, thinking greatly to pleasure him.'[94] Albeit tenuous, this is a valid link and might indeed signal that Fletcher and Massinger did at least have a look at *A Discourse upon the Means of Well Governing* while writing *The False One*.

### THE TITLE

Taken by itself, the title of the play is rather cryptic and would make it impossible for anyone to guess what *The False One* were about if the play-text had not survived to this day. Sometimes puzzled by such an enigmatic title, editors and critics have suggested different possible identifications of the eponymous 'false one'. Among others, John Monck Mason believed that Cleopatra could not be 'the false one' because, 'though haughty, ambitious, and unchaste, [she] is free from falseness'; nor could 'the false one' be one of the 'subordinate characters', that is, Pothinus, Achillas, or Septimius.[95] By inference, then, 'the false one' had to be Caesar, as spelled out more fully by Weber, who thought that 'the scene where [Caesar] is seduced from the affection of Cleopatra by the riches displayed by her brother' exhibits his falsity; at all events, Weber also acknowledged that 'the false one' might well have been Septimius.[96] A. W. Ward was instead confident that the title of the play was a 'reference ... to the wiles of the serpent of old Nile, and not any other of the characters of the drama, though Septimius might be held to have a good claim'.[97] More recently, MacDonald has suggested that 'Cleopatra is perhaps the false one of the title, willing to sacrifice her virginity to Caesar in order to secure her position on the Egyptian throne'.[98]

Even though it is true that several characters are revealed to have been more or less 'false' at some point in the play – as Wiggins succinctly puts it, 'Ptolemy consents to the murder of his guardian, Pompey; Caesar knows his treason caused the civil war, and is temporarily unfaithful to Cleopatra out of avarice; and P[oth]inus rebels against his King' – the critical consensus now seems to be that 'the false one' is Septimius.[99] Even though he is not a high-ranking character, unlike Caesar or Cleopatra, it must be kept in mind that Fletcher and Massinger significantly expanded his role in the story (see SOURCES, above), thus bestowing on him an unhistorical prominence that appears consonant with their decision to name the play after him.

Septimius is repeatedly associated with the notion of falseness in the course of the play. Examples abound: in their first conversation, Acoreus reminds Septimius that 'Truth needs ... no oaths' (1.1.85);

Septimius himself says that he is ready to murder 'A mother or a sister' (2.2.43) or 'to betray a noble friend' (44); Cleopatra's maid Eros places Septimius in the category of 'base betrayers of those men that fed 'em' (3.2.144), which later prompts him to identify himself as 'a traitor and betrayer' (213); when Septimius (apparently) repents of his crimes, he warns the three lame soldiers not to follow his example but to 'take heed of falsehood' (4.3.34); finally, upon resolving to betray Pothinus, Septimius openly acknowledges that 'I in my nature / Was fashioned to be false' (5.3.12-13); Antony later insults him by telling him that he has a mouth 'That never belched but blasphemy and treason / On festival days' (5.3.32-3) and that 'There's no doubt, then, / Thou wilt be false' (39-40).

Hatchuel has advanced a very different interpretation of the title. She argues that it might refer

> not to a character but to the play itself. Written some fifteen years after Shakespeare's *Antony and Cleopatra*, Fletcher and Massinger's *The False One* may introduce itself by openly referring to Shakespeare's original and 'true' work. Through its title, the play immediately claims that it will not follow Shakespeare's plot and that spectators expecting the same kind of material will only deceive themselves. This agenda clearly appears in the Prologue to the play.[100]

Albeit admittedly thought-provoking, Hatchuel's suggestion is not entirely persuasive. For one thing, there is hardly any other title in the entire Fletcher canon that could be said to serve the same function, which would make *The False One* oddly eccentric within a very large corpus of about fifty plays. Second, whereas, as remarked above, the Prologue clearly frames *The False One* as an attempt to offer the audience a different kind of play while still following Shakespeare's path, nothing in the Prologue itself implies that Fletcher and Massinger went so far as to consider Shakespeare's *Julius Caesar* and *Antony and Cleopatra* 'original and "true"' works, while regarding their own, by implication, as derivative and 'false'. In fact, the Prologue oozes with pride at their success in writing a play on familiar topics and characters without aping anyone else's work, which will protect them from any accusations of 'barrenness' (Prol. 11). Finally, if Fletcher and Massinger did feel that they needed a title that would so explicitly connect their own play with Shakespeare's in the eye of the audience as Hatchuel implies, they (or the company) could have more easily opted for a much simpler 'Caesar and Cleopatra' or 'Julius Caesar and Cleopatra'. Such a straightforward title would have far more readily advertised the play's link with

INTRODUCTION 39

Shakespeare's, as was the case with the alternative title of *The Woman's Prize*, that is, *The Tamer Tamed*, which made the Shakespeare–Fletcher connection much more evident by means of openly recalling *The Taming of the Shrew*.

CRITICAL RECEPTION

*Aesthetic judgements*
Notwithstanding the debate regarding its title, the play did not attract much serious critical attention until the end of the twentieth century. In addition, responses to *The False One* before then were highly polarized. Positive judgements came especially from William Hazlitt and from three among the eighteenth- and nineteenth-century editors of the play. For Hazlitt, *The False One* was the play in the canon to come 'nearest in style and manner to Shak[e]speare, not excepting the first act of *The Two Noble Kinsmen*'.[101] Thomas Seward argued that '*Rollo* and *The False One* are two of Fletcher's first-rate plays' and regarded *The False One* as 'a noble emulation of' *Antony and Cleopatra*, 'and the hand as difficult to be distinguished from Shakespear[e]'s, as the works of the very best scholars of Titian and Guido are from those of their masters'.[102] Alexander Dyce believed that 'The portrait of Caesar is equal, if not superior, to any of the representations of him by other dramatists.'[103] In Henry Weber's view, *The False One* was even superior to Shakespeare's *Antony and Cleopatra* 'in point of unity of action and regularity of plot', and he thought that the play had 'such sterling merit, that its utter neglect for many years past must be deplored as another instance of the little attention at present paid to these invaluable treasures of dramatic excellence'.[104] E. H. C. Oliphant regarded *The False One* as an 'admirable tragedy, which has never had justice done it, because it enters into competition with work of Shakespeare's'.[105]

On the opposite side of the fence, it will suffice to quote William W. Appleton and Eugene M. Waith, whose assessments from as late as the 1950s can be taken as representative. For Appleton, *The False One* 'is conceived of in terms that would have appealed to Tiepolo, whose Labia Palace frescoes of Cleopatra evoke much the same atmosphere. The display is sumptuous, the appeal highly theatrical, but it is postured and superficial.'[106] Even worse,

> If *All for Love* represents the *rigor mortis* of tragedy, in *The False One* its death throes have already begun. There is a chill dignity to Massinger's

first and last acts, but neither the magnificence of Fletcher's masque of Nilus nor the rapidity of the action can conceal the play's essential hollowness, its dangerously oversimplified concept of character and situation.[107]

Waith held a similar opinion regarding the alleged superficiality of the play. He argued that '*The False One* seems to pretend to more than it in fact possesses. Its great moments are hollow in spite of every merit.'[108] For Waith, the main problem was that 'the meaning of honor in the play is extremely vague' and 'closely associated with nobility, that other indefinable quality constantly referred to', the 'breadth and haziness' of which concepts made the tragedy 'disappointing'.[109] As a result, Waith concluded that, albeit '[i]nteresting as a link in the development of heroic drama', *The False One* was 'an artistic failure'.[110]

Almost forty years later, however, Waith appeared radically to have changed his mind. Discussing the play again, he wrote that 'It has spectacle, humor, and a greater range of characterization, though every dramatic device is made to serve the play's serious purpose. Expert craftsmanship makes *The False One* a successful, and occasionally even brilliant, play in the Elizabethan mode.'[111] As it happens, Waith's shift in opinion appears to have paved the way for a number of fresh critical takes on *The False One* that will be surveyed in the ensuing section. Scholars have attempted to root the play more firmly in the political context of its first appearance, thereby foregrounding several compelling aspects that had gone largely unnoticed before and contributing as a result to a more favourable overall critical reception.

*Courtiers, Peace, and Empire:* The False One *and Jacobean Politics*

Like other Roman plays of the period, those by Fletcher and Massinger often comment frankly upon such touchy Jacobean issues as absolutism and the limits of the monarch's authority; tyranny and the devastating consequences of tyrannicide; rape and its nefarious repercussions on the individual, the family, and society; and empire and the continued, manifold relevance of the Roman conquests to contemporary foreign and domestic policies. *The False One* is no exception. Fletcher's often critical stance on Jacobean policy was also reflected in his close relationship with his patron Henry Hastings, fifth Earl of Huntingdon. Fletcher seems to have shared the Earl's country-based politics and 'pastoral, anticourt, Protestant [and] anti-Spanish' views, as reflected in the attitude of some of his own plays.[112] As it happens, the earl's sister, Lady Katherine Stanhope, who shared her brother's political outlook, was Massinger's first known patron. Scepticism over James's pacifist policy and pro-Spanish attitude were also issues dear to the heart of William Herbert, third Earl of Pembroke, and his brother Philip, Earl of Montgomery, to whom Massinger presented a bid for patronage as early as 1615, eventually obtaining at least Philip's favour around 1623.

The first scholar to discuss the potential topical resonances of *The False One* was Maxwell, who proposed to interpret the expanded treatment of Septimius in the play as intended to be a veiled allusion to the story of Sir Lewis Stukeley. As James wanted to appease Spain by executing Sir Walter Ralegh, who had infringed the Spanish monopoly in South America, thus compromising the monarch's avowed policy of international peace, the King deployed Stukeley as his instrument in arresting and then having Ralegh executed in 1618. A large section of the English people, who loved Ralegh (and could not attack the King), ended up directing their hatred and anger against 'Judas' Stukeley, whose company was apparently shunned by everyone at court after the deed, and who died in 1620. Maxwell highlights the correspondences between history and fiction as follows: 'Septimius (Stukeley), a Roman (Englishman), at the instigation of Egyptians (Spaniards) and in the hope of reward from Caesar (James), treacherously causes the death of a compatriot and former friend, Pompey (Ralegh), and for his treachery is condemned and despised by all.'[113]

Wiggins rejects Maxwell's argument as 'flawed in two respects': first, Maxwell regards Septimius as an utterly execrable character by ignoring his temporary repentance; second, 'Maxwell does not consider the fact that, as a hired murderer, Septimius is a character in a long tradition', which would have made the audience more readily alert to the similarities between Septimius and the assassins that populate John Webster's tragedies, namely *The White Devil*'s Flamineo and *The Duchess of Malfi*'s Bosola, rather than those between Septimius and Stukeley.[114] In Wiggins's view, Fletcher and Massinger were simply 'tak[ing] advantage of the novel elements in Webster's work' in order 'to cash in on their predecessor's success'.[115]

Wiggins has a point, yet Maxwell does not argue that Fletcher and Massinger *modelled* the story of Septimius after that of Stukeley;

he suggests that, given the popular early modern interest in the extent to which ingratitude might ruin the political hierarchy, the playmakers might have more obliquely 'chose[n] a theme by which they could take advantage of a recent [...] scandal' without arousing any suspicions from the Master of the Revels.[116] Besides, the fact that the characterization of Septimius was influenced by Webster's Flamineo and Bosola does not necessarily exclude simultaneous glances towards contemporary political events. Moreover, the fact that *Sir John Van Olden Barnavelt* was partly meant to allude to Ralegh's death does lend at least a certain degree of plausibility to Maxwell's interpretation.[117] That being said, discussions of the play's engagement with the events of the early 1620s seem more convincing.

1620 was a crucial year for the Jacobean reign. The Elector Palatine Frederick V, who had become James's son-in-law by marrying his daughter Elizabeth in 1613, accepted the crown that had been offered to him by the Protestant nobles of Bohemia, thus defying the Holy Roman Empire. Defeated by Ferdinand II Habsburg at the Battle of White Mountain, Frederick was expelled from Bohemia as well as from his native Palatinate. This was the beginning of what was possibly the worst crisis of James's reign. The fact that James's Protestant daughter and son-in-law had been exiled by the Catholic Habsburgs could not but make his Hispanophile and pacifist attitude even less popular than before, all the more so in light of his current plans to marry his son Charles to the Spanish Infanta. The situation would become even worse for James when the Spanish army invaded the Palatinate in 1621.

While specifying that '*The False One* is not a straightforward political allegory', Kewes suggests that 'To dramatize the fate of the exiled Pompey was surely a deliberate reminder of the fate of another heroic exile, Frederick Elector Palatine', but she does not develop the argument significantly.[118] From a similar standpoint, Marina Hila argues that 'the play is a response to the contemporary controversy surrounding King James's pacifist and Hispanophile foreign policy, echoing the concerns voiced in the anti-Spanish, anti-Catholic pamphlets of the early 1620s'.[119] These pamphlets especially criticized the peace established by James as misguided and 'false', inasmuch as it was not based 'on honour, reciprocal trust, and military preparedness', but 'on unnecessary concessions and a degenerate desire to suffer all for "peace and quiet", which enemies are quick to take advantage of'.[120] James's pacifism was strikingly at odds with the bellicose image the English had of their own country: a foreign policy inspired by the motto *Beati pacifici* made the nation appear to their eye effeminate, weak, and, consequently, more vulnerable to foreign attacks.

At all events, by customarily deploying parallels and correspondences in order 'to generate chains of political associations, rather than individual matches which would be hard to disclaim', in Hila's view the play associates Ptolemy with James 'in his excessive reliance on minions, his predilection for peace and security at any cost, and his use of betrayal as a diplomatic tool. On the other hand, the emasculating effect of peace and sexual pleasure as well as the neglect of national defence are displaced onto Caesar.'[121] Besides, in depicting Ptolemy as a weak, childish king led astray by an all-too-powerful favourite and incapable of handling power as he should, *The False One* broadly meditates on Jacobean politics 'at a time when James had essentially relinquished control of the government to Buckingham', even though the play never posits a one-to-one correspondence between the latter and Pothinus.[122]

Finally, argues Hila, the play also reflects on the popular perception of the proposed Spanish match as an impending threat to England by dramatizing 'the conquest of a nation taking place through feminine control', insofar as 'Cleopatra is a woman who comes complete with her own kingdom, and is aware that she can influence Caesar' by relying 'on her feminine charm' in order to sap his energy through sex, 'so that he quickly loses his martial spirit and becomes effeminate', while Cleopatra's 'masculine constancy' (5.4.18) increases.[123] 'Criticism of foreign policy is thus carefully concealed behind the discourse of misogyny', concludes Hila, in that Caesar is to be blamed as a ruler because he 'neglects the masculine duty of territorial expansion for the individualistic pleasures of his sexual desire for Cleopatra'.[124]

By focusing on certain translation choices made by the playwrights in drawing upon *Pharsalia*, Paleit contends that *The False One* deploys Lucan in order 'to create a resonant historical context for its exploration of courtly vice, overweening ambition, and the dangers of regal absolutism and reason of state', even though the play's 'ability to formulate remedies or alternatives to the ills it diagnoses is limited'.[125] One particularly meaningful example is the expansion of Lucan's *Sceptrorum vis tota* (8.489; i.e., all the power of kings) into 'All the power, / Prerogatives and greatness of a prince' (1.1.307–8) in the speech with which Pothinus convinces

Ptolemy to have Pompey killed. As Paleit points out, 'The word "prerogatives" – areas of discretion outside or above the law – has no clear Roman provenance and derives rather from contemporary English debates concerning the extent of monarchical power', thus alluding to 'a resistance to legal absolutism which was to become more pronounced in Massinger's *The Roman Actor*'.[126] The deployment of this term is especially significant because the Machiavellian Pothinus is implying that 'exercising a royal prerogative necessarily demands rejection of "what's right" [1.1.310]'.[127] *Ragion di stato* is thus conflated with court corruption and ultimately confuted, because the play clearly 'suggests that murdering Pompey has been neither honest *nor* useful'.[128]

That being said, however, Paleit observes that *The False One* should not be seen as a text that is especially critical of the establishment, as it does not offer any radical alternatives but only seems to advocate a system keen 'on containing vices within a relatively stable, hierarchical political order assumed ... to rest on the order of nature'.[129] As a matter of fact, all such potentially 'radical' arguments as the claim that 'kingship rests simply on an originary act of violence or the exercise of brute power' come from Pothinus, thus losing any positive value.[130] *The False One*, adds Paleit, does not advocate an alternative system of government either – not even implicitly – despite the clearly 'sympathetic response to the *Bellum Civile*'s treatment of the loss of republican *libertas*', as demonstrated by the fact that 'the most explicit denunciation of Caesar ... is assigned not to a Roman or even a loyal Egyptian, but the perfidious courtier P[oth]inus after his rebellion against his master's authority'.[131]

Another issue with which the play grapples is that of empire, which Fletcher had already tackled in *Bonduca* and would tackle again in *The Island Princess* (1619–21) and *The Sea Voyage* (1623, with Massinger). As I have argued elsewhere, in *The False One* Fletcher and Massinger seem to foreground Caesar's attraction to material riches in order to voice a series of perplexities raised by British colonial ventures in the New World.[132] In England more than anywhere else, colonizing projects were long dominated by the humanist imagination.[133] As Andrew Fitzmaurice argues, 'humanists were deeply sceptical of profit and nervous of foreign possession at the same time that they saw both as possible sources of glory'.[134] The conceptual framework informing British colonial theory at the time was largely borrowed from classical authorities including Cicero, Sallust, Livy, Tacitus, Juvenal, Quintilian, and Seneca. They showed that the luxury of Rome's Eastern colonies had been a source of feminizing influence as well as the main cause of the decline in martial virtues, the fall of the Republic, and the rise of tyranny. Looking at their own encounters with the New World in light of the experience of Rome, humanists voiced their fears that the inflow of superfluous wealth from the conquered territories might end up weakening the English just as Asiatic riches had enfeebled the warlike temper of the ancient Romans – even though English colonizing projects were persistently unsuccessful in this period, consuming rather than producing resources, through to the first quarter of the seventeenth century.[135]

The depiction of Caesar's greed, lack of self-governance and their consequences in *The False One* is therefore meant to channel this set of anxieties, all the more so given that courage and temperance – which Caesar momentarily loses – were viewed in the early modern imagination as the necessary qualities to overcome disaster and achieve a balance between honour and profit. The crucial segment of the play in which Caesar's love for luxury comes to the fore is the dazzling exhibition of 'the glory / And wealth of Egypt' (3.3.7–8) during the masque in Act 3, scene 4. Caesar's attraction to riches is so unwholesome that he has to leave the room abruptly after crying 'The wonder of this wealth so troubles me / I am not well. Goodnight' (3.4.100–1). In epitomizing the idea of luxury both as a category of infectious goods and as powerful spectacle, the masque represents a decisive turning point in the play. Right in the middle of the show, Caesar, flabbergasted at the sight of the infinite Egyptian riches, proclaims himself ashamed for having embarked on a bloody civil conflict against Pompey when he could have easily taken hold of such staggering sums abroad. He cries out

> I am ashamed I warred at home, my friends,
> When such wealth may be got abroad. What honour,
> Nay, everlasting glory had Rome purchased,
> Had she a just cause but to visit Egypt! (3.4.77–80)

Caesar's words acquire especially bleak overtones for at least two reasons. First, it is possible that Fletcher and Massinger wanted to hint at the now controversial lines of Shakespeare's *Julius Caesar* – 'Know Caesar doth not wrong but with *just cause*, / Nor without cause will he be satisfied' – not as they appear in Shakespeare's First Folio, but as they are mockingly cited in Jonson's *Discoveries* (1641,

480–1) and *The Staple of News* (1626, 6.15–157), and as they have been integrated into the text in the Oxford editions of Shakespeare's complete works since 1986.[136] Fletcher and Massinger might well have chosen a line uttered by Shakespeare's Caesar that had impressed them and stayed with them since they had first heard it, and inserted it at a defining moment in their play. They might have thought that such an allusion – oblique as it is – would hardly escape the most attentive playgoers, who would easily be able to identify the reference to the 'just cause' flaunted by Shakespeare's Caesar. Foregrounding the idea that all Caesar would have needed in order to plunder Egypt without restraint was to find – or, perhaps, to invent – a 'just cause' (like the one Shakespeare's Caesar maintained always to have on his side when 'doing wrong') would set the shamelessly predatory stance of Fletcher and Massinger's Caesar in quite a grim light.

Second, Caesar's exclamation has to be read in the light of an earlier soliloquy, in which he shows no regret for the massacres of foreign populations:

> I am dull and heavy, yet I cannot sleep.
> How happy was I in my lawful wars
> In Germany and Gaul and Britany,
> When every night with pleasure I set down
> What the day ministered! Then sleep came sweetly.
> But since I undertook this home division,
> This civil war, and passed the Rubicon,
> What have I done that speaks an ancient Roman,
> A good, great man? (2.3.29–37)

In the lines that follow, Caesar goes on to express his remorse over the carnage and destruction brought about by internecine strife but shows no regret for the destruction and pillaging of foreign countries and populations: in fact, he considers them absolutely 'lawful'. Combined with Caesar's words during the masque, this soliloquy decisively contributes to casting a negative light on his rapacious and violent expansionism, which is also subjected to harsh criticism by Pothinus and Septimius. Pothinus contemptuously suggests that 'The glebe of empire must be ... manured [in blood]' (5.2.11), while Septimius cynically remarks that the desire to take hold of other peoples' possessions has been inscribed in the Roman people's genetic inheritance since the very foundation of the city:

> Rome, that from Romulus first took her name,
> Had her walls watered with a crimson shower

Drained from a brother's heart; nor was she raised
To this prodigious height that overlooks
Three full parts of the earth that pay her tribute
But by enlarging of her narrow bounds
By the sack of neighbour cities, ne'er made hers
Till they were cemented with the blood of those
That did possess 'em. (5.2.12–20)

Here, Septimius stresses the fact that Roman glory is built on gore and fratricide rather than nobility – blood being metaphorically equated to cement, the material for the actual construction of the city – and maintained through rapine and violence. It is true that Pothinus and Septimius are biased against Caesar and that they are two very despicable characters. Nonetheless, Septimius' words chime with Acoreus' warning to Ptolemy before the masque that there are two main reasons why 'Rome ever raised her mighty armies: / First, for ambition; then, for wealth' (3.3.14–15), and with his later comment to the King that 'I advised your majesty / Never to tempt a conquering guest nor add / A bait to catch a mind bent by his trade / To make the whole world his' (4.1.3–6). Septimius' attack against Rome is also consonant with Achillas' report to Ptolemy that, 'since the masque, [Caesar] sent three of his captains, / Ambitious as himself, to view again / The glory of your wealth' (4.1.44–6). These ideas about Rome's rapacity are also corroborated by Scaeva's utterance immediately before the masque, when he takes pride in his memory that 'In Gaul and Germany we saw such visions / And stood not to admire 'em but possess 'em. / When they are ours, they are worth our admiration' (3.4.4–6). Hence, Pothinus and Septimius do seem to have a point in this case.

As Septimius' words appear to suggest, the play's criticism even seems to extend into a more general preoccupation about the justice of empire and the treatment of other peoples.[137] These kinds of concerns were not uncommon at the time. They also reverberate, for example, in Thomas Kyd's *Cornelia* (1594), in which Cicero seems to regard Caesar's rise to power as deserved retribution for the injustice done by the Romans to foreign populations.[138] As David Armitage remarks, such claims partake of 'an anti-imperial strain within European humanism' that had been alive since 'Erasmus had refused to edit Dante's *Monarchia* in support of Charles V's claims to the Holy Roman Empire'.[139] Similar views had also been expressed by such authors as Sebastian Brant, George Buchanan, Michel de Montaigne, and Francis Bacon. In being informed by both strains of scepticism about colonization – although the issue of the potential dangers posed by luxury is predominant – *The False One* therefore turns out to be even more embroiled in the political context of its time.

### STAGE HISTORY

As remarked above (see A BLACKFRIARS PLAY?), very little information survives regarding early performances of *The False One*. In addition, there appear not to have been any drolls or Restoration adaptations of the play. Colley Cibber's *Caesar in Egypt*, which was performed at Drury Lane in 1724 and is sometimes considered such an adaptation, was in fact mainly inspired by Pierre Corneille's *La Mort de Pompée* (1643) and only lightly borrows from Fletcher and Massinger's play, even though it does very much follow the same plot.

As far as is known, the only occasions on which the play has been revived since the seventeenth century have been two staged readings. One was directed by Lia Wallace at the Blackfriars Playhouse in Staunton, VA, on 4 October 2015 as part of the American Shakespeare Center's Staged Reading Series. The other was directed by Jason Morell at Globe Education Sackler Studios on 19 March 2017 as part of the Shakespeare's Globe 'Read Not Dead' programme, which has been going on since 1995. Both initiatives seek to provide audiences with the opportunity to hear lesser-known and rarely (if ever) performed dramatic works of the early modern English stage.

The American Shakespeare Center reading was included in a 'Roman season' alongside Jonson's *Sejanus His Fall*, Nathanael Richards's *Messalina*, and Chapman's *Caesar and Pompey*. Staged by members of Sweet Wag Shakespeare, *The False One* was described in the press release as 'a surprising, sometimes silly, and all too human story', a 'game of king against queen, Roman against Egyptian, and brother against sister' that 'reveals the fallible human beings behind the legends', teeming as it is 'with uncertainty, intrigue, assassination and seduction'. Wallace interestingly proposed as her concept statement a desire for the performance 'to be about people and not about legends; while at the same time living within the dichotomic reality that these people ARE legends ... So it's like, look at these legends! Look at them fuck up! You fuck up, too! Maybe you could be a legend? Why not!' Put like this, the director's idea might sound somewhat too blunt and forthright, yet

Wallace did capture a crucial hallmark of *The False One*, which is indeed a play that largely explores the notion of cutting great historical personalities down to size by exposing their human weakness and pettiness, aspects that any successful staging of the play ought carefully to take into account.

The performance abided by the general conventions established by the American Shakespeare Center for their staged readings. Hence, the lights remained on for the entire duration of the performance; the script was considerably cut (to roughly 70 per cent of the text) in order to fit a 90-minute slot; costumes were minimalist, with most actors wearing black. Partial exceptions were Cleopatra (Molly Semeret), Achillas (Tyler Bruce Dale), Eros (Ian Charles), and Ptolemy (Patrick Harris), who wore non-black items of clothing as well. Props were used very sparingly: Ptolemy was identified by a crown; Pothinus (Marshall B. Garret) and Scaeva (Aubrey Whitlock) carried swords; a white apron with red stains simulated Labienus' (Jess Hamlet) bloodied armour; Caesar (Zac Harned) sported a helmet with a red crest that hilariously fell down halfway through the performance; Arsinoe (Jess Hamlet again) was holding a plush dog in her lap for most of the performance; a red-and-gold band reaching from across Scaeva's and Antony's (Meredith Johnson) shoulders to their upper waists signalled their higher authority among the Romans.

When not speaking, the actors sat on the stage on gallant stools. Their respective placement emphasized the relationship networks of the play: the audience could see Caesar and his followers on the left, Ptolemy and his entourage on the right, and Cleopatra with her women and Apollodorus (Merlyn Q. Sell) significantly in between. The acting was credible, and the ensemble worked well as a team. George Kendall played a convincingly villainous Septimius, but the most effective rendition was Harned's. His performance as Caesar was especially nuanced: often ironic, it was also intensely heartfelt during the key monologue of Act 2, scene 3, which Harned incisively delivered while sitting on the edge of the stage as a way to capitalize on the audience's proximity. All in all, Harned was able to capture Fletcher and Massinger's Caesar's several moods: now cocky, then clueless; now greedy, then introspective; now authoritative, then oblivious. Despite the omission of the masque, a number of directorial choices were particularly inspired such as Caesar's dragging the rug offstage with Cleopatra still on it at the end of Act 2, scene 3, while giving a wink to the audience, which elicited loud laughter.

The cast was completed by Maria Hart as Acoreus, and by Sophia Beratta, Mary Finch, and Bree Burns as the three lame soldiers.

The 'Read Not Dead' performance was included in a 'Massinger season', which also comprised staged readings of two more Fletcher–Massinger collaborations, namely *The Elder Brother* and *The Custom of the Country*. As Matthew Williamson explained in the theatre programme, this staging also tackled the play's representation of human fallibility in a world 'mired in corruption … in which money displaces honour and obedience as the basis upon which society rests'. By 'subtly disrupt[ing] oppositions between morality and vice', Williamson remarks, *The False One* prevents audiences from forming 'easy judgements or simplistic ethical stances', thus retaining 'its strength as a darkly cynical portrayal of human societ[y]'. These were the aspects that the 2017 performance especially played up.

Simon Jenner's review of the 'spirited' reading directed by Morell provides significant glimpses into the high theatrical potential that the play still retains. Highlights of the show were the interaction between Caroline Faber's 'excellent' Pothinus and Patrick Toomey's Achillas, whose 'incisive voice well complement[ed] Faber's detailed pauses and snake-snatched aplomb', making his 'one of the finest performances'.[140] Peter Bray's rendition of Ptolemy was also particularly successful, blending 'nobility, panic and late resolve in [a] vocally strong performance'.[141] During the masque, the towering position of the lovers was achieved by having Steve Touissant's 'magnificently commanding' Caesar and Madeline Appiah's 'regal' Cleopatra – who was 'festooned in cadmium yellow' during the mattress scene – 'perch on high stepladders', while Daisy Boulton's Arsinoe gave of her utmost on the main stage below and also made 'a tiny nod to the rhythm of Lili Bolero [*sic*] at one point'.[142] A further highlight of the afternoon was Ryan Early's 'super, satyr-snarling performance' as a Scaeva who could not resist his urge to try to dissuade Caesar from being ensnared by Cleopatra, so that, 'Banished from the room, he loll[ed] round a pillar and jump[ed] straight back to rail at Caesar'.[143] All in all, then, Morell 'pace[d] with an alacrity and fine eddy of detail that anchor[ed] memorable scenes'.[144] Other actors were Christian Bradley (Acoreus), Eliza Butterworth (Eros), Jake Harders (Antony), Kyle Lima (Apollodorus), Tama Phethean (Labienus), Edmund Sage Green (Dolabella), and Adam Sabatti and Scott McDowell (soldiers).

## THE TEXT

No manuscript of *The False One* is extant. The copy-text for the present edition is the copy of F1 in the Pennsylvania State University Library (see Figure 4).[145] Whereas the play first appeared in F1 in 1647, it was not assigned to Humphrey Moseley and Humphrey Robinson in the Stationers' Register until 29 June 1660. *The False One* belongs to a group of six plays that were eventually published in F1 but were not in Moseley's possession in September 1646, when the first entry listing thirty 'Beaumont and Fletcher' plays to be included in F1 was made. In fact, Moseley would seem not to have even known of their existence at the time when the first entry was made, which suggests that he probably acquired them after the printing of F1 had already commenced.[146]

Further evidence that this was the case comes from a close examination of the volume itself. In order to have printing proceed as speedily as possible, Moseley divided F1 into eight sections of differing length, which were then sent to different printers, as well as separately signed and paged. *The False One* is in section 2, printed by William Wilson.[147] It occupies 2Q1–2S4 (2S4v blank). The play that precedes *The False One* is *The Coxcomb*, which ends near the top of 2P3; rules and an ornament occupy the rest of the page. The Prologue is printed on 2P3v in a large italic type so that it fills up the entire page. Even the Epilogue, which is much shorter, occupies the whole of 2P4. 2P4v is blank. It is evident that the Prologue and the Epilogue could easily have been made to fit into 2P3 or 2P3v. At all events, it is odd that *The False One* does not begin on 2P4 rather than on 2Q1, and it seems clear that the printer had been trying to stretch the text so as to leave as few blank pages as possible in the final gathering.[148] In addition, the last page of *The Coxcomb* that contains letterpress features the catchword *The Chances*. As this is the play that opens Section 3, it emerges even more evidently that the insertion of *The False One* was late and unexpected.[149] Besides, the fact that some small roman capitals that had not been previously used in the section appear in quire Q suggests that Wilson printed something else between quires P and Q of F1. Yet not much time seems to have passed between the printing of P and Q, because the formes of Section 2 were still used for *The False One*.[150]

Turner's painstaking examination of recurring types in F1 reveals that probably two compositors worked together on *The False One*

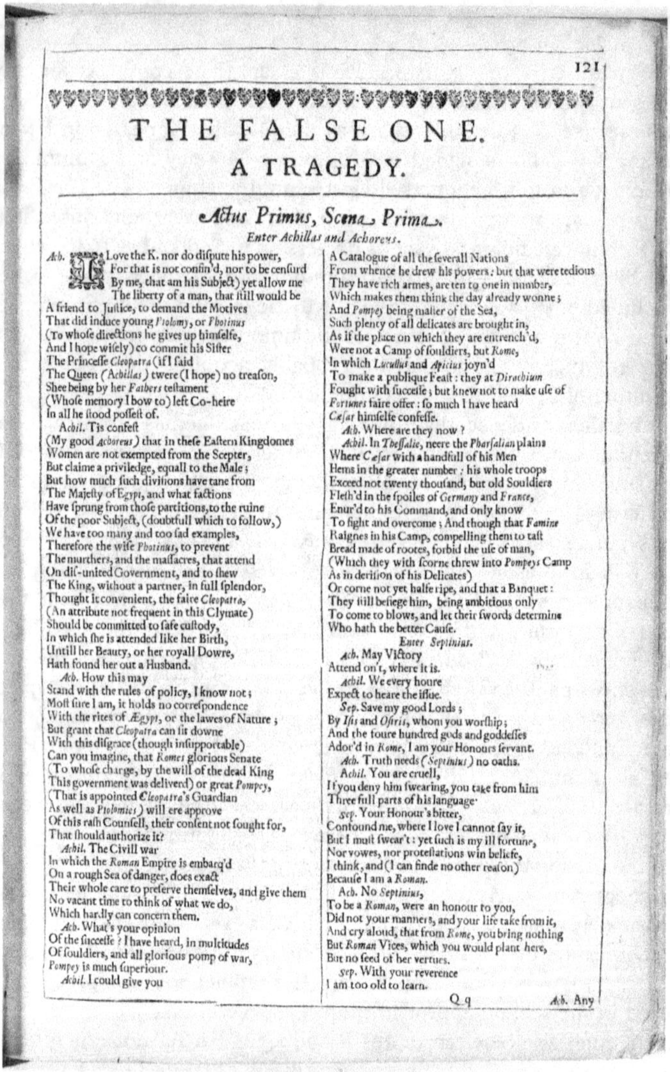

# THE FALSE ONE.
## A TRAGEDY.

*Actus Primus, Scæna Prima.*
*Enter Achillas and Achoreus.*

*Ach.* Love the K. nor do dispute his power,
For that is not confin'd, nor to be censur'd
By me, that am his Subject) yet allow me
The liberty of a man, that still would be
A friend to Justice, to demand the Motives
That did induce young *Ptolomy*, or *Photinus*
(To whose directions he gives up himselfe,
And I hope wisely) to commit his Sister
The Princesse *Cleopatra* (if I said
The Queen (*Achillas*) t'were (I hope) no treason,
Shee being by her *Fathers* testament
(Whose memory I bow to) left Co-heire
In all he stood possest of.
  *Achil.* Tis confest
(My good *Achoreus*) that in these Easterne Kingdomes
Women are not exempted from the Scepter,
But claime a priviledge, equall to the Male;
But how much such divisions have tane from
The Majesty of *Egypt*, and what factions
Have sprung from those partitions, to the ruine
Of the poore Subject, (doubtfull which to follow,)
We have too many and too sad examples,
Therefore the wise *Photinus*, to prevent
The murthers, and the massacres, that attend
On dis-united Government, and to shew
The King, without a partner, in full splendor,
Thought it convenient, the faire *Cleopatra*,
(An attribute not frequent in this Clymate)
Should be committed to safe custody,
In which she is attended like her Birth,
Untill her Beauty, or her royall Dowre,
Hath found her out a Husband.
  *Ach.* How this may
Stand with the rules of policy, I know not;
Most sure I am, it holds no correspondence
With the rites of *Ægypt*, or the lawes of Nature;
But grant that *Cleopatra* can sit downe
With this disgrace (though insupportable)
Can you imagine, that *Romes* glorious Senate
(To whose charge, by the will of the dead King
This government was delivered) or great *Pompey*,
(That is appointed *Cleopatra's* Guardian
As well as *Ptolomies*) will ere approve
Of this rash Counsell, their consent not sought for,
That should authorize it?
  *Achil.* The Civill war
In which the *Roman* Empire is embarq'd
On a rough Sea of danger, does exact
Their whole care to preserve themselves, and give them
No vacant time to think of what we do,
Which hardly can concern them.
  *Ach.* What's your opinion
Of the successe? I have heard, in multitudes
Of souldiers, and all glorious pomp of war,
*Pompey* is much superiour.
  *Achil.* I could give you

A Catalogue of all the severall Nations
From whence he drew his powers: but that were tedious
They have rich armes, are ten to one in number,
Which makes them think the day already wonne;
And *Pompey* being master of the Sea,
Such plenty of all delicates are brought in,
As if the place on which they are entrench'd,
Were not a Camp of souldiers, but *Rome*,
In which *Lucullus* and *Apicius* joyn'd
To make a publique Feast: they at *Dirachium*
Fought with successe; but knew not to make use of
*Fortunes* faire offer: so much I have heard
*Cæsar* himselfe confesse.
  *Ach.* Where are they now?
  *Achil.* In *Thessalie*, neere the *Pharsalian* plains
Where *Cæsar* with a handfull of his Men
Hems in the greater number: his whole troops
Exceed not twenty thousand, but old Souldiers
Flesh'd in the spoiles of *Germany* and *France*,
Enur'd to his Command, and only know
To fight and overcome; And though that Famine
Raignes in his Camp, compelling them to tast
Bread made of rootes, forbid the use of man,
(Which they with scorne threw into *Pompeys* Camp
As in derision of his Delicates)
Or come not yet halfe ripe, and that a Banquet:
They still besiege him, being ambitious only
To come to blowes, and let their swords determine
Who hath the better Cause.
  *Enter Septinius.*
  *Ach.* May Victory
Attend on't, where it is.
  *Achil.* We every houre
Expect to heare the issue.
  *Sep.* Save my good Lords;
By *Isis* and *Osiris*, whom you worship;
And the toure hundred gods and goddesses
Ador'd in *Rome*, I am your Honours servant.
  *Ach.* Truth needs (*Septinius*) no oaths.
  *Achil.* You are cruell,
If you deny him swearing, you take from him
Three full parts of his language.
  *Sep.* Your Honour's bitter,
Confound me, where I love I cannot say it,
But I must swear't: yet such is my ill fortune,
Nor vowes, nor protestations win beliefe,
I think, and (I can finde no other reason)
Because I am a *Roman*.
  *Ach.* No Septinius,
To be a *Roman*, were an honour to you,
Did not your manners, and your life take from it,
And cry aloud, that from *Rome*, you bring nothing
But *Roman* Vices, which you would plant here,
But no seed of her vertues.
  *Sep.* With your reverence
I am too old to learn.

Q q    *Ach.* Any

Figure 4  Opening text of *The False One* in F1

Table 1

| Compositor | A B | A B | A B | A B | B A A B | B A |
|---|---|---|---|---|---|---|
| Forme | Q2v:3 | Q2:3v | Q1v:4 | Q1:4v | R2v:3$a$3$b^1$3$b^2$ | R2:3v |
| Compositor | B A | B A | A B | A B | B A A | A — |
| Forme | R1v:4 | R1:4v | S2v:3 | S2:3v | S1v$a$1v$b$:4 | S1:4v |

according to the pattern shown in Table 1. It is unclear why R3$b$ was divided, but Turner is right to point out that part of the reason might be that 'it contains the lyrics of the masque, all in italics', which were probably separated from the play manuscript.[151] Turner adds that 'Compositor *A* no doubt took S1v$b$, which ordinarily would have been *B*'s, because S4 is a short page.'[152] An examination of the strategies that the compositors deployed to deal with verse-lines too long for the measure reveals that the casting-off of the play-text had probably been done inaccurately. While the compositors' work generally displays a tendency to save space, there is actually much spare space at the end of the text, in particular on S3v and S4, which are only a quarter filled each.[153] Such an inaccurate casting-off might have resulted from the fact that 'Wilson initially anticipated yet another play to be added to his section, or perhaps [from] the pressure of other work in hand when the manuscript of *The False One* was received', which would also chime with the fact that this play shows an 'even more relaxed supervision than that given the rest of the section. The number of typographical errors allowed to stand ... suggests that proof-reading was cursory.'[154] The absence of proofreading seems also to be borne out by the results of Turner's extensive collation of as many as twenty-one copies of the F1 text of *The False One*, which surprisingly returned no press-variants at all.[155] Accordingly, no further collation has been carried out for the present edition.

A number of characteristics of the F1 text of *The False One* would seem to indicate that the play was printed from a private transcript made by the scribe Ralph Crane, who had a documented close connection with the King's Men. First, the F1 text presents an abundance of parentheses that punctuate subordinate constructions, and especially proper names, forms of address, or nouns used in the vocative; second, Fletcher's typical *ye* is very carefully preserved; third, the play is divided into acts and scenes, as was customary in

Crane's transcripts; fourth, F1 seems to maintain Crane's typical hyphenations such as word prefix + stem, word suffix + stem or substantive + modifier(s).[156] It has been suggested that Crane may have had before him an authorial, though not always readily legible, manuscript, owing to the preservation of the stylistic preferences of the playwrights and, at the same time, because of the presence in the text of F1 of around thirty errors that could be attributed to misreading and are about equally distributed between the two compositors.[157] Moreover, Turner notices that 'a surprising number of ordinary words is printed in italics rather than roman, the probable cause being insertions in the Italian hand into blanks left by Crane because he could not decipher his copy'.[158] Since the text in F1 lacks any distinctive signs of theatrical adaptation, this transcript probably belongs to a later stage of Crane's scribal activity, during which he transcribed texts for presentation to patrons on the author's or his own behalf.[159] Yet Crane's collaboration with the King's Men seem to have been terminated during the printing of Shakespeare's First Folio in 1623. How Crane could have accessed the playwrights' manuscripts remains therefore difficult to explain.[160]

*The False One* was included in F2 in 1679 and later appeared in editions of the plays in the (Beaumont and) Fletcher canon in 1711, 1750 (ed. Seward), 1778 (ed. Colman), 1812 (ed. Weber), 1844 (ed. Dyce), 1912 (ed. Luce), and 1996 (ed. Turner). George Darley's 1839 edition reprinted the text established by Weber with very few variations and with no annotation, while the text in the Cambridge edition by Arnold Glover and A. R. Waller (1905–12) simply transcribes F2 with minor typographical corrections. Accordingly, these latter two editions have been excluded from the historical collation. This Revels Plays edition presents readers with the first modern-spelling single-volume annotated edition of John Fletcher and Philip Massinger's *The False One*.

### NOTES

1. On the office-book of Henry Herbert, see Bawcutt, 44, 135–41.
2. Throughout this volume, extant play titles appear in italics; the titles of lost plays are differentiated through the use of quotation marks.
3. Wiggins, *Catalogue*, #1948.
4. Wiggins, *Catalogue*, #1948.
5. Lovascio, *Fletcher's Rome*, 50–1.
6. Bertha Hensman attempted to contribute to the dating of the play by suggesting the presence of a 'veiled allusion' in a speech by Acoreus (1.1.130–7) 'to penalties incurred for indulgence in scurrilous talk

concerning matters of State', which she claimed would have been highly topical in 1620–21 (Hensman, 1.145). However, her contention that Acoreus' words 'are a precise summary of the legislation being passed through Parliament in 1620' and promulgated on 24 December 1620 as *A Proclamation against the Excess of Lavish and Licentious Speech in Matters of State* is not particularly convincing, and it is rather unhelpful in more firmly establishing the date of the play's composition (Hensman, 1.146). A closer examination of the two texts side by side in fact reveals that Acoreus' words only bear an extremely loose and generic resemblance to the contents of the proclamation.

7  Weber, 'Introduction', 3; Hoy, 'Shares', 148–50, 158.
8  Transcribed in Nicoll, 353–4.
9  Dustagheer, 3.
10  Dustagheer, 117.
11  Dustagheer, 118.
12  Dustagheer, 1.
13  Dustagheer, 1.
14  Graves, 125, 153.
15  Graves, 195; White, 'Light'; White, 'Unpicking'.
16  Dustagheer, 135. See also White, 'Light', 128–36.
17  Dustagheer, 5.
18  Dustagheer, 123–4.
19  MacDonald, 59.
20  Hall, 9; Loomba, 60; Holmberg, 119.
21  Karim-Cooper, 11.
22  Wray, 38.
23  Wray, 41.
24  Wray, 43.
25  Poitevin, 17.
26  Jowitt, 294–5.
27  For an insightful discussion of the early modern English conception of 'blushing', see Iyengar, 103–39.
28  Munro, 78. It has to be borne in mind, however, that the shifts in the casting of *Othello* that Munro suggests may reflect concerns about the Blackfriars in the 1630s, and not necessarily also in the late 1610s or early 1620s.
29  Munro, 79.
30  Karim-Cooper, 12.
31  Fletcher and Massinger's *Rollo, or The Bloody Brother* – which is sometimes considered a Roman play, inasmuch as it is largely based on the history of the Roman emperors Antoninus (better known as Caracalla) and his younger brother Geta as reported in *The History of Herodian, a Greek Author Treating of the Roman Emperors after Marcus, Translated out of Greek into Latin by Angelus Politianus and out of Latin into English by Nicholas Smyth* (London, [1556]) – is not included in this list because it is set in medieval France.
32  Wiggins, *Catalogue*, #1799.
33  Owens, 145.
34  Cantor, 27.
35  See Lovascio, *Fletcher's Rome*, 90–3.

36 Paleit, 147.
37 Waith, 'Death of Pompey', 281.
38 Owens, 20.
39 Seward, 'Preface', xii.
40 McDermott, n.p.
41 Weir, 5.
42 Weir, 5.
43 *CWBJ*, 2.192.
44 Donaldson, 356.
45 Kewes, 174.
46 Hensman, 1.128.
47 Waith, *Ideas*, 158. For an extended discussion of Septimius, see Wiggins, *Journeymen*, 198-201.
48 Seward, 124.
49 But see Kewes, 173, who argues that Fletcher and Massinger 'depict [Caesar] as a tyrant in the making and [Cleopatra] as a royal prostitute', and Jensen, *Reading*, 137, who similarly believes that in the play 'Caesar epitomises the ruthless pursuit of power' and is depicted not only as 'a tyrant who causes civil war and destroys the constitution', but also as 'a murderer'.
50 Paleit, 148.
51 Curran, 322.
52 Shepard, 55.
53 Waith, 'Death of Pompey', 279.
54 Hatchuel, 110.
55 Spear, 417.
56 Foucault, 2.78-93; Bushnell, 'Tyranny', 339. See also Breitenberg.
57 Spear, 418.
58 Henderson and McManus, 55; Bushnell, 'Tyranny', 342.
59 Henderson and McManus, 47-59.
60 Spear, 411.
61 Jensen, *Reading*, 110, 169.
62 Curran, 326-7.
63 'Perversely' because the destruction of sceneries was a demonstration of aristocratic conspicuous consumption, the exact opposite of Savonarola's bonfire.
64 Plutarch, 'Caesar', 787A; Suetonius, 26 (57.1); Cassius Dio, 4.42.40.4-5.
65 Waith, *Ideas*, 159.
66 Griffin, 377.
67 Vaught, 13.
68 Cicero, 1.29-30.
69 Curran, 326.
70 Kewes, 178. For Jensen, *Reading*, 137, 'This is a resonant final note, especially when James I's clashes with Parliament during the early 1620s are borne in mind.'
71 The play never fully clarifies whether Cleopatra is actually in love with Caesar, but I do not share the view expressed by Kewes that 'she feels no love or affection for him and is guided *solely* by cold political calculations' (178, my emphasis).
72 Clark, 108-9.

73 Ulrich, 80–98. Ulrich suggests that Fletcher and Massinger may have used Nicolas Coeffeteau's French translation, first published in 1615, but this does not seem particularly likely.
74 Florus, 414 (2.13.52). Cf. Lucan, 8.618–19, 667–74; Plutarch, 'Pompey', 717E.
75 Florus, 415 (2.13.52).
76 Florus, 414 (2.13.52).
77 Florus, 396 (2.13.14). This passage of Florus' *Epitome* was frequently noted down in early modern English commonplace books (see Jensen, 'Florus', 672–3).
78 Florus, 416–17 (2.13.58).
79 Jensen, 'Florus', 660; Woolf, 173.
80 Lovascio, *Fletcher's Rome*, 134–67.
81 Lovascio, *Fletcher's Rome*, 168–70.
82 Lovascio, *Fletcher's Rome*, 170–2.
83 Maxwell, 223.
84 On *The False One* as a prequel to Shakespeare's plays, see Neill, 24; Kewes, 172–3; Hatchuel, 110–12.
85 Hatchuel, 112.
86 Maxwell, 169. McKeithan, 165–6, helpfully groups passages from Shakespeare's *Antony and Cleopatra* exposing her changeability and variety (2.2.245–6; 1.1.50–1; 1.3.3–5; 1.3.71–3; 2.5.1, 3, 9–10) – to which Hatchuel, 110, adds 1.2.137–40.
87 Hatchuel, 111.
88 The lost 'Ptolemy', performed at Bull Inn in 1578, might have included the affair too. See 'Ptolemy', *LPD*, https://lostplays.folger.edu/Ptolemy (accessed 6 October 2020).
89 Caesar's surprising repentance also surfaces in Chapman, *Caesar and Pompey*, 4.4.1–3, and in Alexander, *Julius Caesar*, 1:2.1.411–14. Both plays, however, probably postdate *Caesar's Revenge*.
90 Antony probably became acquainted with Cleopatra while Caesar was still alive, but not on this occasion. See Characters in the Play, n. 2.
91 Ayres, 225 n.1.
92 Hensman, 1.140–1.
93 Turner, 'Introduction', 120 n.5.
94 Gentillet, 271b.
95 Mason, 136–7.
96 Weber, 'Introduction', 5.
97 Ward, 223.
98 MacDonald, 58.
99 Wiggins, *Journeymen*, 199.
100 Hatchuel, 111.
101 Hazlitt, 92.
102 Seward, 'Preface', xii, and first commentary note on the play.
103 Dyce, 'Account', lxii.
104 Weber, 'Introduction', 4.
105 Oliphant, 234.
106 Appleton, 87.
107 Appleton, 88. Ronan, *'Antike Roman'*, 59, similarly argued that 'The whole play is opportunistic and shallow, but the occasional brilliant

shard makes it worth attention today and performed the same function almost four hundred years ago.'
108 Waith, *Pattern*, 124.
109 Waith, *Pattern*, 127.
110 Waith, *Pattern*, 128–9.
111 Waith, 'Death of Pompey', 284.
112 Finkelpearl, 48.
113 Maxwell, 172.
114 Wiggins, *Journeymen*, 201.
115 Wiggins, *Journeymen*, 201.
116 Maxwell, 172.
117 Dutton, *Mastering*, 208–17.
118 Kewes, 174.
119 Hila, 21.
120 Hila, 21.
121 Hila, 24.
122 Hila, 21.
123 Hila, 25.
124 Hila, 26.
125 Paleit, 150.
126 Paleit, 144.
127 Paleit, 144.
128 Paleit, 149.
129 Paleit, 145.
130 Paleit, 145.
131 Paleit, 146–7.
132 For a fuller discussion, see Lovascio, 'She-Tragedy'. Ronan, 'Caesar On and Off', 82, fleetingly suggests that the play seems to host a veiled attack against the 'westward course of the British empire' without developing his argument.
133 See Fitzmaurice, 1–7, 38, 56–8; Armitage, 106.
134 Fitzmaurice, 2.
135 Whitaker, 1–2; Gray, sigs A3r–v.
136 *JC*, ed. Jowett, 3.1.47–8 (my emphasis); *JC*, ed. Neville, 3.1.47–8. For a more detailed discussion of Fletcher and Massinger's use of the phrase, see Lovascio, 'Caesar's "just cause"'.
137 Fitzmaurice, 3.
138 Kyd, *Cornelia*, 1.126–40.
139 Armitage, 109.
140 Jenner, n.p.
141 Jenner, n.p.
142 Jenner, n.p.
143 Jenner, n.p.
144 Jenner, n.p.
145 Available online at https://digital.libraries.psu.edu/digital/collection/emblem/id/5201/rec/4 (accessed 3 December 2020).
146 Bald, 8–10, 13, 34–5.
147 Turner, 'Folio', xxix.
148 Bald, 32–3.
149 Bald, 36; Turner, 'Printers', 44.

150 Turner, 'Introduction', 116.
151 Turner, 'Introduction', 116. Also see Commentary, 3.4.32.
152 Turner, 'Introduction', 116.
153 Turner, 'Introduction', 117.
154 Turner, 'Introduction', 117.
155 Turner, 'Introduction', 120 n.7. The twenty-one copies collated by Turner are: Bodleian B.1.8 Art.; University Library, Cambridge, Aston a.Sel.19 and SSS.10.8; Cyrus Hoy; Newberry Library; University of Illinois, two copies; Boston Public; University of Minnesota; Duke University 429544; Cornell University; Princeton University; Pennsylvania State University; University of Virginia, two copies; University of Washington; University of Wisconsin-Milwaukee, four copies; University of Wisconsin-Madison. The Universal Short Title Catalogue currently records eighty-nine copies of the Folio scattered in libraries around the world: https://www.ustc.ac.uk/editions/3052515 (accessed 10 March 2021).
156 Bald, 113–14; Hoy, 'Shares', 149–50; Turner, 'Introduction', 118–19. On Crane's scribal practices in his dramatic transcripts, see Howard-Hill, *Crane*, 16–68.
157 Hoy, 'Shares', 150; Turner, 'Introduction', 118–19.
158 Turner, 'Introduction', 119.
159 Howard-Hill, 'Crane', 126, 116.
160 Howard-Hill, 'Crane', 128.

# THE FALSE ONE

## [Characters in the Play

Julius CAESAR, dictator of Rome, who defeated Pompey in
the Civil War

---

*No press variants have been found in F1.*

---

1–22.] F1 does not provide a list of roles. F2 gives an incomplete list of the 'Persons Represented in the Play' (lightly emended by Weber, Dyce, and Turner), which offers mostly unsatisfactory descriptions of the characters and abides by the seventeenth-century convention according to which characters were listed based on social rank rather than dramatic prominence. Female roles always came after male ones, often following a space signalling that they belonged to a discrete (and secondary) hierarchy. This conventional subordination was probably strengthened by the fact that female parts were played by young male players. At the end of the list, F2 adds the following information: 'The Scene: Egypt. | The principal actors were: | John Lowin. | John Underwood. | Robert Benfield. | Richard Sharpe. | Joseph Taylor. | Nicholas Tooley. | John Rice. | George Birch.' We cannot know for sure who played which roles. Baldwin (casting-charts between pages 198 and 199) proposed Lowin as Scaeva, Underwood as Septimius, Benfield as Caesar, Sharpe as Cleopatra, Taylor as Pothinus, Tooley as Acoreus, Rice as Antony, and Birch as Achillas. Dutton (pers. comm.) hypothesizes Lowin as Septimius, Taylor as Caesar, and Sharpe as Cleopatra. Further insights on casting are expected to arise from the 'Reading Early Plays' project currently being led by Martin Wiggins.

1. Julius CAESAR] perhaps the most celebrated statesman and military general in Roman history. Born in 100 BCE, quaestor in 69, aedile in 65, praetor in 62, governor of Spain in 61, he formed an important political alliance with Marcus Crassus and Pompey the Great known as the First Triumvirate. He became consul in 59, was governor of Gaul between 58 and 50, and invaded Britain twice in 55 and 54. He defeated Pompey in the civil war and became dictator from 49 to 44 and consul again from 48 to 44. He died that same year, killed by a conspiracy led by Marcus Junius Brutus and Gaius Cassius Longinus. Caesar arrived in Egypt in 48, soon after the victory over Pompey at the Battle of Pharsalus, became involved in the Egyptian civil war, and had an affair with Cleopatra, which resulted in the birth of a son, Caesarion. Their affair continued after Caesar's return to Rome, and Cleopatra herself visited Rome more than once, staying at Caesar's villa just outside Rome.

ANTONY,  
DOLABELLA,  } Caesar's captains  
SCAEVA,  
LABIENUS, a general in Pompey's army, who previously  
    sided with Caesar                                                     5  
Three lame SOLDIERS  
Soldiers

---

2. *ANTONY*] Marcus Antonius (83–30 BCE), commonly known as Mark Antony, served under Caesar in his campaigns in Gaul and in the civil war against Pompey. After Caesar's victory at Pharsalus, he was appointed as Caesar's Master of the Horse (i.e., second in command). Antony may have met a 14-year-old Cleopatra as early as 55 during the Roman campaign in Egypt led by Aulus Gabinius to restore Ptolemy XII to the throne (see 1.1.37–41), although this seems unlikely: see Burstein, 23; Ronan, 'Roman Thoughts', 174, 181 n.5. Certainly, Antony did not follow Caesar to Egypt in 48 after the Battle of Pharsalus but remained in Rome to restore order in Italy, and he had to face opposition from Publius Cornelius Dolabella. Thus, he cannot have met Cleopatra in Alexandria at this time, though he certainly got to know her during her successive visits to Rome. His presence in Egypt with Caesar and Dolabella is unhistorical but curiously shared with the anonymous *Tragedy of Caesar's Revenge*. See Introduction, 35.

3. *DOLABELLA*] Publius Cornelius Dolabella was a Roman general who first took Pompey's side and then went over to Caesar during the civil war. Historically, his relationship with Antony was not friendly but fraught with tension. Though in the play Dolabella criticizes Caesar for his intemperance, he was known historically as a terrible example of profligacy. He did not follow Caesar to Alexandria but was chosen as one of his generals in the expeditions to Africa and Spain. Dolabella's presence in Egypt with Caesar and Antony is unhistorical and curiously shared with the anonymous *Tragedy of Caesar's Revenge*. See Introduction, 35.

4. *SCAEVA*] Marcus Cassius Scaeva, one of Caesar's bravest centurions, managed to resist the assault of Pompey's legions at the Battle of Dyrrachium, though vastly outnumbered. His valour was recalled by Caesar, 3.53.4–5, as well as by Lucan, 6.140–262, and Plutarch, 'Caesar', 770E. On Scaeva, see also Dimitrova.

5. *LABIENUS*] Titus Labienus was an accomplished cavalry commander active during the late republican period. A tribune of the plebs in 63 BCE, he had close ties with Pompey but served as Caesar's senior legate in Gaul. Caesar made him governor of Cisalpine Gaul in 51. Yet, after Caesar crossed the Rubicon, Labienus joined the forces of Pompey, who gave him command of the cavalry. After the defeat at Pharsalus, Labienus did not go to Egypt with Pompey as dramatized in *The False One* but fled to the Greek island of Corcyra. He proceeded to Africa and then to Spain to continue opposing Caesar but died at the Battle of Munda in 45. The name is pronounced as tetrasyllabic ('La-bi-e-nus') throughout. On Labienus, see also Dimitrova.

PTOLEMY, King of Egypt
POTHINUS, a eunuch, chief advisor to Ptolemy
ACOREUS, priest of Isis and advisor to Ptolemy                    10
ACHILLAS, captain of Ptolemy's guard and advisor to
    Ptolemy

---

8. PTOLEMY] Ptolemy XIII Theos Philopator, the son of Ptolemy XII Auletes, was co-ruler of Egypt with his sister (and wife) Cleopatra VII Philopator from 51 to 47 BCE. As he was only 11 years old when he ascended the throne, the eunuch Pothinus acted as a regent for him. In 48, Ptolemy and Pothinus attempted to depose Cleopatra, and a civil war ensued. The situation became even more fraught due to their other sister Arsinoe IV's claim to the throne. When Pompey sought refuge in Egypt after his defeat by Caesar, Ptolemy and Pothinus had him killed by Achillas and Septimius and presented his head to Caesar, hoping to gain his favour. Caesar, however, was far from pleased and later had Pothinus executed and Cleopatra restored to the throne. As Ptolemy still wanted to get rid of Cleopatra, he formed an alliance with Arsinoe and attacked Cleopatra and the Roman troops in Alexandria. The war resulted in Caesar and Cleopatra's victory. Ptolemy drowned while crossing the river Nile, either trying to flee or seeking negotiations. The name is occasionally pronounced as disyllabic ('Ptol'my') in the play.

9. POTHINUS] Pothinus was a powerful eunuch at the court of Ptolemy XIII, for whom he acted as regent with the help of the general Achillas and the rhetorician Theodotus of Chios. He started a civil war by turning Ptolemy against Cleopatra and had Ptolemy order the decapitation of Pompey, himself offering the severed head to Caesar, who later put him to death. This is the first edition of the play to use the spelling Pothinus rather than Photinus as in F1. In line with the editorial guidelines of the series, I have used the present-day form of the name, which has no impact on metre. Both spellings were in use in early modern England: an EEBO-TCP search returns 137 matches for 'Pothinus' and as many as 1,107 matches for 'Photinus'. As Turner illustrates, the spelling 'Pothinus' is be found, for example, in the Life of Caesar 'in North's Plutarch of 1579, 1603 and 1612, as well as in *De bello civili* of 1589'. In Plutarch's 'Life of Antony', however, he is mistakenly made a member of Cleopatra's court in the period before Actium and is accordingly alluded to in *A&C* 3.7.14. Interestingly, the spelling 'Photinus' is also used in the 1619 translation of Florus' *Epitome* by Bolton (p. 418), which Fletcher and Massinger seem to have consulted along other sources (see Introduction, 28–9).

10. ACOREUS] Acoreus is described as the high priest of Memphis in Lucan's *Pharsalia*. In the play he is portrayed as both a priest and a counsellor to Ptolemy. He is not blind as assumed by Weber on the grounds of a literal interpretation of the reference to him as 'the blind priest' at 4.3.78.

11. ACHILLAS] a guardian and general of Ptolemy who killed Pompey with the help of Septimius and later marched against Caesar with the Egyptian army. He occupied most of Alexandria and besieged Caesar, but he was later put to death by Arsinoe.

THE FALSE ONE                           65

SEPTIMIUS, a Roman soldier, formerly in Pompey's army,
        now serving Pothinus
Guard
Soldiers

CLEOPATRA, Queen of Egypt, Ptolemy's sister            15
ARSINOE, Ptolemy's and Cleopatra's sister
EROS, Cleopatra's waiting-woman

---

12. SEPTIMIUS] Lucius Septimius fought under Pompey during the latter's campaign against the pirates. At the time of the events of the play, he was part of the Roman detachment in Egypt and had become military tribune. He is mostly remembered for the assassination of his former commander. According to both Plutarch, 'Pompey', 717A–F, and Caesar, 3.104, Septimius' presence reassured Pompey as he arrived in Egypt, but it was Septimius who first stabbed Pompey in the back, followed by Achillas (and, only in Plutarch, the centurion Salvius), and then decapitated him. F1 offers several instances of the spelling 'Septinius', which is to be found in both Fletcher's and Massinger's shares as well as in both compositor A's and compositor B's shares. Yet the spelling 'Septinius' is to be found in no works that could have served as sources for the play. In Turner's view, 'One can deduce only that "Septimius" ... occurred at least at certain places in the manuscript.' The name is sometimes pronounced as tetrasyllabic ('Sep-ti-mi-us').

15. CLEOPATRA] Born in 69 BCE, the daughter of Ptolemy XII and sister-wife and co-ruler with Ptolemy XIII, Cleopatra VII Philopator was the last ruler of the Ptolemaic dynasty in Egypt. She probably followed her father to Rome in 58 during his exile after an insurrection in Egypt. For her clash against her brother, see PTOLEMY above. The name is pronounced as trisyllabic or tetrasyllabic as the metre requires.

16. ARSINOE] Arsinoe IV reigned between 48 and 47 BCE with her brother Ptolemy XIII in opposition to her half-sister Cleopatra. Following Caesar's decision to give the kingdom of Egypt jointly to Ptolemy and Cleopatra and that of Cyprus to Arsinoe and her other brother Ptolemy XIV, she took command of the Egyptian army, proclaimed herself Queen of Egypt, and besieged the Romans in the palace of Alexandria. After the Roman victory, Arsinoe was taken prisoner and paraded in Caesar's triumph in Rome. She was then executed in 41 on Antony's orders at the instigation of Cleopatra. No diaeresis has been placed on the final '-e' because her name is pronounced as trisyllabic throughout the play (but see 5.4.17).

17. EROS] Cleopatra's maid, and an invention of the playwrights, possibly based on Plutarch's and Shakespeare's Iras, spelled Eras in Mary Sidney's *Antonius* (1592) and in the first edition of Samuel Daniel's *Cleopatra* (1594), but also interestingly bearing the same name as Antony's loyal male follower in *A&C*.

APOLLODORUS, Cleopatra's guardian
A BOY, attending Apollodorus

ISIS                                              } in the masque]          20
NILUS and his Seven Heads
Three LABOURERS

---

18. *APOLLODORUS*] According to Plutarch, 'Caesar', 786D-E, Apollodorus the Sicilian was a follower of Cleopatra who enabled her to meet Caesar in person when he came to Alexandria. Yet the credibility of this episode is now disputed among scholars. There is no other mention of Apollodorus in any other source.
  20. ISIS] A major deity in ancient Egyptian religion, Isis was believed to help the dead enter the afterlife and was regarded as the divine mother of the pharaoh.
  21. NILUS ... *Heads*] a personification of the Nile, the longest river in Africa, which played a crucial role in the development of the Egyptian civilization. As it approaches the Mediterranean Sea, the Nile divides into seven branches, thereby forming the Nile Delta. This was a familiar notion in early modern England, as illustrated by Browne, 312: 'It is generally esteemed, and by most unto our days received, that the river of Nilus hath seven ostiaries, that is, by seven channels disburdeneth itself into the sea.' Since ancient times, however, there had been confusion between the mouths and the springs of the river, which were also often supposed to be seven, their exact location wrapped in mystery and accordingly the object of fervent interest. Hence, the Heads dancing in the masque in Act 3, scene 4, are to be intended as personifications of the fabled headsprings (rather than the mouths) of the river.

# The Prologue

New titles warrant not a play for new,
The subject being old, and 'tis as true
Fresh and neat matter may with ease be framed
Out of their stories that have oft been named
With glory on the stage. What borrows he           5
From him that wrote old Priam's tragedy
That writes his love to Hecuba? Sure, to tell
Of Caesar's amorous heats and how he fell
In the Capitol can never be the same

---

   1. *warrant*] guarantee, authenticate.
   3. *neat*] cleverly contrived.
   4. *their ... that*] the stories of those who.
   5–7. *What ... Hecuba*] Shakespeare is here implicitly put on a par with Homer and Virgil, the main sources of the story of Priam, which was then abundantly drawn upon by successive writers.
   6. *old ... tragedy*] Priam was the legendary King of Troy during the Trojan War. No information is extant regarding any early modern English plays specifically focusing on Priam's death, so that this would seem to be a generic reference to the story of a well-known mythological figure rather than to a specific play. It is striking, however, that in one version of the myth (mentioned by Virgil, *Aeneid*, 2.554–8), Priam was murdered and beheaded on a shore, thus meeting the same fate suffered offstage by Pompey in *The False One*.
   7. *That*] The antecedent is 'he' on l. 5.
   *his*] that is, Priam's.
   *Hecuba*] Priam's wife.
   8. *Caesar's ... heats*] Caesar's liaison with Cleopatra is mentioned several times in *A&C*, but Fletcher and Massinger's is the first play to revolve primarily around it. The anonymous *Tragedy of Caesar's Revenge* dramatizes it too, but only as an episode in an extended series of events. See Introduction, 33–6.
   8–9. *how ... Capitol*] As Caesar was actually killed during a meeting of the Senate at the Theatre of Pompey, and not in the Capitol as dramatized in Shakespeare's tragedy, the reference to Shakespeare becomes all the more specific. Shakespeare seems to have intended the Capitol as the citadel of ancient Rome and to have thought that it was the regular meeting place of the Senate. During this period, however, the Senate most commonly assembled in the Curia Cornelia in the Forum.
   9. *Capitol*] either the Capitoline Hill, one of the seven hills of Rome, or the temple of Jupiter Optimus Maximus erected on that same hill, to which triumphant generals led processions and where they offered sacrifices to the gods.

To the judicious, nor will such blame 10
Those that penned this for barrenness when they find
Young Cleopatra here and her great mind
Expressed to the height, with us a maid and free,
And how he rated her virginity.
We treat not of what boldness she did die 15
Nor of her fatal love to Antony.
What we present and offer to your view,
Upon their faiths, the stage yet never knew.
 Let reason then first to your wills give laws
 And after judge of them and of their cause. 20

---

10. *the judicious*] pronounced 'judicious'; discerning people.
*such*] that is, the judicious.
11. *this*] this play.
12. *Young Cleopatra*] Fletcher and Massinger want to make it clear from the outset that their Cleopatra is not as 'wrinkled deep in time' (*A&C* 1.5.30) as Shakespeare's.
13. *to the height*] to the highest degree.
14. *he*] Caesar.
*rated*] valued.
15. *of ... die*] The most direct reference is to Cleopatra's glorious, solemn suicide as staged by Shakespeare. In *A&C*, Cleopatra dies by applying two asps to her breast in order to defy Octavius Caesar's desire to display her in Rome in his triumph. Her suicide had also been dramatized in Daniel's *Cleopatra*.
16. *fatal ... Antony*] another direct reference to *A&C*.
18. *their*] that is, the playwrights'.
19. *wills*] intentions.
20. *them*] the playwrights.

# The False One

### Act I Scene I

*Enter* ACHILLAS *and* ACOREUS.

*Acoreus.* I love the King nor do dispute his power,
   For that is not confined nor to be censured
   By me, that am his subject. Yet allow me
   The liberty of a man that still would be
   A friend to justice to demand the motives               5
   That did induce young Ptolemy (or Pothinus,
   To whose directions he gives up himself
   And, I hope, wisely) to commit his sister,
   The princess Cleopatra — if I said
   'The Queen', Achillas, 'twere, I hope, no treason,      10
   She being by her father's testament
   (Whose memory I bow to) left coheir
   In all he stood possessed of.
*Achillas.*                           'Tis confessed,
   My good Acoreus, that in these eastern kingdoms
   Women are not exempted from the sceptre            15
   But claim a privilege equal to the male.
   But how much such divisions have ta'en from
   The majesty of Egypt and what factions
   Have sprung from those partitions to the ruin
   Of the poor subject, doubtful which to follow,       20

---

   1.1.0.] Weber adds the setting: '*Alexandria. A hall in the Royal Palace*'.
   2. *confined*] kept within bounds.
*censured*] judged.
   4. *would*] would like to.
   7. *directions*] instructions.
   8. *commit*] 'To imprison or place in custody' (*OED* v. 4a(b)).
  13. *confessed*] acknowledged.
  14. *eastern*] The Egyptians seem unwittingly to have adopted a Eurocentric view.
  17. *divisions*] pronounced 'divisíons'.

> We have too many and too sad examples.
> Therefore, the wise Pothinus, to prevent
> The murders and the massacres that attend
> On disunited government and to show
> The King without a partner in full splendour, 25
> Thought it convenient the fair Cleopatra
> (An attribute not frequent in this climate)
> Should be committed to safe custody,
> In which she is attended like her birth,
> Until her beauty or her royal dower 30
> Hath found her out a husband.
> *Acoreus.*                        How this may
> Stand with the rules of policy I know not;
> Most sure I am it holds no correspondence
> With the rites of Egypt or the laws of nature.
> But grant that Cleopatra can sit down 35
> With this disgrace (though insupportable),
> Can you imagine that Rome's glorious Senate,

---

26. *fair*] beautiful, but also not black. See Introduction, 8–10.
27. *climate*] region.
29. *like*] as befits.
31. *a husband*] Technically, however, Cleopatra would have been her brother Ptolemy's wife according to Egyptian custom. The play makes no mention of such a relationship between them.
35. *grant*] let's suppose.
35–6. *sit down / With*] put up with.
37–41. *Rome's ... Ptolemy's*] Ptolemy XII Auletes, the oldest among Ptolemy IX's illegitimate sons, ascended to the throne in 80 BCE and pursued a pro-Roman policy as a way to secure his position. In 63 he sent riches to Pompey in order to form a patron–client relationship. Five years later he sought refuge in Rome on the occasion of a popular uprising in Egypt, possibly with his daughter Cleopatra, and was succeeded by his other daughter Berenice IV. In Rome, Ptolemy and Cleopatra were sheltered by Pompey, who convinced the Senate to help restore Ptolemy to the throne of Egypt. When rumours of the Romans' possible invasion reached Egypt, a group of one hundred men were sent from Egypt to Rome to present their case against Ptolemy's restoration, but Pompey had their leader poisoned and most of the others murdered before they even reached Rome. As soon as he was restored to the Egyptian throne by a Roman army led by Aulus Gabinius, Ptolemy had Berenice and her supporters put to death, and then ruled Egypt with Cleopatra until 51, when he abdicated due to illness. In his will, he declared that she should rule the kingdom after his abdication together with her brother Ptolemy XIII. The people of Rome were appointed as executors.

>     To whose charge by the will of the dead King
>     This government was delivered, or great Pompey,
>     That is appointed Cleopatra's guardian                40
>     As well as Ptolemy's, will e'er approve
>     Of this rash counsel, their consent not sought for
>     That should authorize it?
> *Achillas.*                    The civil war
>     In which the Roman Empire is embarked
>     On a rough sea of danger does exact                   45
>     Their whole care to preserve themselves and gives them
>     No vacant time to think of what we do,
>     Which hardly can concern them.
> *Acoreus.*                         What's your opinion
>     Of the success? I have heard in multitudes
>     Of soldiers and all glorious pomp of war              50
>     Pompey is much superior.
> *Achillas.*                  I could give you
>     A catalogue of all the several nations
>     From whence he drew his powers, but that were tedious.
>     They have rich arms, are ten to one in number
>     (Which makes them think the day already won),         55
>     And, Pompey being master of the sea,
>     Such plenty of all delicates are brought in
>     As if the place on which they are entrenched
>     Were not a camp of soldiers, but Rome,
>     In which Lucullus and Apicius joined                  60

---

46. *gives*] *F2;* give *F1.*

---

39. *great Pompey*] Gnaeus Pompeius Magnus (106–48 BCE), usually known in English as Pompey or Pompey the Great, was an outstanding general and an important political leader of the late Roman Republic, defeated by Caesar in the civil war.

42. *their ... for*] the consent not asked for of those.

49. *success*] outcome.

59. *soldiers*] pronounced 'soldiers'.

60. *Lucullus and Apicius*] Lucius Licinius Lucullus was a famous gourmand at the time of Pompey and Cicero. Marcus Gavius Apicius was a celebrated epicure in the reigns of Augustus and Tiberius. The two are also paired in *RA* 2.1.29–31: 'Wouldst thou have me / Be an Apicius or a Lucullus, / And riot out my state in curious sauces?' The pairing, however, is here anachronistic.

72 THE FALSE ONE [ACT I

  To make a public feast. They at Dyrrachium
  Fought with success but knew not to make use of
  Fortune's fair offer. So much I have heard
  Caesar himself confessed.
*Acoreus.*       Where are they now?
*Achillas.* In Thessaly, near the Pharsalian plains,    65
  Where Caesar with a handful of his men
  Hems in the greater number. His whole troops
  Exceed not twenty thousand, but old soldiers

---

64. confessed] *Seward;* confesse *F1.*

---

61–4. *They ... confessed*] Dyrrachium is the city of Durrës in present-day Albania, where Caesar and Pompey fought an important battle in the civil war. Pompey's army routed Caesar's troops, but Pompey refrained from pursuing Caesar's fleeing forces, thus mistakenly allowing them to regroup and withdraw to Thessaly. The play seems to echo Suetonius, 16: 'once before Dyrrachium, where being discomfited and put to flight, when he saw that Pompeius followed not on in chase, he said of him that he knew not how to use a victory' (*semel ad Dyrrachium, ubi pulsus non instante Pompeio negavit eum vincere scire*, 36.1). Cf. also Plutarch, 'Pompey', 711A: 'Pompey had valiantly repulsed his men and made them fly, and had slain two thousand of them in the field, but he durst not enter pell-mell with them into their camp as they fled. Whereupon Caesar said to his friends that his enemy had won the victory that day if he had known how to overcome'; 'Caesar', 782D–E: 'Caesar that day was brought unto so great extremity that – if Pompey had not either for fear or spiteful fortune left off to follow his victory and retired into his camp, being contented to have driven his enemies into their camp – returning to his camp with his friends, he said unto them: "The victory this day had been our enemies' if they had had a captain that could have told how to have overcome."'
 64. *confessed*] acknowledged.
 65. *Thessaly*] a region of central Greece, where the plain of Pharsalus was located.
 *Pharsalian plains*] The place where the decisive battle between Caesar and Pompey was fought. Caesar was in a much weaker position, having limited provisions and an army roughly half the size of his opponent's. Pompey intended to refrain from battle in order to starve and exhaust Caesar's troops. Yet he ultimately yielded to the insistence of senators and officers to act immediately, reluctantly decided to engage in battle, and experienced a crushing defeat, which prompted his escape to Egypt, disguised as a private citizen.
 67. *Hems in*] surrounds.

SC I]                   THE FALSE ONE                      73

    Fleshed in the spoils of Germany and France,
    Inured to his command and only know                     70
    To fight and overcome; and, though that famine
    Reigns in his camp, compelling them to taste
    Bread made of roots forbid the use of man
    (Which they with scorn threw into Pompey's camp
    As in derision of his delicates)                        75
    Or corn not yet half ripe, and that a banquet,
    They still besiege him, being ambitious only
    To come to blows and let their swords determine
    Who hath the better cause.

---

  69. *Fleshed in*] hardened in, habituated to.
  *Germany and France*] Caesar subdued Gaul (France) in a series of military campaigns that lasted from 58 to 50 BCE, during which he also campaigned against a number of Germanic tribes in order to secure the eastern border of the new provinces.
  70. *inured*] accustomed.
  *only*] who only.
  71. *though that*] although.
  71–8. *famine ... blows*] Cf. Lucan, 6.108–17: 'but they suffered from the pinch of hunger like men closely besieged. The corn-blades were not yet swelling to the height of harvest; and therefore Caesar saw his wretched men lying on the ground to eat the food of beasts, plucking the bushes, rifling the trees of their leaves, and culling from strange roots suspicious plants that threatened death. The men fought for food – whatever they could soften with fire, or break with their teeth, or swallow down with rasped gullets, and many things never tried before for human consumption; and yet they went on besieging a well-fed foe'; Plutarch, 'Caesar', 782B–C: 'Caesar on th'other side, who had no great plenty of victuals at the first, was in a very hard case, insomuch as his men gathered roots and mingled them with milk, and ate them. Furthermore, they did make bread of it also and sometime, when they skirmished with the enemies and came alongst by them that watched and warded, they cast off their bread into their trenches and said that as long as the earth brought forth such fruits, they would never leave besieging of Pompey.'
  73.] Cf. *A&C* 1.4.62–9: 'Thou didst drink / The stale of horses and the gilded puddle / Which beasts would cough at. Thy palate then did deign / The roughest berry on the rudest hedge. / Yea, like the stag when snow the pasture sheets, / The barks of trees thou browsèd. On the Alps / It is reported thou didst eat strange flesh, / Which some did die to look on.'
  78–9. *determine ... cause*] Cf. Lucan, 7.259–60: 'and this day must decide, on the evidence of destiny, which of the two combatants had justice on his side'.

*Enter* SEPTIMIUS.

*Acoreus.* May victory
    Attend on't, where it is.
*Achillas.* We every hour 80
    Expect to hear the issue.
*Septimius.* Save my good lords!
    By Isis and Osiris, whom you worship,
    And the four hundred gods and goddesses
    Adored in Rome, I am your honours' servant.
*Acoreus.* Truth needs, Septimius, no oaths.
*Achillas.* You are cruel. 85
    If you deny him swearing, you take from him
    Three full parts of his language.
*Septimius.* Your honour's bitter.
    Confound me, where I love I cannot say it,
    But I must swear't. Yet such is my ill fortune
    Nor vows nor protestations win belief; 90
    I think — and I can find no other reason —
    Because I am a Roman.
*Achillas.* No, Septimius,
    To be a Roman were an honour to you,
    Did not your manners and your life take from it
    And cry aloud that from Rome you bring nothing 95
    But Roman vices, which you would plant here,
    But no seed of her virtues.
*Septimius.* With your reverence,
    I am too old to learn —
*Acoreus.* Anything honest.

---

98. learn —] *this edn;* learn. *F1.*

---

80. *on't*] that is, on the better cause.
*where*] (perhaps) where'er.
*every hour*] any minute now.
81. *issue*] result.
82. *Osiris*] A major deity in ancient Egyptian religion, Osiris was the god of fertility, agriculture, and the afterlife.
87. *Three ... parts*] three quarters.
88. *Confound me*] The verb 'confound' was employed in curses or imprecations as an equivalent or substitute for 'bring to perdition' (*OED* v. 2a).
90. *win*] gain.
94. *take*] divert.

SC 1]                    THE FALSE ONE                              75

            That I believe without an oath.
*Septimius.*                      I fear
            Your lordship has slept ill tonight, and that              100
            Invites this sad discourse. 'Twill make you old
            Before your time. Pox o' these virtuous morals
            And old religious principles that fool us.
            I have brought you a new song will make you laugh
            Though you were at your prayers.
*Acoreus.*                        What is the subject?                 105
            Be free, Septimius.
*Septimius.*              'Tis a catalogue
            Of all the gamesters of the court and city,
            Which lord lies with that lady and what gallant
            Sports with that merchant's wife; and does relate
            Who sells her honour for a diamond,                        110
            Who for a tissue robe, whose husband's jealous
            And who so kind that, to share with his wife,
            Will make the match himself. Harmless conceits,
            Though fools say they are dangerous. I sang it
            The last night at my lord Pothinus' table.                 115


102. Pox] *Weber;— F1.*   113.] *Seward; F1 lines* Will ... himselfe? / Harmlesse conceits,.

---

101. *sad*] grave, serious.
102. *Pox*] As this is not a word that would be challenged by the Master of the Revels, who was normally only concerned with references to the deity in its various forms, the deletion is likely to have been made by Crane, who, as Howard-Hill argues, 'apparently did not approve of swearing of any kind' ('Crane', 122). As Richard Dutton (pers. comm.) suggests, Crane seems to have been 'trying to shield the wealthy patrons who bought his copies from the vulgarities of the stage'.
104-45. *I ... thoughts*] Septimius emerges from this exchange as having certain affinities with the character of the licensed fool (e.g., Feste, Lear's Fool etc.), who can get away with all kinds of offence as long as it is entertaining; when it is no longer so, 'Take heed, sirrah, the whip' (*KL* 1.4.108). The entertaining knave, however, will soon prove to be something altogether darker.
106. *Be free*] speak freely.
107. *gamesters*] dissolute men and women.
110. *honour*] virginity, chastity.
112. *share*] participate.

*Acoreus.* How? As a fiddler?
*Septimius.*         No, sir, as a guest,
   A welcome guest too. And it was approved of
   By a dozen of his friends, though they were touched in't.
   For, look you, 'tis a kind of merriment,
   When we have laid by foolish modesty                    120
   (As not a man of fashion will wear it),
   To talk what we have done — at least, to hear it.
   If merrily set down, it fires the blood
   And heightens crest-fall'n appetite.
*Acoreus.*               New doctrine!
*Achillas.* Was't of your own composing?
*Septimius.*             No, I bought it           125
   Of a skulking scribbler for two ptolemies,
   But the hints were mine own. The wretch was fearful,
   But I have damned myself, should it be questioned,
   That I will own it.
*Acoreus.*         And be punished for it.
   Take heed, for you may so long exercise              130
   Your scurrilous wit against authority,
   The kingdom's counsels, and make profane jests —
   Which to you, being an atheist, is nothing —

---

124. fall'n] *1711;* falne *F1.*

---

   116. *fiddler*] 'One who plays on the fiddle; esp. one who does so for hire' (*OED* n. 1a), but perhaps more insultingly meaning 'trifler' (2a), or even 'sexual partner' (Williams, 1.480). There may be also a play on the ancient Greek tradition of reciting to the lyre – words set to (here) vulgar music.
   118. *touched*] alluded to (*OED* v. 26b).
   121. *fashion*] pronounced 'fashion'.
   123. *set down*] composed.
   124. *heightens ... appetite*] literally, stimulates dispirited appetite. The crest is the heraldic device set above the shield and helmet in a coat of arms, but 'crest' is also often allusive of the penis (Williams, 1.331). Hence, the idea here is that this kind of activity is able to make a penis that has lost its erection hard again.
   *doctrine*] teaching, instruction.
   126. *skulking*] sneaking, lurking.
   *ptolemies*] unrecorded in *OED*; probably two low-value coins, even though the coins circulating in ancient Egypt seem not to have been known as 'ptolemies', despite often bearing likenesses of the Ptolemies.
   130. *Take heed*] Be careful.

SC I]                    THE FALSE ONE                        77

    Against religion that your great maintainers,
    Unless they would be thought copartners with you,           135
    Will leave you to the law; and then, Septimius,
    Remember there are whips.
*Septimius.*                 For whores, I grant you,
    When they are out of date; till then, are safe too,
    Or all the gallants of the court are eunuchs.
    And, for mine own defence, I'll only add this:                140
    I'll be admitted for a wanton tale
    To some most private cabinets when your priesthood,
    Though laden with the mysteries of your goddess,
    Shall wait without unnoted. So I leave you
    To your pious thoughts.                 *Exit.*
*Achillas.*                'Tis a strange impudence              145
    This fellow does put on.
*Acoreus.*                The wonder great,
    He is accepted of.
*Achillas.*              Vices for him
    Make as free way as virtues do for others.
    'Tis the times' fault. Yet great ones still have graced,
    To make them sport or rub them o'er with flattery,            150
    Observers of all kinds.

    *Enter* POTHINUS *and* SEPTIMIUS [*stopping some way
        from* ACOREUS *and* ACHILLAS].

---

138. When] *F2;* Till *F1.* are safe] *F1;* they are safe *Weber;* they're safe *Seward.* 149. times'] *Dyce, Luce;* time's *1711, Seward, Weber;* times *F1, F2, Turner.* 151. SD1] *this edn; Enter Photinus and Septinius. F1.*

---

134. *your ... maintainers*] your supporters or those who provide you with the necessaries of life.
138. *are*] they are.
141. *wanton*] lascivious.
142. *cabinets*] apartments.
*when*] while.
144. *without*] outside.
*unnoted*] unnoticed.
145. *strange*] exceptional, surprising.
147. *accepted of*] received, admitted.
149. *still*] always.
150. *To ... flattery*] to be entertained or flattered.
151. *Observers*] followers.

*Acoreus.* [*Aside to* ACHILLAS] No more of him;
    He is not worth our thoughts: a fugitive
    From Pompey's army, and now in a danger
    When he should use his service.
*Achillas.* [*Aside to* ACOREUS] See how he hangs
    On great Pothinus' ear.
*Septimius.* [*To* POTHINUS] Hell and the Furies,   155
    And all the plagues of darkness light upon me:
    You are my god on earth, and, let me have
    Your favour here, fall what can fall hereafter.
*Pothinus.* Thou art believed. Dost thou want money?
*Septimius.*                                 No, sir.
*Pothinus.* Or hast thou any suit? These ever follow   160
    Thy vehement protestations.
*Septimius.*                   You much wrong me.
    How can I want when your beams shine upon me,
    Unless employment to express my zeal
    To do your greatness service? Do but think
    A deed so dark the sun would blush to look on,   165
    For which mankind would curse me, and arm all
    The powers above and those below against me:
    Command me, I will on.
*Pothinus.*                 When I have use,
    I'll put you to the test.
*Septimius.*               May it be speedy,
    And something worth my danger. You are cold   170
    And know not your own powers. This brow was fashioned
    To wear a kingly wreath, and your grave judgement
    Given to dispose of monarchies, not to govern

---

   152–3. *a fugitive ... army*] Cf. Florus, 414: 'Septimius, his fugitive' (*Septimii desertoris sui*, 2.13.52).
   153. *and ... danger*] even in such a dangerous situation as the present one.
   155. *Furies*] three infernal goddesses, also known as Erinyes, who punish the guilty in hell by torturing them to madness: Alecto, Magaera, and Tisiphone.
   156. *light*] fall.
   168. *on*] go on.
   *have use*] need you.
   171. *powers*] strength.
   173. *dispose of*] control, manage.

   A child's affairs. The people's eye's upon you;
   The soldier courts you: will you wear a garment    175
   Of sordid loyalty when 'tis out of fashion?
*Pothinus.* When Pompey was thy general, Septimius,
   Thou saidst as much to him.
*Septimius.*        All my love to him,
   To Caesar, Rome and the whole world is lost
   In the ocean of your bounties. I have no friend,    180
   Project, design or country but your favour,
   Which I'll preserve at any rate.
*Pothinus.*         No more.
   When I call on you, fall not off. Perhaps
   Sooner than you expect I may employ you,
   So leave me for a while.
*Septimius.*        Ever your creature.    *Exit.*   185
*Pothinus.* Good day, Acoreus. — My best friend, Achillas,
   Hath fame delivered yet no certain rumour
   Of the great Roman action?
*Achillas.*         That we are
   To inquire and learn of you, sir, whose grave care
   For Egypt's happiness and great Ptolemy's good    190
   Have eyes and ears in all parts.

    *Enter* PTOLEMY, LABIENUS, [*wounded, and*] Guard.

*Pothinus.*         I'll not boast
   What my intelligence costs me, but ere long
   You shall know more. The King, with him a Roman.

---

174. people's eye's] *Seward;* peoples eye's *F2;* peoples eyes *F1.*   191. SD] *Weber; Enter Ptolomy, Labienus, Guard. F1.*

---

 174. *The ... eye's*] Cf. *3H6* 3.3.117: 'But is he gracious in the people's eye?'
 175. *soldier*] soldiery.
 176. *sordid*] base, squalid.
 182. *at any rate*] at all costs.
 183. *fall not off*] do not desert me.
 187. *fame*] public report, common talk.
 192. *intelligence*] the obtaining of information, espionage.
 *ere*] before.

*Acoreus.* The scarlet livery of unfortunate war
  Dyed deeply on his face.
*Achillas.*           'Tis Labienus, 195
  Caesar's lieutenant in the wars of Gaul
  And fortunate in all his undertakings.
  But, since these civil jars, he turned to Pompey,
  And, though he followèd the better cause,
  Not with the like success.
*Pothinus.*           Such as are wise 200
  Leave falling buildings, fly to those that rise —
  But more of that hereafter.
*Labienus.*           [*To* PTOLEMY] In a word, sir,
  These gaping wounds, not taken as a slave,
  Speak Pompey's loss. To tell you of the battle:
  How many thousand several bloody shapes 205
  Death wore that day in triumph; how we bore
  The shock of Caesar's charge, or with what fury
  His soldiers came on as if they had been
  So many Caesars and like him ambitious
  To tread upon the liberty of Rome; 210
  How fathers killed their sons, or sons their fathers,
  Or how the Roman piles on either side
  Drew Roman blood, which spent, the prince of weapons
  (The sword) succeeded, which in civil wars
  Appoints the tent on which winged victory 215
  Shall make a certain stand; then, how the plains

---

212. *piles*] *F2*; Peils *F1*.

  194–5. *The ... face*] Cf. *Mac* 1.2.1–3: 'What bloody man is that? He can report, / As seemeth by his plight, of the revolt / The newest state.'
  195–8. *'Tis ... Pompey*] Cf. Plutarch, 'Caesar', 780B: 'At that time also Labienus, who was one of Caesar's greatest friends and had been always used as his lieutenant in the wars of Gaul and had valiantly fought in his cause, he likewise forsook him then and fled unto Pompey.'
  203. *gaping*] opening as mouths.
  *not ... slave*] that is, taken in battle.
  204. *loss*] defeat.
  212. *piles*] javelins.
  215. *Appoints*] determines.
  215–16. *the tent ... stand*] a favourite image of Massinger's. Cf. *Duke* 1.1.90: 'on whose fair tent / Winged victory will make her glorious stand'; *MH* 1.2.104–5: 'that plumed victory / Would make her glorious stand upon my tent'; *Pict* 2.2.234–5: 'upon whose tents plumed victory would take / Her glorious stand.'

[SC I]                    THE FALSE ONE

    Flowed o'er with blood, and what a cloud of vultures
    And other birds of prey hung o'er both armies,
    Attending when their ready servitors,
    The soldiers, from whom the angry gods            220
    Had took all sense of reason and of pity,
    Would serve in their own carcasses for a feast;
    How Caesar with his javelin forced them on
    That made the least stop when their angry hands
    Were lifted up against some known friend's face;       225
    Then, coming to the body of the army,
    He shows the sacred Senate and forbids them
    To waste their force upon the common soldier,
    Whom willingly, if e'er he did know pity,
    He would have spared.
*Ptolemy.*                   The reason, Labienus?         230
*Labienus.*  Full well he knows that in their blood he was
    To pass to empire and that through their bowels
    He must invade the laws of Rome and give
    A period to the liberty of the world.
    Then fell the Lepidi and the bold Corvini,          235
    The famed Torquati, Scipios and Marcelli —

---

219. *Attending*] awaiting.
*servitors*] servants.
220. *soldiers*] pronounced 'soldiers'.
223–8.] Cf. Lucan, 7.574–8: 'His hand supplies fresh swords and provides missiles; his voice bids them hack with the steel the faces of the foe. In person he advances the fighting line and urges on his rearguard; he rouses the laggards with blows from the butt-end of his spear. Bidding them spare those of low degree, he points out the senators.'
227. *Senate*] that is, the senators who were present on the battlefield.
*them*] that is, his soldiers.
228. *common soldier*] ordinary soldiers.
231–7.] Cf. Lucan, 7.579–85: 'For he knows where the blood of the empire runs, the [bowels of the laws]; he knows in what quarter Rome must be struck, and the vulnerable points of Liberty now making her last stand on earth. Senators mixed with knights are borne down by the steel, and noble corpses lie low; they slay Lepidi and Metelli, they slay Corvini together with the stock of Torquatus – often leaders of the State, and raised above all men, Magnus alone excepted.'
231. *their*] that is, the senators'.
233. *invade*] assault, violate.
233–4. *give / A period*] put an end.
235–6. *the Lepidi ... Marcelli*] the play follows Lucan, 7.583–4 (quoted above), in listing the names of prestigious senatorial families of Rome. As Roche argues, 'Lucan's thematic emphasis upon Pharsalus as the death of

82  THE FALSE ONE  [ACT I

> Names, next to Pompey's, most renowned on earth.
> The nobles and the commons lay together,
> And Pontic, Punic and Assyrian blood
> Made up one crimson lake, which Pompey seeing        240
> And that his and the fate of Rome had left him,
> Standing upon the rampire of his camp,
> Though scorning all that could fall on himself,
> He pities them whose fortunes are embarked
> In his unlucky quarrel; cries aloud too              245

---

liberty and the equation of the senate with that liberty has compelled him to invent prominent senatorial casualties. He has thus seized upon four emotive names of the republican nobility: the plurals may be taken as generalizing ("men like")' (198). As a matter of fact, the Lepidi were actually supporters of Caesar. The Corvini are best remembered for Marcus Valerius Messala Corvinus, who fought for Cassius at Philippi and for Octavian at Actium but probably would have been too young to fight at Pharsalus. 'Torquati' is a likely allusion to Lucius Manlius Torquatus, who fought against Caesar at Dyrrachium before dying at Thapsus in 47. 'Scipios' is the playwrights' substitution for 'Metelli', the reference clearly being to Quintus Caecilius Metellus Pius Scipio Nasica, Pompey's father-in-law, who survived Pharsalus but later committed suicide in Thapsus. The Marcelli are an addition of the playwrights', probably owing to Gaius Claudius Marcellus having been consul in 49 when Caesar crossed the Rubicon, as well as one of the strongest advocates for the Senate to take extreme measures against him (see 5.2.45).

239–40. *And ... lake*] Cf. Lucan, 7.635–7: 'here the blood of Achaea, Pontus, and Assyria was poured out, and all that bloodshed the torrent of Roman gore forbids to linger and stagnate on the field'.

239. *Pontic ... Assyrian*] that is, of soldiers coming from all those regions: the Kingdom of Pontus, in north-eastern Anatolia, between the rivers Phasys and Halys and the south coast of the Black Sea; the Carthaginian Empire, along the coast of north-west Africa; and the Mesopotamian Kingdom of Assyria, which at the time was largely under the control of the Parthian Empire.

240–9. *which ... misfortunes*] Cf. Lucan, 7.647–51, 654–5, 666–9: 'By now Magnus, unhappy man, was aware that Heaven and the destiny of Rome had gone over to the enemy, though the full extent of the disaster could scarce compel him to despair of his fortunes. Far off on a rising ground he stayed, to see from there the carnage spread through the land of Thessaly ... But he desired not, as the wretched often do, to draw all things in destruction after him and make mankind share his ruin ... and rode round his army and the standards and the troops now shattered on every hand, recalling them from rushing upon instant death, and saying that he was not worth the sacrifice.'

242. *rampire*] rampart.

That they should sound retreat and save themselves,
That he desired not so much noble blood
Should be lost in his service or attend
On his misfortunes; and then, taking horse
With some few of his friends, he came to Lesbos          250
And with Cornelia, his wife, and sons
He touched upon your shore. The King of Parthia,
Famous in his defeature of the Crassi,
Offered him his protection, but Pompey,
Relying on his benefits and your faith,                   255
Hath chosen Egypt for his sanctuary
Till he may recollect his scattered powers
And try a second day. Now, Ptolemy,
Though he appear not like that glorious thing

---

248–9. *attend / On*] accompany.

249. *taking horse*] Labienus' account is here elliptical, not literally implying that Pompey reached the island of Lesbos on horseback, which would have been impossible.

250. *Lesbos*] a Greek island located in the north-eastern Aegean Sea, where Pompey stopped to reunite with his family before proceeding to Egypt while fleeing from Caesar.

251. *Cornelia ... sons*] Cornelia Metella, the daughter of Metellus Scipio and fifth wife of Pompey the Great, and his sons Gnaeus Pompeius (also known as Pompey the Younger), who was rumoured to have had a brief love affair with Cleopatra (see Plutarch, 'Antony', 981C), and Sextus Pompey (who appears in *A&C*). Plutarch, 'Pompey', 715C, however, reports that 'Pompey, passing then by the city of Amphipolis, coasted from thence into the isle of Lesbos to go fetch his wife Cornelia and his son', not sons. The playwrights may have been therefore following Florus' *Epitome*, 415: 'under the eyes of his wife and children he should conclude his days' (*sub oculis uxoris suae liberorumque moreretur*, 2.13.52).

252. *King of Parthia*] Orodes II, King of Kings of the Parthian Empire in Asia from 57 to 37 BCE, at whose court Pompey considered seeking asylum before deciding to head for Egypt according to Plutarch, 'Pompey', 716C–D.

253. *Famous ... Crassi*] Orodes is also remembered for the Parthian victory against Marcus Licinius Crassus at the Battle of Carrhae in 53 BCE. Crassus' defeat at Carrhae was one of the worst military defeats in Roman history. The play uses the plural Crassi because Crassus' son Publius also died in the battle. A powerful Roman politician and general, Crassus had been a member of the First Triumvirate with Caesar and Pompey and was especially famous for his wealth.

*defeature*] defeating.

254. *protection*] pronounced 'protectiòn'.

257. *powers*] forces.

|That three times rode in triumph and gave laws         260
To conquered nations and made crowns his gift —
As this of yours your noble father took
From his victorious hand, and you still wear it
At his devotion — to do you more honour
In his declined estate, as the straightest pine        265
In a full grove of his yet flourishing friends,
He flies to you for succour and expects
The entertainment of your father's friend
And guardian to yourself.
*Ptolemy.*              To say I grieve his fortune
As much as if the crown I wear, his gift,              270
Were ravished from me is a holy truth
Our gods can witness for me. Yet, being young
And not a free disposer of myself,
Let not a few hours borrowed for advice
Beget suspicion of unthankfulness,                     275
Which next to hell I hate. Pray you retire
And take a little rest. [*To* Guard] And let his wounds
Be with that care attended as they were
Carved on my flesh. — Good Labienus, think
The little respite I desire shall be                   280
Wholly employed to find the readiest way
To do great Pompey service.
*Labienus.*                 May the gods,

---

260. *three ... triumph*] Pompey the Great celebrated three triumphs: the first in 79 BCE after his victories in Africa; the second in 71 for his successes in Spain; the third in 61 for his victories in Asia. The association of three triumphs with Pompey was very common among the ancient authorities, and the fact that the three triumphs were celebrated for victories over the three continents made a striking impression, thereby opening up the potential for Pompey to be hailed as the conqueror of the entire world.

264. *devotion*] disposal (*OED* n. 6a).

268. *entertainment*] hospitality.

269. *guardian to yourself*] Cf. Lucan, 8.448–9: 'The sceptre which the boy Ptolemy holds he owes to you, Magnus; it was entrusted to your guardianship.'

271. *ravished*] stolen.

275. *Beget*] engender.

278. *attended*] taken care of.

*as*] as if.

SC I]                    THE FALSE ONE                          85

  As you intend, protect you.   *Exit [with* Guard].
*Ptolemy.*      Sit, sit all: [*They sit.*]
  It is my pleasure. Your advice, and freely.
*Acoreus.* A short deliberation in this        285
  May serve to give you counsel. To be honest,
  Religious and thankful in themselves
  Are forcible motives and can need no flourish
  Or gloss in the persuader. Your kept faith,
  Though Pompey never rise to the height he's fallen from, 290
  Caesar himself will love, and my opinion
  Is, still committing it to graver censure,
  You pay the debt you owe him with the hazard
  Of all you can call yours.
*Ptolemy.*     What's yours, Pothinus?
*Pothinus.* Acoreus, great Ptolemy, hath counselled    295
  Like a religious and honest man,
  Worthy the honour that he justly holds
  In being priest to Isis. But, alas,

---

283. SD] *Dyce; Exit with attendants. Weber; Exit. F1.*

285–94. *A ... yours*] Cf. Lucan, 8.474–6, 480–1: 'There was scarce time to deliberate; yet all the portentous figures of the Macedonian palace assembled. Among them was Acoreus, made mild by age and taught moderation by decrepitude ... He spoke first at the council, dwelling on benefits received and loyalty and the sacred promises of the dead monarch's will.'
 285. *deliberation*] pronounced 'deliberatìon'.
 287. *Religious*] pronounced 'religìous'.
 288–9. *flourish / Or gloss*] rhetorical embellishments.
 292. *committing ... censure*] submitting it to more respected judgement.
 295–312.] Cf. Lucan, 8.482–95: 'But there was one, more fit to counsel wicked kings and know their heart, and a Pothinus dared to sign the death-warrant of a Pompey. He said: "Ptolemy, the laws of God and man make many guilty: we praise loyalty, but it pays the price when it supports those whom Fortune crushes. Take the side of destiny and Heaven, and court the prosperous but shun the afflicted. Expediency is as far from the right as the stars from earth or fire from water. The power of kings is utterly destroyed, once they begin to weigh considerations of justice; and regard for virtue levels the strongholds of tyrants. It is boundless wickedness and unlimited slaughter that protect the unpopularity of a sovereign. If all your deeds are cruel, you will suffer for it the moment you cease from cruelty. If a man would be righteous, let him depart from a court. Virtue is incompatible with absolute power. He who is ashamed to commit cruelty must always fear it."'
 296. *religious*] pronounced 'religìous'.

What in a man sequestered from the world
Or in a private person is preferred                                300
No policy allows of in a king.
To be or just or thankful makes kings guilty,
And faith, though praised, is punished that supports
Such as good fate forsakes. Join with the gods,
Observe the man they favour, leave the wretched:                   305
The stars are not more distant from the earth
Than profit is from honesty. All the power,
Prerogatives and greatness of a prince
Is lost if he descend once but to steer
His course as what's right guides him. Let him leave               310
The sceptre that strives only to be good,
Since kingdoms are maintained by force and blood.
*Acoreus.* Oh, wicked!
*Ptolemy.*             Peace. [*To* POTHINUS] Go on.
*Pothinus.* Proud Pompey shows how much he scorns your
    youth

---

299. *sequestered*] secluded.
302. *or ... or*] either ... or.
311. *that*] The antecedent is 'him' on the previous line.
313.] This is an incomplete line of pentameter, being made up of only six syllables. A significant pause may be intended after Ptolemy's command 'Peace' to capture the tense atmosphere of the final section of the scene.
314–43. *Proud ... Pompey*] Cf. Lucan, 8.496–519: 'Let Magnus suffer for having despised your youth; he thinks you cannot repel even a beaten man from our coast. And, that a stranger may not rob us of the throne, remember that you have others nearer of kin; and, if your crown is uneasy, restore the Nile and Pharos to the sister you have condemned. Let us in any case protect Egypt from the arms of Rome. Whatever did not belong to Pompey during the war will not belong to Caesar either. Driven from all the world, with no reliance left upon his fortunes, he seeks a people to share his fall. He is dragged down by the ghosts of those who fell in civil war. It is not merely Caesar's sword that he flies from: he flies also from the face of the senators, of whom so many are now glutting the vultures of Thessaly; he fears the foreign nations, whom he forsook and left weltering in blood together; he dreads the kings, whose all he destroyed; guilty of Pharsalia and rejected by every country, he troubles our realm which he has not yet destroyed. But we, Ptolemy, can complain more justly of Pompey than he of us: why does he stain secluded and peace-loving Pharos with the guilt of war and bring down Caesar's displeasure on our land? Why when falling did he choose this country of all others to bring to it the curse of Pharsalia and the punishment which he alone should pay? Even now we have incurred guilt, which we cannot purge away except by using the sword. On his motion the Senate granted us the sovereignty of Egypt, and therefore we prayed for his victory.'

                In thinking that you cannot keep your own                    315
                From such as are o'ercome. If you are tired
                With being a king, let not a stranger take
                What nearer pledges challenge: resign rather
                The government of Egypt and of Nile
                To Cleopatra, that has title to them;                         320
                At least defend them from the Roman grip.
                What was not Pompey's while the wars endured
                The conqueror will not challenge. By all the world
                Forsaken and despised, your gentle guardian,
                His hopes and fortunes desperate, makes choice of            325
                What nation he shall fall with and, pursued
                By their pale ghosts slain in this civil war,
                He flies not Caesar only, but the Senate,
                Of which the greater part have cloyed the hunger
                Of sharp Pharsalian fowl; he flies the nations               330
                That he drew to his quarrel, whose estates
                Are sunk in his, and, in no place received,
                Hath found out Egypt, by him yet not ruined.
                And Ptolemy, things considered, justly may
                Complain of Pompey: wherefore should he stain                335
                Our Egypt with the spots of civil war
                Or make the peaceable or quiet Nile
                Doubted of Caesar? Wherefore should he draw
                His loss and overthrow upon our heads
                Or choose this place to suffer in? Already                   340
                We have offended Caesar in our wishes,
                And no way left us to redeem his favour
                But by the head of Pompey.
*Acoreus.*                              Great Osiris,
                Defend thy Egypt from such cruelty

---

321. *grip*] *this edn;* gripe *F1.*   337. *or*] *F1;* and *conj Dyce.*   343. *head*] *F2;* hand *F1.*

315. *your own*] what belongs to you.
318. *pledges*] hostages.
327. *their ... ghosts*] the pale ghosts of those.
329. *cloyed*] satisfied.
330. *sharp*] hungry.
*fowl*] birds.
338. *of*] by.
342. *redeem*] 'To obtain by purchase, to buy' (*OED* v. 9a).

    And barbarous ingratitude!
*Pothinus.*                        Holy trifles,        345
    And not to have place in designs of state.
    This sword, which fate commands me to unsheathe,
                 [*He rises and draws his sword.*]
    I would not draw on Pompey, if not vanquished.
    I grant it rather should have passed through Caesar,
    But we must follow where his fortune leads us.     350
    All provident princes measure their intents
    According to their power and so dispose them.
    And thinkst thou, Ptolemy, that thou canst prop
    His ruins under whom sad Rome now suffers
    Or tempt the conqueror's force when 'tis confirmed?     355

---

   347–62.] Cf. Lucan, 8.520–2, 526–35: 'The sword, which destiny bids me bring forth, I did not intend for Pompey but for the loser, whichever he might be. I shall pierce your heart with it, Magnus; I had rather have slain Caesar; but we are borne by the current that carries the whole world away ... Does he not see our unwarlike population, scarce able to till the fields softened by the falling Nile? We must take the measure of our kingdom and confess our weakness. Are you, Ptolemy, strong enough to prop the fall of Pompey – that fall beneath which Rome is crushed? Dare you disturb the pyre and ashes of Pharsalia, and summon war to your own realms? Before the battle of Pharsalia we took neither side: do we now adopt Pompey's cause when all the world is forsaking it? Do you now challenge the might and proved success of Caesar? To support the loser in adversity is right, but right only for those who have shared in his prosperity; no loyalty ever picked out the wretched as friends.'

   353. *thou ... thou*] Pothinus here shifts from *you* to *thou*. In general, *you* was used by inferiors to address social superiors and less specifically employed to express formality, a respectful distance between speakers, or even, occasionally, a measure of coldness between people supposed to be intimate. *Thou* was usually deployed when addressing family or friends affectionately, or by superiors to address social inferiors; hence, it could also be used to communicate shades of presumption or condescension ranging from the lightly irritating to the extremely offensive. In this case, Pothinus' shift to *thou* would seem to convey his growing insistence in his address to the King, as well as his ill-concealed sense of superiority and patronizing attitude towards the young Ptolemy.

   *prop*] keep from falling.
   354. *whom*] which.
   355. *tempt*] put to the test.
   *confirmed*] firmly established.

SC 1]    THE FALSE ONE    89

    Shall we that in the battle sat as neuters
    Serve him that's overcome? No, no, he's lost.
    And though 'tis noble to a sinking friend
    To lend a helping hand while there is hope
    He may recover, thy part not engaged,                               360
    Though one most dear, when all his hopes are dead,
    To drown him, set thy foot upon his head.
*Acoreus.* Most execrable counsel!
*Achillas.*                        To be followed:
    'Tis for the kingdom's safety.
*Ptolemy.*                [*To* POTHINUS] We give up
    Our absolute power to thee. Dispose of it                          365
    As reason shall direct thee.
*Pothinus.*                        Good Achillas,
    Seek out Septimius. Do you but soothe him:
    He is already wrought. Leave the dispatch
    To me of Labienus. 'Tis determined
    Already how you shall proceed, nor fate                            370
    Shall alter it, since now the die is cast
    But that this hour to Pompey is his last.        [*Exeunt.*]

---

369. me of] *F2;* me; of *F1.*    372. SD] *1711; Exit. F1.*

---

356. *sat as neuters*] remained neutral.
360–1. *thy ... one*] 'If you are not pledged to support his interests, then, though he be one ...' (Luce).
364. *give up*] hand over.
367. *soothe*] blandish, humour.
368. *wrought*] persuaded, prevailed upon.
    *dispatch*] The word is ambiguous. The meaning is probably 'Official dismissal or leave to go, given to an ambassador after completion of his errand; congé' (*OED* n. 2). Yet the verb *dispatch* could also ominously imply that Pothinus will in fact kill Labienus (*OED* n. 4).
371. *the ... cast*] Pothinus appropriates the words that Caesar allegedly pronounced before crossing the Rubicon and moving with his army towards Rome: *alea iacta est* (or, more correctly, *alea iacta esto*, i.e., 'let the die be cast'). See also 5.2.8.
372. *But that*] so that.

## [ACT 1] SCENE 2

*Enter* APOLLODORUS, EROS, ARSINOE [*and a* Boy].

*Apollodorus.* Is the Queen stirring, Eros?
*Eros.* Yes, for, in truth,
    She touched no bed tonight.
*Apollodorus.* I am sorry for it
    And wish it were in me, with my hazard,
    To give her ease.
*Arsinoe.* Sir, she accepts your will
    And does acknowledge she hath found you noble,     5
    So far as, if restraint of liberty
    Could give admission to a thought of mirth,
    She is your debtor for it.
*Apollodorus.* Did you tell her
    Of the sports I have prepared to entertain her?
    She was used to take delight, with her fair hand,     10
    To angle in the Nile, where the glad fish,
    As if they knew who 'twas sought to deceive 'em,
    Contended to be taken; other times,
    To strike the stag, who, wounded by her arrows,
    Forgot his tears in death and, kneeling, thanks her     15
    To his last gasp, then prouder of his fate

---

0.1. SD] *Weber; Enter Apollodorus, Eros, Arsino. F1.*

1.2.0.] Weber adds the setting: '*An Apartment in the Palace of Cleopatra*'.
1. *stirring*] out of bed.
3. *with my hazard*] with the hazard of myself.
4. *will*] intention, purpose.
9. *sports*] entertainments.
10. *fair*] See 1.1.26.
11. *angle*] fish with a hook and bait.
12. *sought*] who sought.
10–13. *She ... taken*] Cf. *A&C* 2.5.10–18: '*Cleopatra.* ... Give me mine angle; we'll to the river. There, / My music playing far off, I will betray / Tawny-finned fishes. My bended hook shall pierce / Their slimy jaws, and as I draw them up / I'll think them every one an Antony, / And say "Aha! You're caught." *Charmian.* 'Twas merry when / You wagered on your angling, when your diver / Did hang a salt fish on his hook, which he / With fervency drew up.'

|  | Than if, with garlands crowned, he had been chosen |  |
|---|---|---|
|  | To fall a sacrifice before the altar |  |
|  | Of the virgin huntress. The King nor great Pothinus |  |
|  | Forbid her any pleasure, and the circuit | 20 |
|  | In which she is confined gladly affords |  |
|  | Variety of pastimes, which I would |  |
|  | Increase with my best service. |  |
| *Eros.* | Oh, but the thought |  |
|  | That she that was born free and to dispense |  |
|  | Restraint or liberty to others should be | 25 |
|  | At the devotion of her brother, whom |  |
|  | She only knows her equal, makes this place |  |
|  | In which she lives, though stored with all delights, |  |
|  | A loathsome dungeon to her. |  |
| *Apollodorus.* | Yet, howe'er |  |
|  | She shall interpret it, I'll not be wanting | 30 |
|  | To do my best to serve her. I have prepared |  |
|  | Choice music near her cabinet and composed |  |
|  | Some few lines, set unto a solemn time, |  |
|  | In the praise of imprisonment. — Begin, boy. |  |

*The Song [by the Boy]*

|  |  |  |
|---|---|---|
|  | Look out, bright eyes, and bless the air: | 35 |
|  | Even in shadows you are fair. |  |
|  | Shut-up beauty is like fire, |  |
|  | That breaks out clearer still and higher. |  |
|  | Though your body be confined |  |
|  | And soft love a prisoner bound, | 40 |
|  | Yet the beauty of your mind |  |
|  | Neither check nor chain hath found. |  |

---

19. *virgin huntress*] that is, Diana, the Roman goddess of hunting, the moon, and chastity.
   20. *circuit*] compass, space.
   22. *would*] would like to.
   26. *devotion*] disposal (*OED* n. 6a).
   30. *wanting*] not forthcoming.
   32. *cabinet*] private apartment, boudoir.
   33. *time*] the rhythmic pattern or character of a piece of music.
   35–44.] See Appendix 2.

Look out nobly, then, and dare
Even the fetters that you wear.
                    [Boy *rejoins* APOLLODORUS.]

         *Enter* CLEOPATRA.

*Cleopatra.* But that we are assured this tastes of duty      45
    And love in you, my guardian, and desire
    In you, my sister, and the rest to please us,
    We should receive this as a saucy rudeness
    Offered our private thoughts. But your intents
    Are to delight us: alas, you wash an Ethiop.              50
    Can Cleopatra, while she does remember
    Whose daughter she is and whose sister — oh,
    I suffer in the name! — and that, in justice,
    There is no place in Egypt where I stand
    But that the tributary earth is proud                     55
    To kiss the foot of her that is her Queen,
    Can she, I say, that is all this, e'er relish
    Of comfort or delight while base Pothinus,

---

44.1. SD] *this edn*; Exit Boy. *Turner; not in F1.*

---

43. *dare*] defy.
44.1. SD] The SD is necessary here to keep track of what the Boy is supposed to do after singing. He might exit here, but Cleopatra's ensuing reference to Apollodorus, Arsinoe, 'and the rest' (i.e., Eros and the Boy) would seem to suggest that that the Boy is still on stage when she enters, and there is no other point in the scene at which it would make sense for him to leave the stage alone. It seems therefore likely that the Boy remains on stage till the end of the scene.
45. *But ... are*] were we not.
47. *the rest*] that is, Eros and the Boy.
48. *saucy*] insolent.
50. *you ... Ethiop*] you labour in vain; a Eurocentric proverb of biblical origin premised on the impossibility of washing a black person's skin white: 'Can the Ethiopian change his skin, or the leopard his spots?' (Jer. 13.23; Dent E186; Aesop, *Fables*, 11). See Hall, 66–7, 107–16. The proverb recurs in *Tamer* 3.2.60; *Cure* 2.2.151; *Bondman* 5.3.144; *Parl* 2.2.70; *RA* 3.2.94. Cf. also *CustCount* 1.2.535: 'The beauteous huntress, fairer far and sweeter / (Diana shows an Ethiop to this beauty), / Protected by two virgin knights'; *Lawyer* 5.1.239–41: 'a French crown will buy / More sport and a companion to whom / You, in your best trim, are an Ethiop'. Cf. also Jonson, *Blackness* 208 and *Beauty* 63.
55. *tributary*] that pays tribute to Cleopatra.

SC 2]                    THE FALSE ONE                              93

     Bondman Achillas and all other monsters
     That reign o'er Ptolemy make that a court                    60
     Where they reside, and this, where I, a prison?
     But there's a Rome, a Senate and a Caesar,
     Though the great Pompey lean to Ptolemy,
     May think of Cleopatra.
*Apollodorus.*              Pompey, madam —
*Cleopatra.* What of him? Speak. If ill, Apollodorus,                  65
     It is my happiness, and for thy news
     Receive a favour kings have kneeled in vain for
     And kiss my hand.
*Apollodorus.*           He's lost.
*Cleopatra.*               Speak it again!
*Apollodorus.* His army routed, he fled, and pursued
     By the all-conquering Caesar.
*Cleopatra.*              Whither bends he?                      70
*Apollodorus.* To Egypt.
*Cleopatra.*       Ha! In person?
*Apollodorus.*              'Tis received
     For an undoubted truth.
*Cleopatra.*           [*Aside*] I live again
     And, if assurance of my love and beauty
     Deceive me not, I now shall find a judge
     To do me right. But how to free myself                        75
     And get access? The guards are strong upon me;
     This door I must pass through. — Apollodorus,
     Thou often hast professed, to do me service,
     Thy life was not thine own.
*Apollodorus.*             I am not altered,

---

61. prison] *F2;* Prisoner *F1.*   64. madam —] *Colman;* Madam?) *F1.*

---

  59. *Bondman*] slave.
  66–8. *and ... hand*] Cf. *A&C* 3.13.82–7: '*Thidias.* ... Give me grace to lay / My duty on your hand. *Cleopatra.* Your Caesar's father oft, / When he hath mused of taking kingdoms in, / Bestowed his lips on that unworthy place, / As it rained kisses.'
  69. *routed*] defeated resoundingly and compelled to retreat in disorder and haste.
  70. *bends*] directs himself.
  71. *received*] believed.
  77. *This ... through*] Cleopatra is here referring to one of the stage doors, a relatively rare example of theatrical self-consciousness in the play.

   And, let your excellency propound a means     80
   In which I may but give the least assistance
   That may restore you to that you were born to —
   Though it call on the anger of the King
   Or, what's more deadly, all his minion
   Pothinus can do to me — I, unmoved,     85
   Offer my throat to serve you, ever provided
   It bear some probable show to be effected.
   To lose myself upon no ground were madness,
   Not loyal duty.
*Cleopatra.* [*To the others*] Stand off. [*They do so.*] — [*To*
   APOLLODORUS] To thee alone
   I will discover what I dare not trust     90
   My sister with. Caesar is amorous
   And taken more with the title of a queen
   Than feature or proportion. He loved Eunoë,
   A moor — deformed too, I have heard — that brought
   No other object to inflame his blood     95
   But that her husband was a king; on both
   He did bestow rich presents. Shall I, then,
   That with a princely birth bring beauty with me,
   That know to prize myself at mine own rate,
   Despair his favour? Art thou mine?
*Apollodorus.*          I am.     100

---

 82. *that*] that which.
 84. *minion*] a court favourite. The word would have carried topical resonance in the Jacobean era in light of James's well-known penchant for male favourites.
 87. *bear ... effected*] displays some probability of success.
 91. *amorous*] devoted to love. Cf. Suetonius, 21: 'An opinion there is constantly received, that he was given to carnal pleasures and that way spent much; also, that he dishonoured many dames and those of noble houses' (*Pronum et sumptuosum in libidines fuisse constans opinio est, plurimasque et illustres feminas corrupisse*, 50.1).
 92. *taken ... with*] attracted by.
 93. *Eunoë*] the wife of Bogudes, King of Western Mauretania. Her affair with Caesar is referred to in passing by Suetonius, 21: 'He was enamoured also upon queens and among them loved Eunoë the Moor, wife of Bogudes, King of Mauretania, upon whom, as also upon her husband, he bestowed very many gifts and of infinite value' (*Dilexit et reginas inter quas Eunoen Mauram Bogudis uxorem, cui maritoque eius plurima et immensa tributi*, 52.1). Historically, the liaison may have actually post-dated Caesar's affair with Cleopatra.

SC 1]                    THE FALSE ONE                    95

*Cleopatra.* I have found out a way shall bring me to him
    Spite of Pothinus' watches. If I prosper,
    As I am confident I shall, expect
    Things greater than thy wishes. [*Aside*] Though I
        purchase
    His grace with loss of my virginity,                      105
    It skills not if it bring home majesty.      *Exeunt.*

                    ACT 2 SCENE 1

*Enter* SEPTIMIUS, *with a head,* ACHILLAS [*and*] Guard.

*Septimius.* 'Tis here! 'Tis done! Behold, you fearful viewers!
    Shake, and behold the model of the world here,
    The pride and strength! Look, look again: 'tis finished!

---

101. *shall*] that shall.
102. *Spite*] in spite.
106. *skills*] matters (*OED* v.1 2b).

2.1.0.] Weber adds the setting: '*Before the Royal Palace*'.
0.1. SD with a head] The head of Pompey is by far the most important prop in the play. How might it have looked in performance? Little information is extant regarding heads as props in the early modern theatre. On most occasions the severed heads would probably have been contained in baskets or sacks (potentially replaced by pumpkins) and would therefore not have been seen by playgoers. Yet there are cases in which, as Michael J. Hirrel argues, 'the balance of the probabilities is that the heads resembled those of the actors who had portrayed the unfortunate characters' (56). Andrew Gurr and Mariko Ichikawa even contend that 'Shakespeare's company must have kept Burbage's head in effigy, for the hero's decapitation at the end of *Macbeth*' (61–2). This kind of interpretation, however, is not universally accepted. Alan Dessen (pers. comm.) is 'dubious about a prop head designed to resemble an individual actor or fictional figure', since 'There are too many of them in use, often multiple examples in a single play'; besides, 'as in today's performances before more squeamish playgoers, some heads could be in a bloody bag'. David McInnis (pers. comm.) similarly believes that heads would have corresponded to roles rather than actual people. In the absence of direct evidence, it is impossible to settle the matter, and every reconstruction of what prop heads looked like on the early modern stage cannot but be conjectural. Yet if we entertain just for a moment the possibility that the heads might indeed have been modelled on the company players' facial features, and if we assume that the King's Men had kept the head that had been modelled on Burbage's for *Macbeth* (if one ever existed), it is striking to imagine the actor playing Septimius appearing on stage with a head looking like Burbage. Pompey's head needs to be that of someone

　　　　That that whole armies, nay, whole nations,
　　　　Many and mighty kings have been struck blind at       5
　　　　And fled before, winged with their fears and terrors;
　　　　That steeled war waited on and fortune courted;
　　　　That high-plumed honour built up for her own;
　　　　Behold that mightiness, behold that fierceness,
　　　　Behold that child of war with all his glories          10
　　　　By this poor hand made breathless! — Here, my Achillas:
　　　　Egypt and Caesar owe me for this service,
　　　　And all the conquered nations.
*Achillas.*　　　　　　　　　　Peace, Septimius.
　　　　Thy words sound more ungrateful than thy actions.
　　　　Though sometimes safety seek an instrument            15
　　　　Of thy unworthy nature, thou loud boaster,
　　　　Think not she is bound to love him too: that's barbarous.
　　　　Why did not I, if this be meritorious
　　　　And binds the King unto me, and his bounties,
　　　　Strike this rude stroke? I'll tell thee, thou poor Roman:  20
　　　　It was a sacred head I durst not heave at,

---

7. steeled war] *conj Sympson and Theobald;* steel-war *conj Mason;* steele warr *F1.*

---

who does not appear on stage, and the late Burbage's head – which the audience would have undoubtedly recognized roughly a year after his death – would have carried an aura of past greatness that would have poignantly conveyed the idea of loss attached to Pompey in the play, and would have made Caesar's horror and incredulity at the sight of it all the more impassioned and relatable. At any rate, Fletcher availed himself of property heads more than once in his theatrical career, but only after the termination of his partnership with Beaumont. Severed heads appear in *Bonduca, Rollo, Sir John Van Olden Barnavelt,* and *The Double Marriage.*

　4. *nations*] pronounced 'nations'.

　7. *steeled war*] As Turner argues, 'F1's "steele" is certainly not impossible, but Theobald and Sympson (in Seward) were probably right to conjecture "steel'd" because of its parallel with "plum'd" (line 8)'. The word recurs at 5.2.21.

　21–2. *It ... thought*] Fletcher and Massinger here seem to have followed Florus, who identifies Septimius as the sole murderer of Pompey (414, 2.13.52), rather than the accounts of Lucan, 8.618–19, 667–74, and Plutarch, 'Pompey', 717E, which place Achillas together with Septimius (Plutarch also mentions the centurion Salvius). See Introduction, 20.

　21. *heave at*] to meditate or threaten an attack upon.

SC I]  THE FALSE ONE  97

   Not heave a thought.
*Septimius.*      It was.
*Achillas.*        I'll tell thee truly
  And, if thou ever yet heardst tell of honour,
  I'll make thee blush: it was thy general's,
  That man's that fed thee once, that man's that bred thee;  25
  The air thou breathedst was his; the fire that warmed thee
  From his care kindled ever; nay, I'll show thee,
  Because I'll make thee sensible of thy business
  And why a noble man durst not touch at it,
  There was no piece of earth thou putst thy foot on  30
  But was his conquest; and he gave thee motion.
  He triumphed three times: who durst touch his person?
  The very walls of Rome bowed to his presence;
  Dear to the gods he was; to them that feared him
  A fair and noble enemy. Didst thou hate him  35
  And for thy love to Caesar sought his ruin?
  Armed in the red Pharsalian fields, Septimius,
  Where killing was in grace and wounds were glorious,
  Where kings were fair competitors for honour,
  Thou shouldst have come up to him, there have fought him,  40
  There, sword to sword.
*Septimius.*     I killed him on commandment.
  If kings' commands be fair, when you all fainted,
  When none of you durst look —
*Achillas.*       On deeds so barbarous.
  What hast thou got?
*Septimius.*     The King's love and his bounty,
  The honour of the service, which, though you rail at,  45
  Or a thousand envious souls fling their foams on me,

---

26. breathedst] *F2;* breath'st *F1.* 28. thy business] *F1;* thy baseness *Seward;* the business *F2.* 37. Armed in] *F2;* Amid *Dyce;* Armed *F1.* 40. fought] *F2;* sought *F1.*

---

 28. *sensible*] aware.
 *business*] task, errand.
 32. *triumphed ... times*] See 1.1.260.
 38. *grace*] favour.
 46. *fling ... foams*] vent their rage.

>     Will dignify the cause and make me glorious,
>     And I shall live —
> *Achillas.*              A miserable villain.
>     What reputation and reward belongs to it
>     Thus with the head I seize on and make mine.       50
>                                   [*He seizes the head.*]
>     And be not impudent to ask me why, sirrah,
>     Nor bold to stay. Read in mine eyes the reason:
>     The shame and obloquy I leave thine own;
>     Inherit those rewards: they are fitter for thee.
>     Your oil's spent, and your snuff stinks. Go out basely.   55
> *Septimius.* The King will yet consider —
>
>              *Enter* PTOLEMY, ACOREUS [*and*] POTHINUS.
>
> *Achillas.*                        Here he comes, sir.
>
>                                   *Exit* [SEPTIMIUS].
> *Acoreus.* [*To* PTOLEMY] Yet if it be undone, hear me, great
>     sir:
>     If this inhuman stroke be yet unstrucken,

---

48. live—] *1711*; live. *F1.*   56. consider—] *Turner*; consider. *F1.*   sir] *F1*; *addressed to Pothinus in Weber; not in Seward.*   56.1. SD] *Turner*; *placed after* consider. *in F1.*

---

  49–50.] Cf. Lucan, 8.674–5: 'But when the neck was severed and parted from the body, the Egyptian minion claims this privilege – to carry it in his right hand.'

  51. *sirrah*] term of address used for servants or social inferiors.

  55. *snuff*] the part of a wick that is consumed by burning and in the case of candles requires to be cut off at intervals. The line is probably reminiscent of Jonson's 'On Spies' (*Epigr* 59): 'Spies, you are lights in state, but of base stuff, / Who, when you've burnt yourselves down to the snuff, / Stink, and are thrown away. End fair enough.'

  56. *sir*] Seward omits and remarks, 'Had Achillas spoke to Septimius, it would have been *sirrah* as before [l. 51]; but he was gone out, and this *sir* seems only to have slipt in from the line below.' Weber has the word 'addressed to P[oth]inus, to whom Achillas shows the head, and with whom he continues in conference during the speech of' Acoreus. As Turner argues, 'F1 does place the exit-direction after "consider —", but this is conventional; Achillas' "Here he comes" ought not to be addressed to vacancy. That "Sir" is an error of anticipation is possible, but the term could be used scornfully and "Sirrah" would have introduced a twelfth syllable.'

  58. *unstrucken*] not struck (only instance recorded in *OED*).

|              If that adorèd head be not yet severed
|              From the most noble body, weigh the miseries,                    60
|              The desolations that this great eclipse works.
|              You are young; be provident: fix not your empire
|              Upon the tomb of him will shake all Egypt,
|              Whose warlike groans will raise ten thousand spirits
|              Great as himself, in every hand a thunder,                       65
|              Destructions darting from their looks, and sorrows
|              That easy women's eyes shall never empty.
*Pothinus.* [*To* PTOLEMY] You have done well, and 'tis done:
    see Achillas
    And in his hand the head.
                       [ACHILLAS *moves towards* PTOLEMY.]
*Ptolemy.*              [*To* ACHILLAS] Stay. Come no nearer.
    Methinks I feel the very earth shake under me.                   70
    I do remember him. He was my guardian,
    Appointed by the Senate to preserve me.
    What a full majesty sits in his face yet!
*Pothinus.* The King is troubled. [*To* PTOLEMY] Be not
    frighted, sir.
    Be not abused with fears: his death was necessary;              75
    If you consider, sir, most necessary,
    Not to be missed. And humbly thank great Isis
    He came so opportunely to your hands.
    Pity must now give place to rules of safety.
    Is not victorious Caesar new arrived                             80
    And entered Alexandria with his friends,
    His navy riding by to wait his charges?
    Did he not beat this Pompey and pursued him?

---

61. *eclipse*] This may be simply metaphorical, but it could also refer to one of the four partial solar eclipses that occurred in 1620: on 4 January, 31 May, 30 June, and 24 November. There had also been a total eclipse on 11 July 1619.

63. *will*] who will.

67. *easy ... eyes*] that is, useless tears.

73.] Cf. Lucan, 8.665–7: 'that the utmost death could do made no alteration in the bearing and countenance of the hero'.

75. *abused with*] deceived by.

80. *new*] newly.

82. *charges*] orders.

100 THE FALSE ONE [ACT 2

    Was not this great man his great enemy,
    This godlike virtuous man, as people held him?    85
    But what fool dare be friend to flying virtue? [*Flourish.*]
    I hear their trumpets.

        *Enter* CAESAR, ANTONY, DOLABELLA [*and*] SCAEVA.

                  'Tis too late to stagger.
    Give me the head [ACHILLAS *does so.*] — [*To*
      PTOLEMY] and be you confident.
    [*To* CAESAR] Hail, conqueror and head of all the world,
    Now this head's off.      [*He shows the head to* CAESAR.]
*Caesar.*              Ha?
*Pothinus.*            Do not shun me, Caesar.    90
    From kingly Ptolemy I bring this present,

---

87. SD] *this edn; placed at line 88.1 in Weber; placed at line 86.1 in F1.*

---

88–90.] Cf. Gentillet, 271b: 'for Caesar soon after arrived in Egypt, unto whom Pothinus and Achillas presented the head of Pompey, thinking greatly to pleasure him'. None of the ancient authorities report that it was Pothinus and Achillas together who presented Caesar with Pompey's head. In Chapman's *Caesar and Pompey*, 5.2.189–202, it is Achillas, Septimius, and Salvius who offer Pompey's head to Caesar.

  89–125.] Cf. Lucan, 9.1014–33: '"Conqueror of the world and mightiest of the Roman race, you are made safe, though you are ignorant of it as yet, by the slaying of your son-in-law. The Macedonian king spares you the toil of war by land and sea, and presents you with the one thing lacking to the victory of Pharsalia. The civil war has been won for you without your presence; when Magnus sought to rebuild the fortunes ruined at Pharsalia, he was laid low by our sword. By so dear a pledge have we bought you, Caesar; by this blood our treaty with you was concluded. We give you the kingdom, to be yours without bloodshed; we give you power over the Nile's waters; we give all that you yourself would have given for Pompey's head; reckon us then as adherents worthy of your army, because Fortune willed that we should have such power against your kinsman. Nor must you undervalue our service, because we conferred it by an execution that cost us nothing. Pompey was our friend of old; he had restored the throne to our king's banished father. Need I say more? You must find a name for this great deed; or else ask what the world says of it. If crime it be, then you admit a greater debt to us, because your own hand is not guilty of the crime." With these words he took off the covering from the head, and held it in his hands.'

> The crown and sweet of thy Pharsalian labour,
> The goal and mark of high ambitious honour.
> Before, thy victory had no name, Caesar,
> Thy travail and thy loss of blood, no recompense;   95
> Thou dreamedst of being worthy and of war,
> And all thy furious conflicts were but slumbers.
> Here they take life, here they inherit honour,
> Grow fixed and shoot up everlasting triumphs.
> Take it and look upon thy humble servant,   100
> With noble eyes look on the princely Ptolemy,
> That offers with this head, most mighty Caesar,
> What thou wouldst once have given for it, all Egypt.

---

92. sweet] *this edn;* sweat *F1.*   96. dreamedst] *Colman;* dreamst *F1.*

---

92. *sweet*] F1 reads 'sweat'. Sympson (in Seward) proposed for the line the emendation 'The crown of thy Pharsalian sweat and labour', which Seward dismissed 'both because labour after sweat, in this position, makes an anti-climax, and as the old text is more poetical; for the sweat of thy labour, put for the end for which thou laboured, is extremely elegant'. The line as printed in F1 may well be elegant, but the meaning of 'end, achievement' for 'sweat' is not attested in *OED*. By contrast, the entry for 'sweet' gives as one of its possible meanings 'something that affords enjoyment or gratifies desire' (*OED* n. 3a). When used in this sense, 'sweet' could be punningly 'Contrasted with sweat' (*OED* n. 3b). John Mason, *The Turk: A Worthy Tragedy* (London, 1610), 5.1, sig. I3, provides a perfect example: 'Ere we had relished the sweet of her sweat, that is, the fruit of her labours'. Given that Pothinus is trying to frame Pompey's death as the gratifying coronation and highest achievement of Caesar's 'labour', it appears justified to emend 'sweat' to 'sweet'. In addition, Pothinus later uses two further pairs of noun phrases – 'goal and mark' (93) and 'Thy travail and thy loss of blood' (95) – that repeat and emphasize the concept of the first one (with an additional chasm between 'crown and sweet' and 'goal and mark'), and also similarly contrasts 'travail' with 'recompense' (95). Fletcher uses 'sweet' as a noun with this meaning elsewhere too: cf. *Val* 4.1.193: 'The sweets of heaven still crown ye'; *NW* 1.8.21-2: 'Is this the sweet of marriage? Have I bred thee / For this reward?'; *Loyal* 4.5: 'These that ye sit a-brooding on like toads, / Sucking from my deserts the sweets and favours, / And render me no pay again but poisons'; *Wife* 3.3.193-4: 'Let's sit together thus, and as we sit / Feed on the sweets of one another's souls.'

*thy*] Here and at 94, 95 (twice), 96, 97, 103, 120, 122, 123, and 125, Pothinus' addressing Caesar with *thou* rather than the more appropriate *you* may be an indication either of his desire to be considered Caesar's equal or of his contempt for Caesar, or both.

95. *travail*] with the common pun on 'travel'.

*Achillas.* Nor do not question it, most royal conqueror,
   Nor disesteem the benefit that meets thee            105
   Because 'tis easily got: it comes the safer.
   Yet let me tell thee, most imperious Caesar,
   Though he opposed no strength of swords to win this
   Nor laboured through no showers of darts and lances,
   Yet here [*Pointing to* PTOLEMY's *breast*] he found a fort
      that faced him strongly,                          110
   An inward war: he [*Pointing to* POMPEY's *head*] was his
      grandsire's guest,
   Friend to his father, and when he was expelled
   And beaten from this kingdom by strong hand
   And had none left him to restore his honour,
   No hope to find a friend in such a misery,           115
   Then in stepped Pompey, took his feeble fortune,
   Strengthened and cherished it and set it right again.
   This was a love to Caesar.
*Scaeva.*                    Give me hate, gods!
*Pothinus.* This Caesar may account a little wicked,
   But yet remember: if thine own hands, conqueror,     120
   Had fallen upon him, what it had been then?
   If thine own sword had touched his throat, what that
      way?
   He was thy son-in-law: there to be tainted
   Had been most terrible. Let the worst be rendered:
   We have deserved for keeping thy hands innocent.     125

---

104. SP *Achillas*] *conj* Theobald; *Ach.* F1.

108. *he*] that is, Ptolemy.
111. *grandsire*] grandfather, that is, Ptolemy IX Soter II, who reigned from 116 to 107 BCE and then from 88 to 81. Pompey, however, was never his guest in Egypt. Ptolemy IX did receive an embassy from Rome in 86, but the embassy was led by Lucius Licinius Lucullus, who was trying to secure ships from Egypt in support of Lucius Cornelius Sulla in the First Mithridatic War, and did not include Pompey. The playwrights' choice seems intended to intensify the bonds that linked the Ptolemaic dynasty to Pompey.
112. *he*] that is, Ptolemy's father.
113. *by strong hand*] by the use of force.
116. *his*] that is, of Ptolemy's father.
123. *son-in-law*] Pompey had been married to Caesar's daughter Julia.
124. *Let … rendered*] Let the worst part of what happened be spelled out.

SC 1]                    THE FALSE ONE                           103

*Caesar.* O Scaeva, Scaeva, see that head! See, captains,
   The head of godlike Pompey!
*Scaeva.*                          He was basely ruined,
   But let the gods be grieved that suffered it,
   And be you Caesar.
*Caesar.*                    O thou conqueror,
   Thou glory of the world once, now the pity,                    130
   Thou awe of nations, wherefore didst thou fall thus?
   What poor fate followed thee and plucked thee on
   To trust thy sacred life to an Egyptian?
   The life and light of Rome to a blind stranger
   That honourable war ne'er taught a nobleness,                  135
   Nor worthy circumstance showed what a man was?
   That never heard thy name sung but in banquets
   And loose lascivious pleasures? To a boy
   That had no faith to comprehend thy greatness,
   No study of thy life to know thy goodness?                    140
   And leave thy nation, nay, thy noble friend,
   Leave him distrusted that in tears falls with thee,
   In soft relenting tears? Hear me, great Pompey,
   If thy great spirit can hear, I must task thee:
   Thou hast most unnobly robbed me of my victory,                145
   My love and mercy.
*Antony.* [*To* DOLABELLA] Oh, how brave these tears show!
   How excellent is sorrow in an enemy!

---

129. Caesar.] *Colman;* Caesar — *F1.*    137. sung] *F2;* sang *F1.*

---

129–31. *O ... thus*] Cf. *JC* 3.1.148–50: 'O mighty Caesar! Dost thou lie so low? / Are all thy conquests, glories, triumphs, spoils, / Shrunk to this little measure?'

129. *thou*] Caesar's insistence on *thou/thee/thy*, used seventeen times over seventeen lines – here and at 130, 131 (twice), 132 (twice), 133, 137, 139, 140 (twice), 141 (twice), 142, 144 (twice), and 145 – is meant to suggest his intimacy with Pompey, as well as the extent to which he is moved by the sight of his rival's head.

134. *blind*] lacking in discernment.

142. *Leave ... distrusted*] Withhold your trust or confidence from him.

144. *task*] reprehend.

145–6. *Thou ... mercy*] Cf. Lucan, 9.1066–8: 'you have taken from me the one privilege of civil war – the power of granting life to the defeated'.

*Dolabella.* [*To* ANTONY] Glory appears not greater than this
    goodness.
*Caesar.* Egyptians, dare you think your high pyramids,
    Built to outdare the sun (as you suppose),                         150
    Where your unworthy kings lie raked in ashes,
    Are monuments fit for him? No, brood of Nilus,
    Nothing can cover his high fame but heaven,
    No pyramids set off his memories
    But the eternal substance of his greatness,                           155
    To which I leave him. [*To* Guard] Take the head away
    And, with the body, give it noble burial. —
                          [*Exit* Guard, *with the head.*]
    Your earth shall now be blessed to hold a Roman
    Whose braveries all the world's earth cannot balance.
*Scaeva.* [*Aside*] If thou be'st thus loving, I shall honour thee.    160
    But great men may dissemble ('tis held possible)
    And be right glad of what they seem to weep for;
    There are such kind of philosophers. Now do I wonder

---

150. outdare] *F1;* out-dure *Seward.*    157.1. SD] *this edn; not in F1.*

---

  149. *pyramids*] As Dyce makes clear, 'though both the folios have pyra-mides, there can be no doubt that the poet intended the word to consist of only three syllables'; also at 154. 'Egyptians' at the beginning of the line probably needs to be pronounced 'Egyptians'.
  150. *outdare*] exceed in daring.
  151. *raked in*] covered with.
  159. *braveries*] acts of bravery.
  *world's earth*] a rendering of the Latin phrase *orbis terrarum.*
  160–5. *If ... face*] Scaeva is sceptical regarding the sincerity of Caesar's tears over Pompey's head, a controversial issue since antiquity (see Appian, 2.86; Plutarch, 'Pompey', 718B–C; Lucan, 8.663–91; Florus, 2.13.54; Cassius Dio, 42.4–5; Canfora, 213–17; Jensen, *Reading*, 138), and manages to instil doubt in the audience about whether they should be taken as a manifestation of hypocrisy. However, this possibility is not endorsed anywhere else in the play. True, Pothinus does corroborate this (cf. 236–40), but his stance is far too partial to be taken seriously into account. Caesar's tears over Pompey also figure as a prominent concern at the beginning of Cary's *Mariam* 1.1–4, 9–14: 'How oft have I with public voice run on / To censure Rome's last hero for deceit / Because he wept when Pompey's life was gone, / Yet when he lived, he thought his name too great? / ... / Now do I find, by self-experience taught, / One object yields both grief and joy: / You wept indeed when on his worth you thought, / But joyed that slaughter did your foe destroy. / So at his death your eyes' true drops did rain, / Whom, dead, you did not wish alive again.'

SC 1]                    THE FALSE ONE                              105

      How he would look if Pompey were alive again,
      But how he would set his face.
Caesar.                              You look now, King,                165
      And you, that have been agents in this glory,
      For our especial favour.
Ptolemy.                   We desire it.
Caesar. And doubtless you expect rewards.
Scaeva.                                       Let me give 'em.
      I'll give 'em such as nature never dreamt of,
      I'll beat him and his agents in a mortar                          170
      Into one man, and that one man I'll bake then.
Caesar. Peace. [*To all Egyptians*] I forgive you all: that's
         recompense.
      [*To* PTOLEMY] You are young and ignorant — that
         pleads your pardon —
      And fear it may be more than hate provoked ye.
      Your ministers, I must think, wanted judgement,                   175
      And so they erred. [*To all Egyptians*] I am bountiful to
         think this,
      Believe me, most bountiful; be you most thankful.
      That bounty share amongst ye. [*To* PTOLEMY] If I
         knew
      What to send you for a present, King of Egypt —
      I mean a head of equal reputation                                 180
      And that you loved — though it were your brightest
         sister's
      (But her you hate), I would not be behind ye.
Ptolemy. Hear me, great Caesar —
Caesar.                              I have heard too much.

---

183. Caesar —] *this edn*; Caesar? *Luce;* Caesar! *Colman; Cesar. F1.* have heard] *F2;* heave hard *F1.*

    166. *glory*] glorious enterprise (meant sarcastically).
    172-3. *I ... pardon*] Cf. Lucan, 9.1087-9: 'Yet I spare his youth and pardon his crime. Let your master learn that pardon is the highest reward this shedding of blood can earn.'
    175. *judgement*] discernment.
    178-82. *If ... ye*] Cf. Lucan, 9.1068-71: 'If the king of Egypt did not hate his sister, I might have made a fitting return for such a gift by sending him the head of Cleopatra.'
    182. *behind ye*] slow in repaying you.

  And study not with smooth shows to invade
  My noble mind as you have done my conquest:  185
  Ye are poor and open. I must tell you roundly:
  That man that could not recompense the benefits,
  The great and bounteous services of Pompey
  Can never dote upon the name of Caesar.
  Though I had hated Pompey and allowed his ruin,  190
  I gave you no commission to perform it.
  Hasty to please in blood are seldom trusty,
  And, but I stand environed with my victories —
  My fortune never failing to befriend me,
  My noble strengths and friends about my person —  195
  I durst not try ye nor expect a courtesy
  Above the pious love you showed to Pompey.
  You have found me merciful in arguing with ye:
  Swords, hangmen, fires, destructions of all natures,
  Demolishments of kingdoms and whole ruins  200

---

199. hangmen] *F2;* hungers *Dyce;* Hangers *F1.*

---

 184. *study]* try.
  *smooth]* specious.
  *invade]* encroach upon.
 186. *open]* liberal.
 189. *dote]* bestow love.
  *upon ... Caesar]* the first of the dozen instances in the play of Caesar's historically attested habit of referring to himself in the third person.
  191–7.] Cf. Lucan, 9.1071-2, 1081-4: 'Why did he draw the sword independently and thrust his weapon into the conflict of Romans? ... Do not fancy that you deceive the conqueror: the same reception on the shore was prepared for me too, and I may thank Pharsalia that my head is not carried like his.'
 192. *trusty]* trustworthy.
 193. *but ... with]* were I not surrounded by.
 194.] The notion that Caesar had a privileged relationship with fortune was commonplace in the early modern imagination. Caesar was often described as the prime example of the *fortunatus*, that is, a man markedly favoured by fortune. See Tappan, 3-14; Soellner, 151 n.30.
 195. *about]* around.
 196. *try]* put to the test.
 197. *pious love]* (meant sarcastically).
 199. *hangmen]* F2's reading makes perfect sense, all the more so given that Septimius is indeed hanged on Caesar's orders in Act 5, scene 3. Dyce's emendation to 'hungers' appears unnecessary.

Are wont to be my orators. Turn to tears,
You wretched and poor seeds of sunburnt Egypt,
And, now you have found the nature of a conqueror
That you cannot decline with all your flatteries,
That where the day gives light will be himself still,     205
Know how to meet his worth with humane courtesies:
Go and embalm those bones of that great soldier,
Howl round about his pile, fling on your spices,
Make a Sabaean bed and place this phoenix
Where the hot sun may emulate his virtues,               210
And draw another Pompey from his ashes,
Divinely great, and fix him 'mongst the worthies.
*Ptolemy.* We will do all.
*Caesar.*           You have robbed him of those tears
His kindred and his friends kept sacred for him;
The virgins of their funeral lamentations;               215
And that kind earth that thought to cover him,
His country's earth, will cry out 'gainst your cruelty
And weep unto the ocean for revenge
Till Nilus raise his seven heads and devour ye.

---

206. *humane*] *F1*; human *1711*.

201. *wont*] accustomed.
204. *decline*] divert from his course.
205. *still*] always.
207–12.] Cf. Lucan, 9.1089–93: 'You must lay in the grave the head of the great general, and not in such a way that the earth merely hides your guilt: give incense to fitting sepulture, ask pardon of the head, collect the ashes strewn on the shore, and let the scattered remains meet in a single urn.'
209. *Sabaean bed*] a layer of the renowned spices (especially frankincense and myrrh) that were regularly brought to Europe from Yemen in Arabia, where the people of the Sabei used to live.
209–11. *phoenix ... ashes*] The phoenix was a mythical Arabian bird that was believed to be reborn out of its own funeral pyre. As only one existed at any given time, it was also a byword for uniqueness.
212. *worthies*] heroes, perhaps with an anachronistic allusion to the Nine Worthies, a group of nine characters drawn from history, the Bible, and legend, and regarded as constituting the supreme embodiment of the chivalric ideals established in the Middle Ages. Still popular in the Renaissance, this group usually included three pagan generals (Hector, Alexander the Great, and Julius Caesar), three Old Testament heroes (David, Joshua, and Judas Maccabeus), and three Christian warriors (King Arthur, Charlemagne, and Godfrey of Bouillon). Interestingly, sometimes Pompey replaced Caesar (cf. *LLL* 5.1.122).

My grief has stopped the rest. When Pompey lived, 220
He used you nobly; now he is dead, use him so.
        *Exit [with* ANTONY, DOLABELLA *and* SCAEVA].
*Ptolemy.* Now where's your confidence, your aim, Pothinus,
    The oracles and fair favours from the conqueror
    You rung into mine ears? How stand I now?
    You see the tempest of his stern displeasure. 225
    The death of him you urged a sacrifice
    To stop his rage presaging a full ruin.
    Where are your counsels now?
*Acoreus.*            I told ye, sir
    (And told the truth), what danger would fly after.
    And, though an enemy, I satisfied you 230
    He was a Roman, and the top of honour,
    And howsoever this might please great Caesar,
    I told ye that the foulness of his death,
    The impious baseness —
*Pothinus.*            Peace, ye are a fool.
    Men of deep ends must tread as deep ways to 'em. 235
    Caesar I know is pleased, and, for all his sorrows,
    Which are put on for forms and mere dissemblings,
    I am confident he's glad. To have told ye so
    And thanked ye outwardly had been too open
    And taken from the wisdom of a conqueror. 240
    Be confident and proud ye have done this service:
    Ye have deserved, and (ye will find it) highly.
    Make bold use of this benefit and be sure
    You keep your sister, the high-souled Cleopatra,
    Both close and short enough she may not see him. 245
    The rest, if I may counsel, sir —
*Ptolemy.*            Do all,
    For in thy faithful service rests my safety.   [*Exeunt.*]

221.1. SD] Dyce; *Exit with* ANTONY, DOLABELLA, SCEVA, *and Soldiers.*
Weber; *Exit.* F1.   235. to 'em] F2; to'm F1.   239. thanked] *1711*; thanke
F1.   247. SD] F2; *Exit.* F1.

221. *used*] treated.
226. *him*] that is, Pompey.
227. *his*] that is, Caesar's
233. *his*] that is, Pompey's.
245. *Both ... enough*] so rigidly confined that.

## [ACT 2] SCENE 2

*Enter* SEPTIMIUS.

*Septimius.* Here's a strange alteration in the court:
Men's faces are of other sets and motions,
Their minds of subtler stuff. I pass by now
As though I were a rascal: no man knows me;
No eye looks after; as I were a plague, 5
Their doors shut close against me and I wondered at
Because I have done a meritorious murder.
Because I have pleased the time, does the time plague me?
I have known the day they would have hugged me for it,
For a less stroke than this have done me reverence, 10
Opened their hearts and secret closets to me,
Their purses and their pleasures, and bid me wallow.
I now perceive the great thieves eat the less,
And the huge Leviathans of villainy
Sup up the merits, nay, the men and all 15
That do them service, and spout 'em out again
Into the air, as thin and unregarded
As drops of water that are lost i'th' ocean.
I was loved once for swearing and for drinking,
And for other principal qualities that became me. 20
Now a foolish unthankful murder has undone me
If my lord Pothinus be not merciful
That set me on.

---

2.2.0.] Weber adds the setting: '*Before the Palace*'. Dyce sets the scene in '*An apartment in the Palace*'. It could be either, but I would incline towards Dyce's hypothesis.

2.] The people's facial expressions are now different.

3. *of ... stuff*] more perceptive.

5. *as*] as if.

13. *the less*] the lesser thieves.

14. *Leviathans*] The Leviathan is an enormous creature with the form of a sea serpent referenced in the Hebrew Bible. Its name is here used with the meaning of 'man of vast and formidable power or enormous wealth' (*OED* n. 1c).

21. *unthankful*] unappreciated, disagreeable.

*Enter* POTHINUS.

      And he comes: now, fortune!
*Pothinus.* Caesar's unthankfulness a little stirs me,
 A little frets my blood. Take heed, proud Roman,      25
 Provoke me not, stir not my anger farther:
 I may find out a way unto thy life too,
 Though armed in all thy victories, and seize it.
 A conqueror has a heart, and I may hit it.
*Septimius.* May it please your lordship?
*Pothinus.*          O Septimius!      30
*Septimius.* Your lordship knows my wrongs.
*Pothinus.*           Wrongs?
*Septimius.*             Yes, my lord,
 How the captain of the guard, Achillas, slights me.
*Pothinus.* Think better of him: he has much befriended thee,
 Showed thee much love in taking the head from thee.
 The times are altered, soldier: Caesar's angry,      35
 And our design to please him lost and perished.
 Be glad thou art unnamed: 'tis not worth the owning.
 Yet, that thou mayst be useful —
       [*He shows* SEPTIMIUS *a purse.*]
*Septimius.*            Yes, my lord,
 I shall be ready.
*Pothinus.*      For I may employ thee
 To take a rub or two out of my way         40
 As time shall serve. Say that it be a brother

---

23. SD] *this edn; placed at line 23.1 in 1711; placed at line 22.1 in F2; placed at the margin on line 22 in F1.*

---

24. *unthankfulness*] ingratitude.
25. *frets*] stirs.
*Take heed*] Be careful.
25–9. *Take ... hit it*] Pothinus is here implicitly addressing the absent Caesar.
27–9.] Cf. Plutarch, 'Caesar', 786B–C: 'Pothinus the Eunuch ... after he had caused Pompey to be slain and driven Cleopatra from the court, secretly laid wait all the ways he could how he might likewise kill Caesar.'
28. *seize*] There may be a pun here between 'Caesar' and 'seizer': Pothinus fantasizes about becoming the 'seizer' of 'Caesar'. On the 'Caesar/seizer' pun potential, esp. in Jonson's *Sejanus*, see Hopkins, 163.
37. *unnamed*] unmentioned.
40. *rub*] snag, obstacle.

SC 2]　　　　　　THE FALSE ONE　　　　　　　111

　　Or a hard father —
Septimius.　　　　　　'Tis most necessary:
　　A mother or a sister or whom you please, sir.
Pothinus. Or to betray a noble friend —
Septimius.　　　　　　　　　　'Tis all one.
Pothinus. I know thou will stir for gold.
Septimius.　　　　　　　　　　'Tis all my motion.　　45
Pothinus. [*Giving* SEPTIMIUS *the purse*] There, take that for
　　thy service, and farewell.
　　I have greater business now.
Septimius.　　　　　　　I am still your own, sir.
Pothinus. One thing I charge thee: see me no more, Septimius,
　　Unless I send.
Septimius.　　　I shall observe your honour.
　　　　　　　　　　　　　　　　　*Exit* [POTHINUS].
　　So, this brings something in the mouth, some savour.　　50
　　This is the lord I serve, the power I worship,
　　My friends, allies, and here lies my allegiance.
　　Let people talk as they please of my rudeness
　　And shun me for my deed: bring but this to 'em,
　　Let me be damned for blood, yet still I am honourable.　　55
　　This god creates new tongues and new affections,
　　And though I had killed my father, give me gold,
　　I'll make men swear I have done a pious sacrifice.
　　Now I will outbrave all, make all my servants,
　　And my brave deed shall be writ in wine for virtuous.　　60
　　　　　　　　　　　　　　　　　　　　*Exit*.

---

42. father —] *this edn*; Father. *1711*; Father? *F1*. 44. friend —] *this edn*; Friend? *F2*; friend. *F1*. 49. honour] *Turner*; houre *F1*. 49.1. SD] *Weber*; *placed after* send. *in F1*.

---

44. *'Tis all one*] It's all the same.
45. *all my motion*] the only thing that moves me.
49. *observe*] obey.
60. *writ in wine*] written by drunk people.

## [ACT 2] Scene 3

*Enter* CAESAR, ANTONY, DOLABELLA [*and*] SCAEVA.

*Caesar.* Keep strong guards, and with wary eyes, my friends.
There is no trusting to these base Egyptians:
They that are false to pious benefits
And make compelled necessities their faiths
Are traitors to the gods.
*Antony.*                    We'll call ashore 5
A legion of the best.
*Caesar.*                    Not a man, Antony.
That were to show our fears and dim our greatness.
No, 'tis enough my name's ashore.
*Scaeva.*                    Too much too:
A sleeping Caesar is enough to shake them.
There are some two or three malicious rascals 10
Trained up in villainy, besides that Cerberus,
That Roman dog that licked the blood of Pompey.
*Dolabella.* 'Tis strange, a Roman soldier?
*Scaeva.*                    You are cozened.
There be of us, as be of all other nations,

---

2.3.0.] Weber adds the setting: 'Caesar's *Apartments in the Palace*'.

3. *false*] treacherous, faithless.

6–7. *Not ... greatness*] Cf. *JC* 1.2.210–11: 'I rather tell thee what is to be feared / Than what I fear: for always I am Caesar.'

8. *'tis ... ashore*] Cf. *JC* 1.2.197–200: 'I fear him not: / Yet if my name were liable to fear / I do not know the man I should avoid / So soon as that spare Cassius.' Just as in Shakespeare's play Caesar ignores Antony's advice regarding the threat posed by Cassius, here Caesar deliberately ignores Antony's proposal to station a military garrison on the coast because he trusts the power of his own name to the point of considering it sufficient to ward off the danger of an enemy attack.

10. *malicious*] full of hate.

11. *Cerberus*] in Greek and Latin mythology, the multi-headed dog guarding the entrance to the underworld in order to prevent the dead from leaving, sometimes described as having snakes growing out from multiple parts of its body, and accordingly venomous (Horace gives him a single dog head and one hundred snake heads). Calling a traitor such as Septimius 'Cerberus' might therefore seem an odd choice, but Cerberus is probably alluded to here as a kind of pre-Christian devil, which is consonant with other references to Septimius as a devil or worse than a devil in the play (3.2.113, 5.3.37–8, 54).

13. *cozened*] deceived.

|  |  |  |
|---|---|---|
| | Villains and knaves: 'tis not the name contains him | 15 |
| | But the obedience. When that's once forgotten, | |
| | And duty flung away, then welcome, devil. | |
| | Pothinus and Achillas, and this vermin, | |
| | That's now become a natural crocodile, | |
| | Must be with care observed. | |
| *Antony.* | And 'tis well counselled. | 20 |
| | No confidence, nor trust — | |
| *Scaeva.* | I'll trust the sea first | |
| | When with her hollow murmurs she invites me | |
| | And clutches in her storms as politic lions | |
| | Conceal their claws. I'll trust the devil first: | |
| | The rule of ill I'll trust before the doer. | 25 |
| *Caesar.* | Go to your rests and follow your own wisdoms, | |
| | And leave me to my thoughts. Pray, no more compliment. | |
| | Once more, strong watches. | |
| *Dolabella.* | All shall be observed, sir. | |
| | [*Exeunt all but* CAESAR.] | |
| *Caesar.* | I am dull and heavy, yet I cannot sleep. | |

25. The ... doer] *F1; not in F2*. doer] *1711;* dore *F1*. 28.1. SD] *Weber; Exeunt. / Manet Caesar (centred) Colman; Exit. F1*.

---

15. *contains*] restrains.
17. *flung*] cast.
18. *vermin*] creeping insect, but also parasite.
19. *a ... crocodile*] a crocodile native of the place, that is, a true Egyptian, given that for early moderns the crocodile (along with the pyramids and the Nile) stood for Egypt as a whole.
23. *clutches in*] holds tightly.
*politic*] cunning.
25.] I'll rather trust the touchstone of evil than its agent. Seward: 'as God is the rule of good or virtue, so is the devil of ill'.
27. *compliment*] ceremony.
29–61.] Unlike Shakespeare's Caesar, who is denied even the shortest soliloquy or the least significant aside, Fletcher and Massinger's Caesar has more than one. This one is particularly poignant, in that it enables Caesar to express his feelings of grief and remorse at his past actions against Rome. Caesar's repentance has no authority in the historical record: if anything, classical sources say the opposite. Compare 'The exclamation attributed to [Caesar] by Asinius [Pollio], as he viewed the battlefield of Pharsalus strewn with the bodies of the slain – "They would have it so!"' (Canfora, 70). Besides, Caesar never mentions any regrets in his *Commentarii de bello civili*. Interestingly, Caesar's repentance is a motif shared by three other early modern English plays, the anonymous *Caesar's Revenge*, William Alexander's *Julius Caesar*, and Chapman's *Caesar and Pompey*. See Lovascio, 'Caesar'.

> How happy was I in my lawful wars 30
> In Germany and Gaul and Britany,
> When every night with pleasure I set down
> What the day ministered! Then sleep came sweetly.
> But since I undertook this home division,
> This civil war, and passed the Rubicon, 35
> What have I done that speaks an ancient Roman,
> A good, great man? I have entered Rome by force
> And on her tender womb, that gave me life,
> Let my insulting soldiers rudely trample.
> The dear veins of my country I have opened, 40
> And sailed upon the torrents that flowed from her,
> The bloody streams that in their confluence
> Carried before 'em thousand desolations.
> I robbed the treasury and at one grip
> Snatched all the wealth so many worthy triumphs 45
> Placed there as sacred to the peace of Rome.
> I razed Massilia in my wanton anger,

---

32. set] *F2;* sat *F1.* 33. Then] *Turner;* the *F1.* 44. grip] *this edn;* gripe *F1.* 47. razed] *F2;* raiz'd *F1.*

---

31. *Germany*] See 1.1.69.
*Gaul*] See 1.1.69.
*Britany*] During his Gallic Wars, Caesar invaded Britain twice: in 55 and 54 BCE. Jasper Fisher's play *Fuimus Troes, or The True Trojans* (publ. 1633) depicts Caesar's invasions of Britain. The early modern spelling of the word has been retained for the sake of the metre.

32–3. *When ... ministered*] Caesar is here reflecting on his writing of the *Commentarii* (Mason).

35. *Rubicon*] a river in north-eastern Italy that marked the boundary between the Roman province of Cisalpine Gaul and Italy proper. At the time, Caesar was the proconsul of Gaul, so he had *imperium* (that is, the right to command an army) in that province, but not in Rome. Only consuls and praetors were allowed to exercise *imperium* in Rome; anyone else attempting to do so would commit a capital crime. When Caesar led a legion south over the Rubicon from Cisalpine Gaul to Rome in 48 BCE he deliberately broke the law on *imperium*, thereby making armed conflict inevitable.

36. *speaks*] shows me to be.

44. *at one grip*] with a single movement of my hand.

47. *Massilia*] the French city of Marseilles, which had sided with Pompey in the civil war and was therefore besieged and subdued by Caesar. The early modern spelling of the city's name has been retained for the sake of the metre.
*wanton*] reckless, showing no regard for justice.

>     Petreius and Afranius I defeated,
>     Pompey I overthrew. What did that get me?
>     The slubbered name of an authorized enemy.                50
>                                     *Noise within.*
>     I hear some noise: they are the watches, sure.
>     What friends have I tied fast by these ambitions?
>     Cato, the lover of his country's freedom,

---

48. Afranius] *F2; Affrinius F1.*   50. slubbered] *F2;* slubbord *F1.*   51. noise] *F2;* noises *F1.*

---

48. *Petreius and Afranius*] Marcus Petreius and Lucius Afranius were Roman politicians and generals. From 55 BCE onwards they administered the Spanish provinces as legates of Pompey. They fought against Caesar in the civil war and were defeated, after some initial successes, at the Battle of Pharsalus in 48. After this defeat, they fled to North Africa, where they continued to fight in the resistance to Caesar and achieved several victories until the Pompeians' ultimate defeat at Thapsus in 46.

49. *What ... me*] Caesar's question to himself, which occupies the second half of the line, is entirely made up of monosyllables, which seems to confer on it a certain emphasis and urgency. Caesar's question is also foregrounded, and its rhythmical effectiveness heightened, by being surrounded by what seems to be an unusual concentration of long words in 48–50 ('Petreius', 'Afranius', 'defeated', 'overthrew', 'slubbered', 'authorized').

50. *slubbered*] sullied.

*an ... enemy*] Editors have widely commented upon this phrase. Seward glosses it as 'an enemy to his country pronounced so by the authority of the whole Senate', but also suggests that it might be read as 'an unauthorized enemy', that is, 'an enemy without a legal cause or legal authority'. For Colman, it 'seems to mean only successful', while Mason believes that 'Caesar's meaning appears to be this. Soon after he had passed the Rubicon, Pompey fled from Rome, and was followed by the greater part of the Senate. When Caesar arrived there he was named dictator by such of the senators as remained in the city, and chosen consul for the ensuing year. Invested with these offices, which entitled him to the legitimate command of the Republic, he subverted the liberties of his country.' At any rate, this oxymoronic phrase is especially interesting because, together with the following 'honourable rebel' (59), it embodies textually Caesar's inner conflict while simultaneously highlighting the substantial difference between Caesar's power and its legitimacy.

52. *fast*] tightly.

53. *Cato*] Marcus Porcius Cato, the great-grandson of the more famous Cato 'the Censor', was quaestor in 65 BCE, tribune of the plebs in 62, and praetor in 54. A man of extraordinary moral rigour and integrity, a staunch defender of the republican institution and an admirer of the Stoic philosophy, he vehemently opposed Caesar's politics and sided with Pompey in the civil war. He committed suicide in Utica in 46 after the Pompeians' defeat at Thapsus. His suicide earned him the glory of a martyr and is gruesomely depicted in Chapman's *Caesar and Pompey*, 5.2.151–77.

Is passed now into Afric to affront me;
Juba, that killed my friend, is up in arms too;   55
The sons of Pompey are masters of the sea,
And from the relics of their scattered faction
A new head's sprung. Say I defeat all these too:
I come home crowned an honourable rebel.
I hear the noise still, and it comes still nearer.   60
Are the guards fast? Who waits there?

*Enter* SCAEVA *with a packet,* CLEOPATRA *in it.*

*Scaeva.*                              Are ye awake, sir?

---

54. *Afric*] The early modern spelling has been retained for the sake of the metre.
    *affront*] oppose.
55. *Juba ... friend*] Juba I, King of Numidia between 60 and 46 BCE, was an ally of Pompey's. In 49 Caesar sent his friend, the praetor Gaius Scribonius Curio, to Africa in order to take that province from the republicans. Curio died during the Second Battle of the Bagradas River fought against Juba.
56. *The ... Pompey*] After Pompey's death, his sons Gnaeus and Sextus continued to fight against Caesar. Defeated at Thapsus, they crossed over to the province of Hispania and raised another army, which Caesar defeated at the Battle of Munda in 45 BCE. Gnaeus was killed, while Sextus survived.
57. *relics*] remains.
58. *A ... sprung*] a reference to the Hydra, the mythological monster depicted as a many-headed serpent. If a head was cut off, two more would spring up. Interestingly, this is another multi-headed horror, after Cerberus. The play's preoccupation with the head of Pompey and the heads of the Nile seems to have a bearing on these mythological references to creatures with several heads.
60. *still nearer*] nearer and nearer.
61. *fast*] firmly in position.
61. SD] From Scaeva's entry onwards, the scene seems to be in direct conversation with *A&C*, insofar as it stages the delivery of Cleopatra to Caesar in a '*packet*' (also containing a 'litter'), which theatrically develops the passing allusion to the episode in *A&C* 2.6.68–70. See Introduction, 32. Scaeva's reiterated interruptions of the couple's dialogue bestow distinctively comic overtones to the scene, which is largely taken up by 'an antiphon of coarse, soldierly observations from Scaeva and enraptured comments from Caesar' (Waith, *Pattern*, 125). The source of the anecdote is Plutarch, 'Caesar', 786D–E: 'Caesar ... secretly sent for Cleopatra, which was in the country, to come unto him. She, only taking Apollodorus Sicilian of all her friends, took a little boat and went away with him in it in the night, and came and landed hard by the foot of the castle. Then, having no other mean

SC 3]                    THE FALSE ONE                    117

*Caesar.* I'th' name of wonder.
*Scaeva.*                    Nay, I am a porter,
  A strong one too, or else my sides would crack, sir.
  An my sins were as weighty, I should scarce walk with
      'em.
*Caesar.* What hast thou there?
*Scaeva.*                Ask them which stay without      65
  And brought it hither. Your presence I denied 'em
  And, put 'em by, took up the load myself.
  They say 'tis rich and valued at the kingdom.
  I am sure 'tis heavy: if you like to see it,
  You may; if not, I'll give it back.
*Caesar.*                    Stay, Scaeva,                70

---

to come into the court without being known, she laid herself down upon a mattress or flock bed, which Apollodorus her friend tied and bound up together like a bundle with a great leather thong, and so took her upon his back and brought her thus hampered in this fardel unto Caesar in at the castle gate. This was the first occasion – as it is reported – that made Caesar to love her, but afterwards, when he saw her sweet conversation and pleasant entertainment, he fell then in further liking with her and did reconcile her again unto her brother the King, with condition that they two jointly should reign together.' In the play, however, Cleopatra acts on her own initiative, for which the playwrights seem to have followed Lucan, 10.56–8: 'But then Cleopatra, having bribed the guards to undo the chain across the harbour of Pharos, sailed in a small two-banked ship and entered the Macedonian palace without Caesar's knowledge.'

packet] Although clearly it must have been large enough to contain Cleopatra but small enough to be carried by Scaeva, it is difficult to determine exactly what the '*packet*' might have looked like in the first performance, especially because 'packet' is an unusual word in early modern stage directions: there is no entry for it in Dessen and Thomson's *Dictionary*. Scaeva points out to Caesar that Cleopatra 'brings her bed along' and 'Carries her litter to lie soft' (112–13), while Achillas later refers to the '*packet*' as 'a pack of bedding / Or a small truss of household furniture' (3.1.18–19). In the absence of other evidence, it appears plausible to suppose that the King's Men might have followed Plutarch's above-mentioned description by having 'a mattress or flock bed ... tied and bound up together like a bundle with a great leather thong' carried onstage upon Scaeva's back.

63. *or else*] otherwise.
64. *An*] if.
   *should*] would be able to.
65. *them which*] those who.
   *without*] outside.

I would fain see it.
*Scaeva.* I'll begin to work, then.
        [*He starts undoing the packet.*]
No doubt to flatter ye, they have sent ye something
Of a rich value, jewels or some treasure,
Maybe a rogue within, to do a mischief.
I pray you stand farther off. If there be villainy,         75
Better my danger first: he shall 'scape hard too. —

        [*The packet having been opened,*
        CLEOPATRA *is discovered.*]

Ha? What art thou?
*Caesar.* Stand farther off, good Scaeva.
What heavenly vision! Do I wake or slumber?
Farther off that hand, friend.
*Scaeva.* What apparition,
What spirit have I raised? Sure, 'tis a woman:         80
She looks like one. Now she begins to move too:
A tempting devil, on my life. Go off, Caesar,
Bless thyself off! A bawd grown in mine old days?

---

76. too. —] *this edn;* too, — *Turner;* too. *Colman;* too; *1711;* too, *F1.*

71. *fain*] like to.
76. *he*] Scaeva assumes that, if the packet contains a person, it must be a *man* sent to murder Caesar. As a result, the surprise effect on both characters and audience is increased when Cleopatra springs out.
    *'scape*] escape.
77–132.] After coming out of the '*packet*', Cleopatra remains silent for as many as fifty-six lines, while Caesar and Scaeva talk about (and to) her, which makes one wonder what she might have been supposed to do during such a long silence. Make eyes and bat her eyelashes at Caesar? Roll her eyes at Scaeva's offences? Look for the audience's complicity? Express boredom through body language? There can be no definitive answer, but these all seem plausible options.
77. *thou*] Scaeva's use of *thou* to address Cleopatra, here and elsewhere, expresses his scorn for her.
79–82. *apparition ... spirit ... devil*] Cf. *A&C*: 'my *charm*' (4.12.16), 'This grave *charm*' (4.12.25), 'Ah, thou *spell*! Avaunt! (4.12.30), 'The *witch* shall die' (4.12.37). Emphases mine.
82. *Go off*] leave, go away.
83. *Bless ... off*] guard yourself from it, or (perhaps) sanctify yourself from it by (anachronistically) making the sign of the cross.

Bawdry advanced upon my back? 'Tis noble.
Sir, if you be a soldier, come no nearer.                               85
She is sent to dispossess you of your honour,
A sponge, a sponge to wipe away your victories.
An she would be cooled, sir, let the soldiers trim her:
They'll give her that she came for and dispatch her.
Be loyal to yourself. [*To* CLEOPATRA] Thou damned
    woman,                                                              90
Dost thou come hither with thy flourishes,
Thy flaunts and faces to abuse men's manners?
And am I made the instrument of bawdry?
I'll find a lover for ye, one shall hug ye —
                                            [*He draws his sword.*]
*Caesar.* Hold, on thy life, and be more temperate,                     95
    Thou beast.
*Scaeva.*              Thou beast?
*Caesar.*                          Couldst thou be so inhuman,
    So far from noble men to draw thy weapon
    Upon a thing divine?
*Scaeva.*                  Divine or human,
    They are never better pleased nor more at heart's ease
    Than when we draw with full intent upon 'em.                        100
*Caesar.* [*To* CLEOPATRA] Move this way, lady; pray ye, let
    me speak to ye.

---

94. ye —] *this edn;* you! *Colman;* ye. *F2;* ye; *F1.* 96. inhuman] *1711;* inhumane *F1.* 97. men] *F1;* Man *1711.* 101.] *Colman; F1 lines* Move ... (Lady) / Pray ... ye.

---

84. *Bawdry*] the practice of a bawd.
*noble*] splendid (meant sarcastically).
86. *dispossess*] deprive.
88. *An*] if.
*trim*] a slang term for 'deflower' (Farmer and Henley, 7.204).
89. *that*] what.
*dispatch*] send away.
91. *flourishes*] showy movements of the body or limbs (*OED* n. 6a).
92. *flaunts*] ostentatious displays.
*faces*] outward shows, pretences.
*abuse*] pervert.
94. *one*] one that.
100. *when ... draw*] the sword, but also implying a bawdy reference to the penis.

*Scaeva.* [*To* CLEOPATRA] And, woman, you had best stand —
*Caesar.*                                    By the gods,
 But that I see her here and hope her mortal,
 I should imagine some celestial sweetness,
 The treasure of soft love —
*Scaeva.*                    Oh, this sounds mangily,            105
 Poorly and scurvily in a soldier's mouth.
 You had best be troubled with the toothache too,
 For lovers ever are, and let your nose drop
 That your celestial beauty may befriend ye.
 At these years do you learn to be fantastical?            110
 After so many bloody fields, a fool?
 She brings her bed along too: she'll lose no time.
 Carries her litter to lie soft: do you see that?
 Invites ye like a gamester: note that impudence.
 For shame, reflect upon yourself, your honour,            115
 Look back into your noble parts and blush.
 Let not the dear sweat of the hot Pharsalia

---

102. stand —] *Seward;* stand. *F1.*   105. love —] *this edn;* love! *Colman;* love. *F1.*

---

102–5. *By ... love*] Caesar starts to describe Cleopatra in language characterized by the stylistic features typical of the conventions of courtly love, which adds to the comic overtones of the scene.

105. *mangily*] in a mangy or unworthy manner; shabbily (*OED*).

106. *scurvily*] in a rude, mean, sour way.

107. *toothache*] In the early modern era, toothache was believed to be caused by humours descending from the head or by worms that could penetrate the teeth. Moreover, toothache and love were regarded as associated ailments. Compare *MAdo* 3.2.20–7: 'Benedick. I have the toothache. / Don Pedro. Draw it. / Benedick. Hang it! / Claudio. You must hang it first and draw it afterwards. / Don Pedro. What? Sigh for the toothache? / Leonato. Where is but a humour or a worm. / Benedick. Well, every one can master a grief but he that has it. / Claudio. Yet, say I, he is in love'; and Massinger, *Parl* 2.113: 'I am troubled / With the toothache or with love, / I know not whether: / There is a worm in both.'

110. *At ... years*] Caesar was 52 years old at the time, and therefore already old by early modern standards, while Cleopatra was about 21.

*fantastical*] fanciful, full of wild ideas.

113. *litter*] bed.

114. *gamester*] prostitute.

116. *parts*] pieces of conduct, acts (*OED* n. 14).

117. *Pharsalia*] the decisive Battle of Pharsalus, at which Caesar defeated Pompey.

SC 3]                    THE FALSE ONE                           121

 Mingle with base embraces. Am I he
That have received so many wounds for Caesar,
Upon my target groves of darts still growing?    120
Have I endured all hungers, colds, distresses
And, as I had been bred that iron that armed me,
Stood out all weathers now to curse my fortune?
To ban the blood I lost for such a general?
*Caesar.* Offend no more. Be gone.
*Scaeva.*        I will, and leave ye,  125
Leave ye to women's wars. That will proclaim ye.
You'll conquer Rome now, and the Capitol,
With fans and looking glasses. Farewell, Caesar.
            [*He begins to leave.*]
*Cleopatra.* [*To* CAESAR] Now I am private, sir, I dare speak
 to ye,
But thus low first, for as a god I honour ye.    130
            [*She kneels.*]
*Scaeva.* Lower you'll be anon.
*Caesar.*      Away.
*Scaeva.*       [*To* CLEOPATRA] And privater,
 For that you covet all.
*Caesar.*      Tempt me no farther.
            *Exit* [SCAEVA].

---

132.1. SD] *Weber; placed after* all. *in F1.*

 120.] A target is a light round shield or buckler; a small targe (*OED* n.1 1). Plutarch, 'Caesar', 770E, recounts that Scaeva fought 'in a conflict before the city of Dyrrachium, having one of his eyes put out with an arrow, his shoulder stricken through with a dart, and his thigh with another, and having received thirty arrows upon his shield'.
 122. *as*] as if.
 124. *ban*] curse.
 126. *proclaim ye*] show who you really are.
 129. *private*] removed from public view or knowledge (*OED* adj.1 6), but also (sexually) intimate (*OED* adj.1 7b).
 131.] Scaeva's barbed remark – which plays both on the image of Cleopatra under Caesar ('lower') and on the polysemy of the adjective 'private' – though predictable enough, effectively emphasizes the sexual overtones of this first meeting between Caesar and Cleopatra, thus mocking the romance-like register that Caesar deployed earlier.
 132. *all*] that is, all women.

122                    THE FALSE ONE                    [ACT 2

*Cleopatra.* Contemn me not because I kneel thus, Caesar.
　　I am a queen and coheir to this country,
　　The sister to the mighty Ptolemy,                                 135
　　Yet one distressed that flies unto thy justice,
　　One that lays sacred hold on thy protection
　　As on a holy altar to preserve me.
*Caesar.* Speak, queen of beauty, and stand up.
*Cleopatra.*　　　　　　　　　　　　　　　　I dare not.
　　Till I have found that favour in thine eyes,                      140
　　That godlike great humanity to help me,
　　Thus to thy knees must I grow, sacred Caesar.
　　And if it be not in thy will to right me
　　And raise me like a queen from my sad ruins,
　　If these soft tears cannot sink to thy pity                       145
　　And waken with their murmurs thy compassions,
　　Yet for thy nobleness, for virtue's sake

---

133. kneel] *F2;* know *F1.*

---

　　133–8, 139–55. *Contemn ... preserve me, I dare ... world*] Cleopatra's speeches, Caesar's eventual agreement to help her, and their spending the night together are based on Lucan, 10.82–99, 104–6: 'Trusting in her beauty, Cleopatra approached him, in sorrow but not in tears: she had decked out her feigned grief, and her hair, as far as became her, was disordered, as if she had torn it; and thus she began: "Mighty Caesar, if birth counts for aught, I am the noble daughter of Lagus, king of Egypt; but I have been driven from my father's throne and shall be an exile for ever, unless your right hand restores me to my former destiny; and therefore I, a queen, embrace your feet. Appear as a benign star and assist our nation. I shall not be the first woman to rule the cities of the Nile: Egypt is accustomed to put up with a queen and make no distinction of sex. Read the last words of my dead father: he gave me an equal share of the royal power with my brother ... The boy himself loves his sister, if only he were free; but his feelings and his soldiers are alike controlled by Pothinus. I do not myself ask to be admitted to any share of my father's power; I beg you only to free our house from such guilt and shame; destroy the dangerous strength of the favourite, and bid the king be a king indeed..." Vain would have been her appeal to the stern ear of Caesar; but her face supported her petition, and her wicked beauty gained her suit.'
　　133. *Contemn*] scorn, despise.
　　136. *thy*] While petitioning Caesar, Cleopatra switches from *you* to *thou.* Having already kneeled in front of him, she no longer needs to express her obedience and subservience through forms of address, which she uses in order to establish special intimacy with him instead. She uses eleven singular forms across twenty lines (136, 137, 140, 142, 143, 145, 146, 147, 148, 149, and 155) and reverts to the plural after she stands up again.
　　142. *grow*] lower myself.

And, if thou be'st a man, for despised beauty,
For honourable conquest, which thou dot'st on,
Let not those cankers of this flourishing kingdom, 150
Pothinus and Achillas, the one a eunuch,
The other a base bondman, thus reign over me,
Seize my inheritance and leave my brother
Nothing of what he should be but the title.
As thou art wonder of the world —

*Caesar.*                                    Stand up, then, 155
                                           [*He raises her.*]
And be a queen: this hand shall give it to ye.
Or choose a greater name, worthy my bounty.
A common love makes queens: choose to be worshipped,
To be divinely great, and I dare promise it.
A suitor of your sort and blessèd sweetness 160
That hath adventured thus to see great Caesar
Must never be denied. You have found a patron
That dare not in his private honour suffer
So great a blemish to the heaven of beauty:
The god of love would clap his angry wings 165
And from his singing bow let fly those arrows
Headed with burning griefs and pining sorrows,
Should I neglect your cause, would make me monstrous,
To whom, and to your service, I devote me.

---

155. world —] *Seward;* world. *F1.*

---

149. *dot'st on*] love.
150. *cankers*] malignant or destructive influences that corrode or corrupt and are difficult to eradicate (*OED* n. 4a).
152. *bondman*] slave.
158. *A ... queens*] The love of a common man would make you a queen; Caesar's love can do much more than that.
165. *The ... love*] The reference seems to be to Cupid, often depicted as carrying the bow and arrow that are his source of power: anyone shot by one of his arrows was believed to be instantly filled with unrestrainable desire.
167. *burning ... sorrows*] generated if desire is not reciprocated.
*pining*] painful, tormenting.
168. *would*] that would.
169. *whom*] that is, the god of love.
*me*] myself.

*Enter* SCAEVA [*again*].

Cleopatra. [*Aside*] He is my conquest now, and so I'll work
    him     170
    The conqueror of the world will I lead captive.
Scaeva. [*To* CAESAR] Still with this woman? Tilting still
    with babies?
    As you are honest, think the enemy,
    Some valiant foe indeed now charging on ye,
    Ready to break your ranks, and fling these —
Caesar.                            Hear me,     175
    But tell me true: if thou hadst such a treasure —
    And, as thou art a soldier, do not flatter me —
    Such a bright gem brought to thee, wouldst thou not
    Most greedily accept?
Scaeva.              Not as an emperor,
    A man that first should rule himself, then others.     180
    As a poor hungry soldier, I might bite, sir,
    Yet that's a weakness too.
              [*To* CLEOPATRA] Hear me, thou tempter,

---

169.1. SD] *this edn; Re-enter* SCAEVA. *Dyce; Enter Sceva.* F1. 180. should]
F2; would F1.

---

    170–1.] He is my conquest now, and I will fashion him in such a way as
to lead the conqueror of the world captive. The most immediate source of
Cleopatra's aside is Lucan, 10.65: 'hoping to head an Egyptian triumph and
lead a Caesar captive'. However, there also seems to be a nod to Caesar's
depiction as a slave to love in Petrarch's *Triumphi*. In the *Triumphus Famae*,
Caesar is described as inferior to Scipio Africanus only because he let himself
be conquered by Cleopatra (ll. 89–90).
    172. *Tilting*] jousting, possibly with an allusion to sexual intercourse.
    *babies*] the small reflections that lovers were believed to see in each other's
eyes when they gazed into them (*OED* n. 4).
    177. *do ... me*] Cf. *JC* 2.1.206–7: 'But when I tell him he hates flatterers,
/ He says he does, being then most flattered.'
    179–80. *Not ... others*] Scaeva's lucid reply openly sets out one of the
crucial questions posed by the play: how can Caesar wield power over others
when he is not even able to govern his own appetites? In the early modern
social imagination, the self-governance demanded of men was also the
ground of their claim to authority (see Introduction, 24–5; Shepard, 70;
Bushnell, *Tyrants*, 15; Jensen, *Reading*, 169).

[*To* CAESAR] And hear, thou Caesar, too, for it
   concerns thee,
And if thy flesh be deaf, yet let thine honour,
The soul of a commander, give ear to me: 185
[*To* CLEOPATRA] Thou wanton bane of war, thou
   gilded lethargy,
In whose embraces ease, the rust of arms,
And pleasure, that makes soldiers poor, inhabits —
*Caesar.* Fie, thou blasphem'st.
*Scaeva.*             I do, when she is a goddess.
[*To* CLEOPATRA] Thou melter of strong minds, dar'st
   thou presume 190
To smother all his triumphs with thy vanities
And tie him like a slave to thy proud beauties?
To thy imperious looks? That kings have followed
Proud of their chains? Have waited on? [*To* CAESAR] I
   shame, sir.
*Caesar.* Alas, thou art rather mad. Take thy rest, Scaeva. 195
Thy duty makes thee err, but I forgive thee.
Go. Go, I say! Show me no disobedience.
'Tis well, farewell. —         *Exit* [SCAEVA].
         The day will break, dear lady.
My soldiers will come in. Please you retire
And think upon your servant?
*Cleopatra.*       Pray you, sir, know me 200
And what I am.
*Caesar.*      The greater I more love ye,

---

188. inhabits —] *Dyce;* inhabits! *Colman;* inhabites. *F1.*   198. SD] *Turner; placed at line 197 in Seward; placed at line 194 in F1.*

---

183. *thou Caesar*] the only instance in the whole play of Scaeva's using *thou* to address Caesar, sharply signalling the urgency with which the centurion feels the need to guard his general from the danger that he thinks Cleopatra embodies.
  186. *wanton*] reckless, but also lustful.
  *bane*] that which causes death or ruin.
  *gilded*] adorned or embellished so as to seem attractive (*OED* adj. 3).
  190. *melter*] weakener.
  193. *That*] The antecedent is 'him' on the previous line.
  194. *Have ... on*] The subject of the verb is 'kings' in the previous line.
  *shame*] feel ashamed.
  196. *duty*] sense of duty.
  200. *know*] get to know.

And you must know me too. [*He offers to embrace her.*]
*Cleopatra.* So far as modesty
And majesty gives leave, sir; ye are too violent.
[*She gently thrusts him away.*]
*Caesar.* You are too cold to my desires.
*Cleopatra.* Swear to me,
And by yourself — for I hold that oath sacred —  205
You will right me as a queen —
*Caesar.* These lips be witness,
[*He kisses her.*]
And, if I break that oath —
*Cleopatra.* You make me blush, sir,
And in that blush interpret me.
*Caesar.* I will do.
Come, let's go in, and blush again: this one word
You shall believe.
*Cleopatra.* I must: you are a conqueror. *Exeunt.* 210

## ACT 3 SCENE I

*Enter* PTOLEMY [*and*] POTHINUS.

*Pothinus.* Good sir, but hear —
*Ptolemy.* No more. You have undone me.
That that I hourly feared is fall'n upon me,
And heavily, and deadly.
*Pothinus.* Hear a remedy.
*Ptolemy.* A remedy now the disease is ulcerous
And has infected all? Your secure negligence  5
Has broke through all the hopes I have and ruined me.
My sister is with Caesar in his chamber;

---

1. hear —] *this edn;* hear! *Colman;* heare. *F1.*   2. fall'n] *Colman;* falne *F1.*

---

202. *know*] with the secondary meaning of having sexual intercourse with.
206. *right*] do justice to.
207. *blush*] another indication that Cleopatra is not black. See Introduction, 9.
3.1.0.] Weber adds the setting: '*A Room in the Palace*'.
5. *secure*] overconfident.

|          | All night she has been with him, and no doubt |    |
|          | Much to her honour.                            |    |
| *Pothinus.* |                     Would that were the worst, sir. |    |
|          | That will repair itself, but I fear mainly     | 10 |
|          | She has made her peace with Caesar.            |    |
| *Ptolemy.* |                                'Tis most likely, |    |
|          | And what am I then?                            |    |
| *Pothinus.* |                     Plague upon that rascal,  |    |
|          | Apollodorus, under whose command,              |    |
|          | Under whose eye —                              |    |

*Enter* ACHILLAS.

*Ptolemy.*                    Curse on you all, ye are wretches.
*Pothinus.* 'Twas providently done, Achillas.
*Achillas.*                              Pardon me.                15
*Pothinus.* Your guards were rarely wise and wondrous
        watchful.
*Achillas.* I could not help it if my life had lain for't.
    Alas, who would suspect a pack of bedding
    Or a small truss of household furniture,
    And (as they said) for Caesar's use? Or who durst,            20
    Being for his private chamber, seek to stop it?
    I was abused.

*Enter* ACOREUS.

*Acoreus.*         'Tis no hour now for anger;
    No wisdom to debate with fruitless choler.
    Let us consider timely what we must do,
    Since she is flown to his protection,                         25
    From whom we have no power to sever her

---

  15. *providently*] judiciously (meant sarcastically).
  16. *rarely*] extraordinarily (meant sarcastically).
  *wondrous*] marvellously (meant sarcastically).
  17.] I wouldn't have been able to do anything about it even if my life had depended on it.
  22. *abused*] deceived.
  *hour*] time.
  25. *she*] that is, Cleopatra.
  *his*] that is, Caesar's.
  *protection*] pronounced 'protection'.

    Nor force conditions —
*Ptolemy.*                   Speak, good Acoreus.
*Acoreus.* Let indirect and crooked counsels vanish,
    And straight and fair directions —
*Ptolemy.*                   Speak your mind, sir.
*Acoreus.* Let us choose Caesar and endear him to us     30
    An arbitrator in all differences
    Betwixt you and your sister: this is safe now
    And will show off most honourable.
*Pothinus.*                Base,
    Most base and poor, a servile, cold submission.
    Hear me and pluck your hearts up like stout counsellors:    35
    Since we are sensible this Caesar loathes us
    And have begun our fortune with great Pompey,
    Be of my mind.
*Acoreus.*          'Tis most uncomely spoken,
    And, if I say 'most bloodily', I lie not:
    The law of hospitality it poisons     40
    And calls the gods in question that dwell in us.
    Be wise, O King.
*Ptolemy.*         I will be. Go, my counsellor,
    To Caesar go and do my humble service,
    To my fair sister my commends negotiate,
    And here I ratify whate'er thou treatst on.     45
*Acoreus.* Crowned with fair peace, I go.
*Ptolemy.*                 My love go with thee.

                        *Exit* [ACOREUS].
[*To* POTHINUS *and* ACHILLAS] And from my love go
    you, you cruel vipers. —

---

36. loathes] *F2;* loades *F1.*    46.1. SD] *Dyce; placed after* I go. *in F1.*

---

27–9. *Speak ... Speak*] Acoreus' circumlocutions soon make Ptolemy impatient, as the reiteration of the imperative 'Speak' suggests.
    33. *show off*] appear by contrast.
    34. *servile*] slavish.
    *cold*] apathetic.
    35. *stout*] valiant, brave.
    36. *sensible*] aware.
    38. *Be ... mind*] agree with me.
    *uncomely*] unsuitably.
    44. *commends*] greetings, compliments.

sc 2]                    THE FALSE ONE                        129

        You shall know now I am no ward, Pothinus.    *Exit.*
*Pothinus.* This for our service? Princes do their pleasures,
        And they that serve obey in all disgraces.                50
        The lowest we can fall to is our graves.
        There we shall know no difference. Hark, Achillas,
        I may do something yet, when times are ripe,
        To tell this rare unthankful King —
*Achillas.*                              Pothinus,
        Whate'er it be, I shall make one, and zealously,          55
        For better die attempting something nobly
        Than fall disgraced.
*Pothinus.*              Thou lov'st me, and I thank thee.
                                                *Exeunt.*

                        [ACT 3] SCENE 2

            *Enter* ANTONY, DOLABELLA [*and*] SCAEVA.

*Dolabella.* Nay, there's no rousing him; he is bewitched, sure,
        His noble blood curdled and cold within him,
        Grown now a woman's warrior.
*Scaeva.*                              And a tall one:
        Studies her fortifications and her breaches,

---

49.] *Seward; F1 lines* This ... service? | Princes ... pleasures,.   54. rare] *F1;* raw *F2.*   King —] *Colman;* King. *F1.*

2. curdled] *F2;* crudled *F1.*

---

48. *ward*] one who is under the protection or control of another (*OED* n.2 6b).
54. *rare*] truly, extremely; 'Used as an intensifier modifying adjectives or nouns' (*OED* adj. 5d).
55. *make one*] take part in your enterprise.
3.2.0.] Weber adds the setting: '*Before the Palace*'.
1. *Nay*] The Roman soldiers' discussion regarding the extent to which their general's relationship with Cleopatra reduces and emasculates him (which occupies the first fifty lines of the scene) significantly starts with 'Nay', thus appearing intended to elicit in the audience a recollection of Philo's famous opening speech in *A&C* 1.1.1–2: 'Nay, but this dotage of our general's / O'erflows the measure.' The initial use of 'Nay' also signals that the conversation has started offstage.
3. *tall*] bold, valiant.

    And how he may advance his ram to batter
    The bulwark of her chastity.
*Antony.*        Be not too angry,
    For, by this light, the woman's a rare woman,
    A lady of that catching youth and beauty,
    That unmatched sweetness —
*Dolabella.*      But why should he be fooled so?
    Let her be what she will, why should his wisdom,
    His age and honour —
*Antony.*       Say it were your own case
    Or mine or any man's that has heat in him.
    'Tis true at this time, when he has no promise
    Of more security than his sword can cut through,
    I do not hold it so discreet, but a good face, gentlemen,
    And eyes that are the winningest orators,
    A youth that opens like perpetual spring
    And, to all these, a tongue that can deliver
    The oracles of love —
*Scaeva.*       I would you had her
    With all her oracles and miracles:
    She were fitter for your turn.
*Antony.*       Would I had, Scaeva,
    With all her faults too. Let me alone to mend 'em.

---

15. gentlemen] *F2;* Gentleman *F1.*

---

 6. *bulwark*] rampart.
 6–9. *Be ... sweetness*] Antony's words here and later at 15–19 and 21–3 suggest that he, too, has started to be infatuated with Cleopatra. This seems intended to make Cleopatra's allure appear all the more irresistible but has no authority in the sources. It does, however, have a striking parallel in the anonymous *Tragedy of Caesar's Revenge*, in which Antony's love is even more evident. See Introduction, 35.
 7. *rare*] exceptional.
 8. *catching*] captivating.
 11. *case*] perhaps with a pun on vagina (Williams, 1.211).
 15. *gentlemen*] It is not unusual for Fletcher to append the vocative 'gentlemen' to lines that already possess their five feet. See also 28.
 16. *winningest*] most persuasive.
 17. *like ... spring*] Cf. *A&C* 2.2.245: 'Age cannot wither her.'
 19. *would*] wish.
 21. *fitter ... turn*] more suitable for your purpose.
 *Would I had*] I wish I had her.

SC 2]                THE FALSE ONE                    131

  O' that condition I make thee mine heir.
Scaeva. I had rather have your black horse than your
  harlots.
Dolabella. Caesar writes sonnets now; the sound of war      25
  Is grown too boisterous for his mouth. He sighs too.
Scaeva. And learns to fiddle most melodiously,
  And sings: 'twould make your ears prick up to hear
  him, gentlemen.

---

23. make] *Turner;* made *F1.*   24. harlots] *F1;* harlot *Turner.*

---

  23. *make*] 'Antony is jokingly making a promise to Sc[a]eva now; he did not do so in the past, as F1's "made" indicates' (Turner).
  24. *horse*] perhaps with a pun on 'whores'.
  27. *fiddle*] play the violin, but also slang for copulate (Williams, 1.479–80). It could also obliquely reference 1.1.16 – when Acoreus had called Septimius 'a fiddler' – thus fostering an implicit comparison between Caesar with Septimius for the Roman general's being 'false' to himself under Cleopatra's spell.
  28–31.] Editors have found these lines metrically challenging. It is not necessary, however, to emend the lineation as Seward and later editors did. Following Turner, I have kept Scaeva's speech as arranged in F1. The extrametrical 'gentlemen' (28) should be left where it is (cf. 15); line 29 could be viewed as a headless line, i.e., a line with a missing unstressed syllable before the first stressed one, or, alternatively, expanding "tis' to 'it is' would make it a ten-syllable line; in l. 30, 'admirable' could be 'reduced to one heavy and two light syllables (ād-mĭ-răl)' (Turner) and 'He will' may be read as 'He'll'. Turner argues that 'Line 31 remains ragged', but, if 'be in' is read as a single syllable and 'general' is pronounced as disyllabic ('gen'ral'), the problems in this line are solved too. Yet it is crucial to remember that Fletcher employed blank verse rather loosely, with an abundance of trisyllabic feet or implied elisions (I have counted over 500 throughout the play, which has deterred me from noting them all down in the Commentary), and a particular fondness for supernumerary syllables at the end of the line: his plays give ample evidence of his penchant for double, triple, and even quadruple endings, side by side with the occasional use of alexandrines (see Gayley, 243–59; Lewis, 265–86; Tarlinskaja, 200–20). Hence, it is generally not particularly productive to attempt artificially to squeeze Fletcher's lines into a metrical straitjacket by trying to make them perfectly fit the standard blank verse measure. Moreover, most metrically 'problematic' lines in *The False One* are delivered by Scaeva, a character who is portrayed as particularly outspoken and irritable. The list of the 'Persons Represented in the Play' in F2 aptly styles him as 'a free speaker'. His excessively long lines crop up when he is particularly outraged at Caesar's conduct: his difficulty in restraining his own anger thus seems to be reflected in his inability to make his lines fit the standard iambic pentameter grid. Cf. 4.2.158, 170–1, 185, 187.

                Shortly she'll make him spin, and 'tis thought
                He will prove an admirable maker of bone lace,       30
                And what a rare gift will that be in a general?
*Antony.* I would he could abstain.
*Scaeva.*                         She is a witch, sure,
                And works upon him with some damned enchantment.
*Dolabella.* How cunning she will carry her behaviours
                And set her countenance in a thousand postures       35
                To catch her ends!
*Scaeva.*                         She will be sick, well, sullen,
                Merry, coy, overjoyed and seem to die,
                All in one half an hour, to make an ass of him.
                I make no doubt she will be drunk too, damnably,
                And in her drink will fight: then she fits him.      40

---

29–30.] *F1; Seward lines* Shortly ... he'll prove / An ... Bonelace.

29. *she'll ... spin*] The allusion is to the classical myth of Hercules' subjugation by Omphale, the Amazonian Queen of Lydia. Omphale bought Hercules as a slave, became his lover, and forced him to wear her clothes and spin wool with the women of her court, while she wore his lion's skin and armed herself with his club. The story was frequently represented in Renaissance painting to show the dangers of woman's domination of man. Hercules, carrying a distaff (a tool used in spinning), and Omphale, with a club in her hand and a lion's skin on her back, appear in the dumb show and prologue that precede Act 4 of the anonymous *Locrine* (1595). Hercules follows Omphale, and she turns and strikes him on his head with her pantofle.

30. *bone lace*] a type of fine lace originally made using threads wound on bone or ivory bobbins, also known as bobbin lace or pillow lace. As the crafting of bone lace originated in the Renaissance, the allusion is anachronistic. The 'bone' perhaps also has bawdy connotations, in that Caesar's 'sword' is now reduced to lacemaking.

32–3. *witch ... enchantment*] See 2.3.79–82.

34–40.] Cf. *A&C* 1.3.3–5: 'If you find him sad, / Say I am dancing; if in mirth, report / That I am sudden sick'; 1.3.13: 'I am sick and sullen'; 1.2.137–8, 139–40: 'I have seen her die twenty times upon far poorer moment ... she hath such a celerity in dying.'

34. *cunning*] cunningly.

35. *countenance*] face.

*postures*] expressions, perhaps with an innuendo on sexual positions (Williams, 3.1066–7).

36. *catch her ends*] achieve her goals.

SC 2]                    THE FALSE ONE                    133

*Antony.* That thou shouldst bring her in!
*Scaeva.*                              'Twas my blind fortune.
  My shoulders told me by the weight 'twas wicked.
  Would I had carried Milo's bull a furlong
  When I brought in this cow-calf. He has advanced me
  From an old soldier to a bawd of memory.                45
  Oh, that the sons of Pompey were behind him,
  The honoured Cato and fierce Juba with 'em,
  That they might whip him from his whore and rouse him,
  That their fierce trumpets from his wanton trances
  Might shake him like an earthquake.

            *Enter* SEPTIMIUS [*richly dressed*].

*Antony.*                             What's this fellow?    50
*Dolabella.* Why, a brave fellow, if we judge men by their clothes.
*Antony.* By my faith, he is brave indeed. He's no commander?
*Scaeva.* Yes, he has a Roman face. He has been at fair wars,

---

42. shoulders] *Dyce;* Souldiers *F1.*   50. SD] *Dyce; Enter Septinius. F1.*
52. commander?] *F2;* cõmander. *F1.*

---

41. *blind fortune*] The Roman goddess *Fortuna* was often depicted blindfolded to represent the idea that she bestows luck on mortals and removes it from them without discretion or prejudice. Scaeva's comment is ironic.
  43. *Milo's bull*] Milo of Croton was a hugely successful wrestler from the Magna Graecian city of Croton who was said to have carried a bull on his shoulders.
  *furlong*] an eighth of a mile, 660 feet, 220 yards, or approximately 201 metres.
  44. *cow-calf*] a female calf (a derogatory synonym for women). Cf. *Woman* 3.1.133–5: 'Merchant. ... they worship / Nothing with so much service, as the cow-calves. / Paulo. What do mean you by cow-calves? Merchant. Why, their women.'
  45. *of memory*] memorable, notorious.
  46. *Pompey*] See 2.3.56.
  47. *Cato*] See 2.3.53.
  *Juba*] See 2.3.55.
  49. *wanton*] lascivious.
  51. *brave*] 'a quibble upon the usual acceptation of the word brave, and that which it bore anciently, gorgeous, gallantly attired' (Weber).
  53. *fair*] considerable.

And plenteous too, and rich: his trappings show it.
*Septimius.* [*Aside*] An they will not know me now, they'll
   never know me. 55
Who dare blush now at my acquaintance? Ha!
Am I not totally a span-new gallant
Fit for the choicest eyes? Have I not gold,
                          [*He pulls out a purse.*]
The friendship of the world? If they shun me now,
Though I were the arrantest rogue (as I am well
   forward), 60
Mine own curse, and the devil's too, light on me.
*Antony.* Is't not Septimius?
*Scaeva.*                  Yes.
*Dolabella.*               He that killed Pompey?
*Scaeva.* The same dog, scab, that gilded botch, that rascal!
*Dolabella.* How glorious villainy appears in Egypt!
*Septimius.* Gallants, and soldiers! [*Aside*] Sure, they do
   admire me. 65
*Scaeva.* Stand further off: thou stinkst.
*Septimius.*                A likely matter.
These clothes smell mustily, do they not, gallants?
They stink, they stink, alas, poor things, contemptible.
By all the gods in Egypt, the perfumes
That went to trimming these clothes cost me —
*Scaeva.*                      Thou stinkst still. 70

---

61. the devil's too, light] *F2;* the devil's are light *Dyce;* the devil's are lit *Colman;* the Devil's too light *1711;* the Devills are light *F1.*

---

54. *plenteous*] yielding abundant spoil.
*trappings*] embellishments, ornaments.
55. *An*] if.
57. *span-new*] perfectly new.
60. *arrantest*] most notorious, most downright.
*I ... forward*] I am progressing speedily towards that goal.
61. *light*] will fall.
63. *scab*] rascal, scoundrel.
*gilded*] adorned or embellished so as to seem reputable (*OED* adj. 3).
*botch*] goitre, bubo.
64. *glorious*] splendid (meant sarcastically).
67. *mustily*] 'with a taint of mustiness or mould' (*OED* adv. 2).

*Septimius.* The powdering of this head too —
*Scaeva.*                                    If thou hast it,
    I'll tell thee all the gums in sweet Arabia
    Are not sufficient, were they burnt about thee,
    To purge the scent of a rank rascal from thee.
*Antony.* I smell him now. Fie! How the knave perfumes
        him!                                                           75
    How strong he scents of traitor!
*Dolabella.*                      You had an ill milliner:
    He laid too much of the gum of ingratitude
    Upon your coat. You should have washed off that, sir.
    Fie! How it chokes! Too little of your loyalty,
    Your honesty, your faith, that are pure ambers.                    80
    I smell the rotten smell of a hired coward.
    A dead dog is sweeter.
*Septimius.*              Ye are merry gentlemen,
    And, by my troth, such harmless mirth takes me too.
    You speak like good blunt soldiers, and 'tis well enough.
    But did you live at court as I do, gallants,                       85
    You would refine, and learn an apter language.
    I have done ye simple service on your Pompey.
    You might have looked him yet this brace of
        twelvemonths

---

71–4. *If ... thee*] Cf. *Mac* 5.1.50–1: 'Here's the smell of the blood still. All the perfumes of Arabia will not sweeten this little hand.'

72. *the ... Arabia*] Arabia had been a source of perfumes to the West since the Middle Ages. It was particularly well known for this kind of gum, largely burnt as incense.

75. *How ... him*] How much he smells of knave!

76. *strong*] intensely.
*milliner*] 'a seller of fancy wares, accessories, and articles of (female) apparel, esp. such as were originally made in Milan' (*OED* n. 2).

80. *ambers*] pieces of amber.

81. *hired*] mercenary.

82–3. *Ye ... too*] I know you gentlemen are joking at my expense, but I won't take offence.

83. *by my troth*] on my word, by my faith.

86. *refine*] become more polished.

88. *looked*] looked for.
*brace of twelvemonths*] couple of years.

    And hunted after him like foundered beagles,
    Had not this fortunate hand —
*Antony.*                      He brags on't too;
    By the good gods, rejoices in't. [*To* SEPTIMIUS] Thou wretch,
    Thou most contemptible slave.
*Scaeva.*                 Dog, mangy mongrel,
    Thou murdering mischief in the shape of soldier
    To make all soldiers hateful, thou disease
    That nothing but the gallows can give ease to.
*Dolabella.* Thou art so impudent that I admire thee
    And know not what to say.
*Septimius.*             I know your anger
    And why you prate thus. I have found your melancholy:
    Ye all want money, and you are liberal captains,
    And in this want will talk a little desperately.
    [*Offering the purse to them*] Here's gold: come, share. I
        love a brave commander.
    And be not peevish, do as Caesar does.
    He's merry with his wench now; be you jovial,
    And let's all laugh and drink. Would ye have partners?
    I do consider all your wants and weigh 'em.
    He has the mistress; you shall have the maids.
    I'll bring 'em to ye, to your arms.
*Antony.*                     I blush,
    All over me I blush and sweat to hear him.
    Upon my conscience, if my arms were on now,
    Through them I should blush too. [*To* SCAEVA *and*
        DOLABELLA] Pray ye, let's be walking.
*Scaeva.* Yes, yes, but ere we go, I'll leave this lesson
    And let him study it. [*To* SEPTIMIUS] First, rogue; then, pander;
    Next, devil that will be! Get thee from men's presence,

---

95. to.] *this edn;* to — *Turner;* to! *Colman;* to. — *F1.*

---

  89. *foundered*] crippled.
  99. *liberal*] generous, free-spending.
102. *peevish*] senseless, foolish.
108. *me*] myself.

SC 2]           THE FALSE ONE                    137

    And where the name of soldier has been heard of
    Be sure thou live not. To some hungry desert,         115
    Where thou canst meet with nothing but thy
      conscience —
    And that in all the shapes of all thy villainies
    Attend thee still — where brute beasts will abhor thee
    And even the sun will shame to give thee light,
    Go hide thy head or, if thou thinkst it fitter,         120
    Go hang thyself.
*Dolabella.*          Hark to that clause.
*Scaeva.*                            And that speedily,
    That nature may be eased of such a monster.
                      [*Exeunt all but* SEPTIMIUS.]
*Septimius.* Yet all this moves not me nor reflects on me.
    I keep my god still, and my confidence.
    Their want of breeding makes these fellows murmur.   125
    Rude valours, so I let 'em pass, rude honours.
    There is a wench yet that I know affects me,
    And company for a king: a young plump villain
    That, [*Shaking the purse*] when she sees this gold, she'll
      leap upon me.

                    *Enter* EROS.

---

122.1. SD] *Weber; Exe.* / *Manet Septimius (centred) Colman; Exe. 1711; Exit. F1.* 124. god] *F1;* gold *F2.*

---

118. *Attend ... still*] That always accompany you.

121. *hang thyself*] According to Matt. 27.3–10, Judas hanged himself; hence, this might be a covert way of drawing an analogy between Septimius and Stukeley, who was widely branded a 'Judas' as a consequence of his involvement in Ralegh's arrest. See Introduction, 41–2.

123–9.] In this soliloquy it seems to be implied that Septimius is addressing the audience in order to share his thoughts (and hopes) with them. The same occurs at 151–5.

124. *god*] 'F2 reads gold, but, as Seward recognizes, gold is Septimius' god' (Turner).

125. *breeding*] good manners.

127. *affects*] likes.

128. *plump*] plumpness was seen as attractive and an indication of vitality in the early modern era.

    *villain*] 'used playfully, or without serious imputation of bad qualities' (*OED* n. 1c).

    And here she comes. I am sure of her at midnight —   130
    My pretty Eros, welcome.
*Eros.*         I have business.
*Septimius.* Above my love, thou canst not.
*Eros.*          Yes. Indeed, sir,
    Far, far above.
*Septimius.*    Why, why so coy? Pray ye, tell me.
    We are alone.
*Eros.*      I am much ashamed we are so.
*Septimius.* You want a new gown now, and a handsome
    petticoat,                 135
    A scarf and some odd toys. I have gold here ready:
           [*He shows her the purse*]
    Thou shalt have anything.
*Eros.*         I want your absence.
    Keep on your way. I care not for your company.
*Septimius.* How? How? You are very short. Do you know
    me, Eros,
    And what I have been to ye?
*Eros.*         Yes, I know ye,     140
    And I hope I shall forget ye. Whilst you were honest,
    I loved ye too.
*Septimius.*    Honest? Come, prithee, kiss me.
       [*He embraces her and tries to kiss her.*]
*Eros.* I kiss no knaves, no murderers, no beasts,
    No base betrayers of those men that fed 'em;
    I hate their looks. And, though I may be wanton,   145
    I scorn to nourish it with bloody purchase,
    Purchase so foully got. I pray ye, unhand me:
          [*She thrusts him away.*]
    I had rather touch the plague than one unworthy.
    Go, seek some mistress that a horse may marry
    And keep her company: she is too good for ye.  *Exit.*   150

---

146. bloody] *F2*; blood *F1*.

---

 136. *toys*] trinkets.
 139. *short*] 'rudely or angrily curt in expression; returning short answers; snappish' (*OED* adj. 10a).
 145. *wanton*] lascivious.
 146. *it*] that is, my lust.
 *purchase*] gain, spoil.

SC 2]                    THE FALSE ONE                        139

*Septimius.* Marry, this goes near. Now I perceive I am
    hateful.
  When this light stuff can distinguish, it grows dangerous.
  For money seldom they refuse a leper,
  But sure I am more odious, more diseased too.
  It sits cold here.

              *Enter three lame* Soldiers.

            [*Aside*] What are these? Three poor soldiers?   155
  Both poor and lame: their misery may make 'em
  A little look upon me and adore me.
  If these will keep me company, I am made yet.
*1 Soldier.* [*To* Soldiers] The pleasure Caesar sleeps in makes
    us miserable.
  We are forgot, our maims and dangers laughed at.       160
  He banquets, and we beg.
*2 Soldier.*              He was not wont
  To let poor soldiers that have spent their fortunes,
  Their bloods and limbs walk up and down like
    vagabonds.
*Septimius.* Save ye, good soldiers! Good poor men, heaven
    help ye.
  You have borne the brunt of war and show the story.   165
*1 Soldier.* [*To* Soldiers] Some new commander, sure.
*Septimius.*              You look, my good friends,
  By your thin faces, as you would be suitors.

---

152. this light stuff] *F2;* these light Stuffs *Seward;* this light stuffes *F1.*
153. leper] *F2;* Leaper *F1.*   155. SD] *Weber; placed at line 154.1 in F1.*

---

  151. *Marry*] indeed; a corruption of 'by the Virgin Mary', a mild interjection.
*goes near*] touches me closely.
  152. *this ... stuff*] such a frivolous woman.
*distinguish*] discriminate.
  155. *It ... here*] An oppressive feeling of gloom and despondency weighs heavily here (perhaps with Septimius indicating his heart).
  158. *I ... yet*] My happiness is still assured.
  160. *forgot*] forgotten. Also at 169.
  161. *wont*] accustomed.
  165. *brunt*] shock, violence.
  167. *suitors*] suppliants.

140        THE FALSE ONE        [ACT 3

*2 Soldier.* To Caesar, for our means, sir.
*Septimius.*                              And 'tis fit, sir.
*3 Soldier.* We are poor men and long forgot.
*Septimius.*                              I grieve for it.
    Good soldiers should have good rewards and favours.    170
    I'll give up your petitions, for I pity ye,
    And freely speak to Caesar.
*All Soldiers.*                          Oh, we honour ye.
*1 Soldier.* A good man sure ye are: the gods preserve ye.
*Septimius.* And, to relieve your wants the while, hold, soldiers.
                              [*He gives them gold.*]
    Nay, 'tis no dream: 'tis good gold. Take it freely;    175
    'Twill keep ye in good heart.
*2 Soldier.*                          Now goodness quit ye.
*Septimius.* I'll be a friend to your afflictions,
    And eat and drink with ye too, and we'll be merry,
    And everyday I'll see ye.
*1 Soldier.*                          You are a soldier,
    And one sent from the gods, I think.
*Septimius.*                              I'll clothe ye    180
    (Ye are lame) and then provide good lodging for ye,
    And at my table, where no want shall meet ye —

                *Enter* SCAEVA [*again*].

*All Soldiers.* Was never such a man!
*1 Soldier.*                          Dear honoured sir,
    Let us but know your name, that we may worship ye.
*2 Soldier.* That we may ever thank.
*Septimius.*                          Why, call me anything.    185
    No matter for my name. [*Aside*] That may betray me.

---

168. To] *F2; not in F1.* 182. ye —] *Dyce;* you. — *Weber;* ye. *F1.* 182.1. SD] *this edn; Enter Sceva. F1.* 185. thank.] *1711;* thank — *Seward;* thank? *F1.*

---

   171. *give up*] present, deliver.
   172. SP All Soldiers] Probably one soldier speaks, while others indicate agreement (see Honigmann, 120–3). Also at 183.
   176. *quit*] repay.
   177. *afflictions*] pronounced 'afflictïons'.
   181. *Ye are lame*] This parenthesis is probably intended as Septimius' way of explaining why the soldiers cannot be expected to fend for themselves, and accordingly showing that he is apparently acting out of genuine concern.

SC 2]            THE FALSE ONE                    141

*Scaeva.* A cunning thief. — Call him Septimius, soldiers,
    The villain that killed Pompey.
*All Soldiers.*                    How?
*Scaeva.* Call him the shame of men.              *Exit.*
*1 Soldier.*        [*To* SEPTIMIUS] Oh, that this money
    Were weight enough to break thy brains out. Fling all,    190
                            [*They fling the gold at him.*]
    And fling our curses next: let them be mortal.
    Out, bloody wolf, dost thou come gilded over
    And painted with thy charities to poison us?
*2 Soldier.* I know him now. May never father own thee
    But as a monstrous birth shun thy base memory,           195
    And, if thou hadst a mother — as I cannot
    Believe thou wert a natural burden — let her womb
    Be cursed of women for a bed of vipers.
*3 Soldier.* Methinks the ground shakes to devour this rascal,
    And the kind air turns into fogs and vapours             200
    Infectious mists to crown his villainies.
    Thou mayst go wander like a thing heaven hated.
*1 Soldier.* And valiant minds hold poisonous to remember.
    The hangman will not keep thee company:
    He has an honourable house to thine.                     205
    No, not a thief, though thou couldst save his life for't,
    Will eat thy bread, nor one for thirst starved drink with
        thee.

---

193. thy] *F2;* the *F1.* 201. Infectious] *F2;* To infectious *Turner;* Th'infectious *Seward;* The infectious *F1.*

---

188.] This is an incomplete line of pentameter, being made up of only eight syllables. This might indicate a longer break immediately before or after the Soldiers' 'How?' as a way to accentuate the impression of their dismay. In this case the SP might indeed indicate that the three soldiers speak in unison, unlike what occurs at 172 and 183 above.
    192. *thou*] Though the three soldiers have used *you* to address Septimius so far, they start to deploy *thou* contemptuously as soon as they learn who he really is.
    *gilded over*] covered with gilding.
    197. *natural burden*] child delivered naturally.
    200. *vapours*] used as a transitive verb, with the meaning of 'to send forth, out, or up, to emit or discharge, to disperse, etc., in the form of vapour' (*OED* v. 3a).
    205. *to*] as compared with.

*2 Soldier.* Thou art no company for an honest dog,
    And so we'll leave thee to a ditch, thy destiny.
                      *[They kick him to the ground.]*
                              *Exeunt* [Soldiers].
*Septimius.* Contemned of all, and kicked too? Now I find it:   210
    My valour's fled too with mine honesty,
    For since I would be knave I must be coward;
    This 'tis to be a traitor and betrayer.
    What a deformity dwells round about me!
    How monstrous shows that man that is ungrateful!   215
    I am afraid the very beasts will tear me,
    Inspired with what I have done; the winds will blast me.
    Now I am paid, and my reward dwells in me,
    The wages of my fact. My soul's oppressed.
    Honest and noble minds, you find most rest.   *Exit.*   220

## [ACT 3] SCENE 3

*Enter* PTOLEMY, ACOREUS, POTHINUS [*and*] ACHILLAS.

*Ptolemy.* I have commanded, and it shall be so.
    A preparation I have set o'foot,
    Worthy the friendship and the fame of Caesar.
    My sister's favours shall seem poor and withered;
    Nay, she herself, trimmed up in all her beauties,   5
    Compared to what I'll take his eyes withal,
    Shall be a dream.
*Pothinus.*             Do you mean to show the glory

---

209.2. SD] *Dyce; Exeunt. F1.*

210. *Contemned*] scorned, despised.
217. *Inspired with*] animated by.
219. *wages*] reward.
    *fact*] deed.

3.3.0.] Weber adds the setting: '*A Room in the Palace*'.
4. *withered*] Cf. *A&C* 2.2.245: 'Age cannot wither her.'
5. *trimmed up*] adorned.
6. *take*] captivate, delight.
    *withal*] with.
7. *dream*] idle fantasy.

And wealth of Egypt?
*Ptolemy.* Yes, and in that lustre
Rome shall appear, in all her famous conquests
And all her riches, of no note unto it.                                  10
*Acoreus.* Now you are reconciled to your fair sister,
Take heed, sir, how you step into a danger,
A danger of this precipice. But note, sir,
For what Rome ever raised her mighty armies:
First, for ambition; then, for wealth. 'Tis madness,                     15
Nay, more, a secure impotence to tempt
An armèd guest. Feed not an eye that conquers
Nor teach a fortunate sword the way to be covetous.
*Ptolemy.* Ye judge amiss and far too wide to alter me.
Let all be ready as I gave direction,                                    20
The secret way of all our wealth appearing
Newly and handsomely, and all about it.
No more dissuading: 'tis my will.
*Acoreus.* I grieve for't.
*Ptolemy.* I will dazzle Caesar with excess of glory.
*Pothinus.* I fear you'll curse your will. We must obey ye.              25
                                                              [*Exeunt.*]

---

20. Let] *Seward;* Yet *F1.* 25.1. SD] *Seward; Ex. F1.*

---

10. *unto*] as compared with.

12. *Take heed*] Be careful.

13. *precipice*] 'loftiness as of a precipice; precipitousness' (*OED* n. 3). The first recorded example in *OED* is dated 1650.

15–17. *'Tis ... guest*] Cf. Lucan, 10.146–9: 'What blindness, what madness for display, to reveal their wealth to the general in a civil war, and to kindle the avarice of a guest in arms!'

16. *secure*] overconfident.

*impotence*] 'lack of self-restraint, violent passion' (*OED* n. 3). Cf. *Woman* 2.1.51–2: 'The being your sister would anew inflame me / With much more impotence to dote upon her.'

18. *fortunate*] See 2.1.194.

19. *wide*] mistakenly.

22. *Newly*] for the first time.

*about*] set about.

25. *will*] wilfulness.

## [ACT 3] SCENE 4

*Enter* CAESAR, ANTONY, DOLABELLA [*and*] SCAEVA,
*above.*

*Caesar.* I wonder at the glory of this kingdom
And the most bounteous preparation,
Still as I pass, they court me with.
*Scaeva.*                      I'll tell ye:
In Gaul and Germany we saw such visions
And stood not to admire 'em but possess 'em.     5
When they are ours, they are worth our admiration.

*Enter* CLEOPATRA [*above*].

*Antony.* The young Queen comes: give room.
*Caesar.*                      Welcome, my dearest.
Come, bless my side.
*Scaeva.*                Ay, marry, here's a wonder:
As she appears now, I am no true soldier

---

6.1. SD] Dyce; *Enter Cleopatra. F1.*

3.4.0.] Weber adds the setting: '*Another [room] in the same with a Gallery*'. The scene is very loosely based on Lucan, 10.107–331. The passage in *Pharsalia* describes the banquet with which Cleopatra celebrates her political alliance with Caesar and reports a lengthy conversation between Caesar and Acoreus, the former seeking to learn from the latter about Egypt in general and about the sources of the Nile in particular, which become in the play the subject matter of the masque.
  2. *bounteous*] bountiful.
  *preparation*] pronounced 'preparation'.
  3. *Still as*] whenever.
  6.1. SD] Turner (quoting Gurr's suggestion in private conversation) argues that 'Antony could be trying to make space in a crowded area to encourage [Cleopatra] to ascend and Caesar's words could be an invitation to which she does not respond. When Caesar turns away from her, her isolation would be emphasized if she were at one side of the stage below.' This is possible, and it is always difficult to give a definitive answer to such questions of staging. That being said, it seems to me that Antony's and Caesar's speeches at 7–8 rather clearly suggest otherwise. The Romans above move to make room for Cleopatra, and she sits next to Caesar, who then utterly ignores her in favour of the masque despite having her *right next to him*, which enrages Cleopatra even more.
  8. *marry*] indeed; a corruption of 'by the Virgin Mary', a mild interjection.

SC 4]               THE FALSE ONE                    145

    If I be not readiest to recant.
*Cleopatra.*                    [*To* CAESAR] Be merry, sir:      10
    My brother will be proud to do you honour
    That now appears himself.
        *Enter* PTOLEMY, ACOREUS, ACHILLAS, POTHINUS
            [*and*] APOLLODORUS [*below*].
*Ptolemy.*                       Hail to great Caesar!
    My royal guest, first I will feast thine eyes
    With wealthy Egypt's store, and then thy palate,
    And wait myself upon thee.
                  *Treasure brought in* [*below*].
*Caesar.*                     What rich service!                   15
    What mines of treasure! Richer still!
*Cleopatra.*                       My Caesar,
    What do you admire? Pray ye, turn and let me talk to ye.
    Have ye forgot me, sir? How, a new object?
    Am I grown old o'th' sudden, Caesar?
*Caesar.*                             Tell me
    From whence comes all this wealth.
*Cleopatra.*                        Is your eye that way,        20
    And all my beauties banished?
*Ptolemy.*                       I'll tell thee, Caesar.
    We owe for all this wealth to the old Nilus.
    We need no dropping rain to cheer the husbandman,
    Nor merchant that ploughs up the sea to seek us.
    Within the wealthy womb of reverend Nilus           25
    All this is nourished, who, to do thee honour,
    Comes to discover his seven deities,
    His concealed heads, unto thee: see with pleasure

---

12. SD] *conj Turner; Enter* PTOLEMY, ACOREUS, ACHILLAS, POTHINUS, *and* APOLLODORUS, *above. Weber, Dyce, Luce; Enter Ptolomy, Achoreus, Achillas, Photinus, Apollodorus. F1, F2, 1711, Seward, Colman.*

---

  13. *feast*] provide a feast for.
  15. *wait ... thee*] attend personally as a servant to your requests and needs.
*service*] homage, ceremony.
  16. *Richer still*] richer and richer.
  18. *forgot*] forgotten.
*object*] that is, object of desire.
  19. *old*] tiresome.

                    The matchless wealth of this land!
*Cleopatra.*             [*To* CAESAR] Come, ye shall hear.
*Caesar.* Away. Let me imagine.
*Cleopatra.*                How? Frown on me?                    30
    The eyes of Caesar wrapped in storms?
*Caesar.*                          I am sorry,
    But let me think —
*Cleopatra.*            A little dross betray me?

                        *Music.*

            Enter ISIS *and three* Labourers [*below*].

                        *Song.*

*Isis.*     Isis, the goddess of this land,
            Bids thee, great Caesar, understand
            And mark our customs. And first know        35
            [*Pointing to the* Labourers] With greedy eyes these
                watch the flow
            Of plenteous Nilus: when he comes,
            With songs, with dances, timbrels, drums,
            They entertain him. [*To the* Labourers] Cut his way,

---

29. The ... land!] *Turner; assigned to Caesar in F1.* hear] *F1;* heare me *F2.*
32. Cleopatra. A ... me?] *Turner; after line 76 in F1.* 32.2. SD] *Weber (subst); Enter Isis, and three Labourers. F1.* 32.3. SD] *Weber; not in Colman; placed as 32.1 in F1.* 33. SP Isis] *Colman; not in F1.*

---

29. *The ... land*] As Turner illustrates, 'F1 is wrong in either omitting a stop after "pleasure" or in supplying a speech-prefix to "The ... Land." Of the two it is certainly easier to think the punctuation overlooked. Yet because terminal punctuation is rarely omitted elsewhere in F1, I believe the scribe, prompted either by an authorial false start or by Caesar's exclamations at lines 15–16, added the prefix.'
   31. *wrapped in storms*] thundering against me.
   32. *A ... me*] As Turner usefully explains, 'Cleopatra, as in F1, could speak this line during the masque. It does, however, exactly fit the stichomythic passage preceding the masque; moreover, the separation of a divided pentameter by forty-three lines of text is extraordinary. F1's drastic misplacement of this line indicates that it was originally misplaced by Crane, and that in turn indicates that the text of the original masque was separated from the text of the play.'
   36. *greedy*] eager, zealous.
   37. *plenteous*] prolific, bountiful.
   39. *Cut his way*] Open a passage for him.

|  |  |  |
|---|---|---|
| | And give his proud heads leave to play: | 40 |
| | Nilus himself shall rise and show | |
| | His matchless wealth in overflow. | |

[*The*] Labourers' Song

*Labourers.* Come, let us help the reverend Nile:
He's very old; alas the while!
Let us dig him easy ways                    45
And prepare a thousand plays.
To delight his streams, let's sing
A loud welcome to our spring.
This way let his curling heads
Fall into our new-made beds.                50
This way let his wanton spawns
Frisk and glide it o'er the lawns.
This way profit comes, and gain:
How he tumbles here amain!
How his waters haste to fall                55
Into our channels! Labour all
And let him in: let Nilus flow
And perpetual plenty show.
With incense let us bless the brim
And, as the wanton fishes swim,             60
Let us gums and garlands fling
And loud our timbrels ring.
    Come, old father, come away;
    Our labour is our holiday.
*Isis.* Here comes the agèd river now,      65

[*Enter* NILUS.]

---

48. A loud] *F2;* Aloud *F1*.   65.1. SD] *Dyce; placed at line 64.1 in Colman; not in F1.*

---

49. *curling*] having curls.
51. *wanton*] frisky, frolicsome. Also at 60.
   *spawns*] offspring.
52. *Frisk ... it*] Dance and move smoothly.
54. *amain*] with full force.
57. *flow*] rise to a great height and overflow.
59. *brim*] shore.
62. *timbrels*] tambourines or similar musical instrument of percussion that could be held up in the hand (*OED* n.1 a).

148                    THE FALSE ONE                    [ACT 3

    With garlands of great pearl his brow
    Begirt and rounded. In his flow
    All things take life, and all things grow.
    A thousand wealthy treasures still,
    To do him service at his will,      70
    Follow his rising flood and pour
    Perpetual blessings in our store.
    Hear him, and next there will advance
    His sacred heads to tread a dance
    In honour of my royal guest.      75
    Mark them too, and you have a feast.
*Caesar.* I am ashamed I warred at home, my friends,
  When such wealth may be got abroad. What honour,
  Nay, everlasting glory had Rome purchased,
  Had she a just cause but to visit Egypt!    80

    [*Song.*]

*Nilus.*  Make room for my rich waters' fall
      and bless my flood.
    Nilus comes flowing, to you all
      increase and good.
    Now the plants and flowers shall spring,  85
    And the merry ploughman sing.
    In my hidden waves I bring
    Bread and wine and everything.
    Let the damsels sing me in,
    Sing aloud that I may rise.      90
    Your holy feasts and hours begin,
    And each hand bring a sacrifice.
      Now my wanton pearls I show

---

80.1.] *this edn;* Nilus' SONG. *Luce;* SONG *by* NILUS. *Dyce;* NILUS *sings. Weber; not in Colman;* Nylus SONG, and Dance. *F1.* 81. SP *Nilus*] *Colman; not in F1.*

---

 67. *Begirt*] girded around.
 77–80.] Cf. Lucan, 10.169–71: 'Caesar learns to squander the wealth of a plundered world; he is ashamed to have made war against one so poor as Pompey, and desires a pretext for war with the Egyptians.'
 80. *just cause*] See Introduction, 45–6.
 93. *wanton*] luxurious.

> That to ladies' fair necks grow.
>                     Now my gold                              95
> And treasures that can ne'er be told
> Shall bless this land by my rich flow,
>     And after this, to crown your eyes,
>     My hidden holy heads arise.

[*Enter* NILUS' Seven Heads *and dance, and exeunt masquers.*]

*Caesar.* The wonder of this wealth so troubles me    100
   I am not well. Goodnight.
*Scaeva.*                        I am glad ye have it:
   Now we shall stir again.
*Ptolemy.*             [*Aside*] Thou, wealth, still haunt him.
*Scaeva.* A greedy spirit set thee on: we are happy.
*Ptolemy.* Lights, lights for Caesar, and attendance.
*Cleopatra.*                           [*Aside*] Well,
   I shall yet find a time to tell thee, Caesar,    105
   Thou hast wronged her love. The rest here.
*Ptolemy.*                          Lights along still.
   Music and sacrifice to sleep for Caesar.   *Exeunt.*

---

99. heads] *Dyce;* head *F1.* 99.1. SD] *Dyce (subst); The Masquers dance, and exeunt. Weber; not in F1.* 102. SP *Ptolemy*] *F1; Dol. Seward.* 106. The rest] *F1;* disgrac'd *Turner.*

---

102. *Thou ... him*] As Turner illustrates, 'Thinking the speech must belong to a Roman because it continues Sc[a]eva's wish that Caesar's greed will "occasion a new war", Seward changed the prefix to *Dol.*, "as the nearest in the trace of the letters to *Ptol.*" The speech does follow from Sc[a]eva's, but ironically. Ptol[e]my thinks the wonder of Egypt's wealth will win him Caesar's favour; Sc[a]eva knows that the time for action has come again because gold is the one thing that will drive Cleopatra from Caesar's mind.'
   103. *set thee on*] has incited you.
   106. *The rest here*] 'The meaning of the last sentence may be: *The rest of what I intend to do and say, I keep to myself till a fit opportunity*' (Seward). Turner emended to 'disgrac'd here' because he found the interpretation unsatisfactory, but I consider F1's reading acceptable, if a little obscure, on the basis of Seward's gloss. Perhaps Cleopatra here is meant to point to her bosom.

## ACT 4 SCENE 1

*Enter* PTOLEMY, POTHINUS, ACHILLAS [*and*]
ACOREUS.

*Acoreus.* [*To* PTOLEMY] I told ye carefully what this would
    prove to,
What this inestimable wealth and glory
Would draw upon ye. I advised your majesty
Never to tempt a conquering guest nor add
A bait to catch a mind bent by his trade 5
To make the whole world his.
*Pothinus.*          [*To* PTOLEMY] I was not heard, sir,
Or what I said lost and contemned. I dare say,
And freshly now, 'twas a poor weakness in ye,
A glorious childishness. I watched his eye
And saw how falcon-like it tow'red and flew 10
Upon the wealthy quarry, how round it marked it.
I observed his words and to what it tended,
How greedily he asked from whence it came
And what commerce we held for such abundance.
The show of Nilus how he laboured at 15
To find the secret ways the song delivered!
*Acoreus.* [*To* PTOLEMY] He never smiled, I noted, at the
    pleasures
But fixed his constant eyes upon the treasure.
I do not think his ears had so much leisure,
After the wealth appeared, to hear the music. 20
Most sure, he has not slept since, for minds troubled
With objects they would make their own still labour.

---

21. for] *Dyce;* his *F1.*

---

4.1.0.] Weber adds the setting: '*A Room in the Royal Palace*'.
1. *what ... to*] how this would turn out.
5. *bent*] inclined.
   *trade*] habitual course of action (*OED* n. 3b).
7. *contemned*] scorned, despised.
8. *freshly*] with renewed vigour.
9. *glorious*] vainglorious.
11. *quarry*] prey.
22. *still*] always.

SC I]                    THE FALSE ONE                    151

*Pothinus.* [*To* PTOLEMY] Your sister he ne'er gazed on.
  That's a main note:
  The prime beauty of the world had no power over him.
*Ptolemy.* Where was his mind the whilst?
*Pothinus.*                    Where was your carefulness,      25
  To show an armèd thief the way to rob ye?
  Nay, would you give him this, it will excite him
  To seek the rest. Ambition feels no gift
  Nor knows no bounds. Indeed, ye have done most
    weakly.
*Ptolemy.* Can I be too kind to my noble friend?               30
*Pothinus.* To be unkind unto your noble self but savours
  Of indiscretion, and your friend has found it.
  Had ye been trained up in the wants and miseries
  A soldier marches through, and known his temperance
  In offered courtesies, you would have made              35
  A wiser master of your own, and stronger.
*Ptolemy.* Why, should I give him all, he would return it.
  'Tis more to him to make kings.
*Pothinus.*                    Pray thee, be wiser
  And trust not, with your lost wealth, your loved liberty:
  To be a king still at your own discretion              40

---

25. SP *Ptolemy*] this edn; *Ach. F1*.   27. it will] *Colman*; 'twill *F1*.   29. bounds. Indeed] *F2 (subst)*; bounds indeed: *F1*.

---

  23. *a ... note*] an important sign.
  25. SP Ptolemy] F1 and all subsequent editions assign the question 'Where was his mind the whilst?' to Acoreus. There seems to be no compelling reason, however, for Acoreus to ask such a question, given that he already knows that Caesar's mind was set on Egypt's wealth, as he himself has just made clear. Besides, Pothinus' ensuing question must be directed at Ptolemy, who is the one who decided 'To show an armèd thief the way to rob ye' despite Acoreus' attempts in the previous scene to dissuade him from doing so.
  28. *Ambition ... gift*] 'Ambition does not look on anything it has power to seize as a gift from the owner; no present you can make Caesar will affect him with gratitude: his sword is the arbitrator of right and wrong, and he acknowledges no other law' (Seward).
    31. *savours*] tastes.
    32. *indiscretion*] lack of discernment.
    33. *wants*] straits, hardship.
    35. *courtesies*] courteous acts.
    39. *trust*] entrust.

    Is like a king; to be at his, a vassal.
    Now take good counsel or no more take to ye
    The freedom of a prince.
*Achillas.*                 'Twill be too late else,
    For, since the masque, he sent three of his captains,
    Ambitious as himself, to view again           45
    The glory of your wealth.
*Pothinus.*                The next himself comes,
    Not staying for your courtesy, and takes it.
*Ptolemy.* What counsel, my Acoreus?
*Acoreus.*                I'll go pray, sir,
    For that is best counsel now. The gods may help ye.
                                            *Exit.*
*Pothinus.* I found ye out a way, but 'twas not credited,     50
    A most secure way. Whither will ye fly now?
*Achillas.* For when your wealth is gone, your power must
        follow.
*Pothinus.* And that diminished also, what's your life worth?
    Who would regard it?
*Ptolemy.*             You say true.
*Achillas.*                 What eye
    Will look upon King Ptolemy? If they do look,        55
    It must be in scorn, for a poor king is a monster.
    What ear remember ye? 'Twill be then a courtesy,
    A noble one, to take your life too from ye.
    But, if reserved, you stand to fill a victory,
    As who knows conquerors' minds, though outwardly     60
    They bear fair streams? O sir, does this not shake ye?

---

49.1. SD] *Seward; Ex. F1.* 56.] *Seward; F1 lines* It ... scorne: / For ... monster;. 61.] *Seward; F1 lines* They ... streames. / O ... ye?.

---

    43. *else*] otherwise.
    44. *three ... captains*] perhaps Antony, Dolabella, and Scaeva.
    47. *staying*] waiting.
    50. *credited*] given credence to.
    54. *regard*] respect.
    59. *reserved ... victory*] preserved from death, you will be used to make the Roman victory perfect, that is, you will be left alive to suffer the humiliation of taking part in the Roman triumph as a captive.
    61. *bear ... streams*] put on a friendly face.

SC 2]                    THE FALSE ONE                    153

 If to be honeyed on to these afflictions —
*Ptolemy.* I never will. I was a fool.
*Pothinus.*      For then, sir,
 Your country's cause falls with ye too, and fettered:
 All Egypt shall be ploughed up with dishonour.   65
*Ptolemy.* No more. I am sensible, and now my spirit
 Burns hot within me.
*Achillas.*     Keep it warm and fiery.
*Pothinus.* At last, be counselled.
*Ptolemy.*     I will, though I perish.
*Pothinus.* Go in. We'll tell you all, and then we'll execute.
              *Exeunt.*

## [ACT 4] SCENE 2

*Enter* CLEOPATRA, ARSINOE [*and*] EROS.

*Arsinoe.* You are so impatient.
*Cleopatra.*     Have I not cause?
 Women of common beauties and low births,
 When they are slighted, are allowed their angers.
 Why should not I, a princess, make him know
 The baseness of his usage?
*Arsinoe.*      Yes, 'tis fit,   5
 But, then again, you know what man —
*Cleopatra.*      He is no man.
 The shadow of a greatness hangs upon him,
 And not the virtue. He is no conqueror:

---

68. At] *Turner;* And *F1.*

6. man —] *Colman;* man. *F1.*

---

  62. *honeyed on*] 'allured by sweet speeches' (Luce).
  64. *fettered*] bound in chains.
  66. *sensible*] aware of the situation.
  68. *At last*] As Turner argues, 'F1's "And last" implies an enumeration or a series, but there has been neither. Ptol[e]my is now "sensible" ...; his regal spirit will no longer submit to Caesar. He is thus ready for P[oth]inus' counsel at last – finally.'

 4.2.0.] Weber adds the setting: '*The Apartment of* Cleopatra *in the Palace*'.
 1. *impatient*] probably pronounced 'impatìent'.
 5. *usage*] conduct.

    He's suffered under the base dross of nature,
    Poorly delivered up his power to wealth, 10
    The god of bedrid men, taught his eyes treason.
    Against the truth of love he has raised rebellion,
    Defied his holy flames.
*Eros.*                He will fall back again
    And satisfy your grace.
*Cleopatra.*         Had I been old
    Or blasted in my bud, he might have showed 15
    Some shadow of dislike, but to prefer
    The lustre of a little art, Arsinoe,
    And the poor glow-worm light of some faint jewels
    Before the life of love and soul of beauty?
    Oh, how it vexes me! He is no soldier: 20
    All honourable soldiers are love's servants.
    He is a merchant, a mere wandering merchant,
    Servile to gain. He trades for poor commodities
    And makes his conquests thefts. Some fortunate captains
    That quarter with him and are truly valiant 25
    Have flung the name of 'happy Caesar' on him;
    Himself ne'er won it. He is so base and covetous
    He'll sell his sword for gold.
*Arsinoe.*               This is too bitter.
*Cleopatra.* Oh, I could curse myself, that was so foolish,
    So fondly childish to believe his tongue, 30
    His promising tongue, ere I could catch his temper.

---

21. love's] *F2;* Lovers *F1.*

---

11. *bedrid*] confined to bed through sickness or infirmity.
*taught*] which taught.
13. *fall ... again*] return to his former practice.
15. *blasted ... bud*] already deprived of my virginity.
17. *art*] cunning, artfulness, artifice.
18. *glow-worm*] that is, faint.
*faint*] sickly.
23. *Servile*] slavishly devoted.
31. *promising*] that makes promises.
*ere*] before.
*catch ... temper*] get to know his actual attitude of mind.

I had trash enough to have cloyed his eyes withal —
His covetous eyes — such as I scorn to tread on,
Richer than e'er he saw yet, and more tempting.
Had I known he had stooped at that, I had saved mine
    honour,                                                    35
I had been happy still. But let him take it
And let him brag how poorly I am rewarded.
Let him go conquer still weak, wretched ladies.
Love has his angry quiver too, his deadly,
And, when he finds scorn, armèd at the strongest.              40
I am a fool to fret thus for a fool,
An old blind fool too. I lose my health? I will not.
I will not cry. I will not honour him
With tears diviner than the gods he worships,
I will not take the pains to curse a poor thing.               45
*Eros.* Do not: you shall not need.
*Cleopatra.*          Would I were prisoner
To one I hate, that I might anger him.
I will love any man to break the heart of him,
Any that has the heart and will to kill him.
*Arsinoe.* Take some fair truce.
*Cleopatra.*          I will go study mischief                 50
And put a look on, armed with all my cunnings,
Shall meet him like a basilisk and strike him.

---

39. his] *F1*; is *conj Dutton.*   42. health?] *F2*; health: *F1.*   46. Do] *F2*; Dye *F1*.

---

32. *trash*] worthless stuff, dross (often contemptuously applied to money; cf. *JC* 4.3.73–4: 'wring / From the hands of peasants their vile trash').
*cloyed*] satiated.
*withal*] with.
35. *had ... honour*] would have preserved my chastity.
36. *had*] would have.
38. *still*] always.
41.] Fletcher's customary use of alliteration is here coupled with an entirely monosyllabic delivery that makes this (and the following) line particularly effective in channelling Cleopatra's anger.
42. *old*] See 2.3.110.
51. *cunnings*] skills (in deceit).
52. *basilisk*] mythical reptile (sometimes identified with the cockatrice), allegedly hatched by a serpent from a cock's egg and supposed to kill by gazing.

Love, put destroying flames into mine eyes;
Into my smiles, deceits, that I may torture him,
That I may make him love to death, and laugh at him. 55

*Enter* APOLLODORUS.

*Apollodorus.* Caesar commends his service to your grace.
*Cleopatra.* His service? What's his service?
*Eros.* Pray ye, be patient.
　　The noble Caesar loves still.
*Cleopatra.* What's his will?
*Apollodorus.* He craves access unto your highness.
*Cleopatra.* No.
　　Say 'no'. I will have none to trouble me. 60
*Arsinoe.* Good sister —
*Cleopatra.* None, I say. I will be private.
　　Would thou hadst flung me into Nilus, keeper,
　　When first thou gav'st consent to bring my body
　　To this unthankful Caesar.
*Apollodorus.* 'Twas your will, madam;
　　Nay, more, your charge upon me, as I honoured ye. 65
　　You know what danger I endured.
*Cleopatra.* Take this
　　　　　　　　　　　　　　　　　[*She gives him a jewel.*]
　　And carry it to that lordly Caesar sent thee.
　　There's a new love, a handsome one, a rich one,
　　One that will hug his mind. Bid him make love to it,
　　Tell the ambitious broker this will suffer — 70

---

61. sister —] *Dyce;* sister! *Colman;* Sister. *F2;* Sister: *F1.*

56. *commends*] presents (for favourable acceptance).
　*service*] probably with the secondary meaning of sexual action (see Williams, 3.1220–1), though it starts from the faux-chivalry of the knight abasing himself to his lady.
　59. *craves*] asks, begs.
　60. *will*] wish to.
　61. *private*] alone, undisturbed.
　63. *body*] as opposed to her mind and soul.
　65. *charge*] order.
　66. *endured*] underwent.
　70. *broker*] pawnbroker.
　*suffer*] allow, permit.

*Enter* CAESAR.

*Apollodorus.* He enters.
*Cleopatra.* How?
*Caesar.* I do not use to wait, lady.
    Where I am, all the doors are free and open.
*Cleopatra.* I guess so, by your rudeness.
*Caesar.* Ye are not angry?
    Things of your tender mould should be most gentle.
    Why do you frown? Good gods, what a set anger    75
    Have you forced into your face! Come, I must temper
      ye.
    What a coy smile was there, and a disdainful!
    How like an ominous flash it broke out from ye!
    Defend me, love! Sweet, who has angered ye?
*Cleopatra.* Show him a glass: that false face has betrayed
      me,    80
    That base heart wronged me.
*Caesar.* Be more sweetly angry.
    I wronged ye, fair?
*Cleopatra.* Away with your foul flatteries:
    They are too gross. But that I dare be angry,
    And with as great a god as Caesar is,
    To show how poorly I respect his memory,    85
    I would not speak to ye.
*Caesar.* Pray ye, undo this riddle
    And tell me how I have vexed ye.
*Cleopatra.* Let me think first
    Whether I may put on a patience

---

81. wronged me.] *Dyce;* wrong'd me — *Turner;* wronged me! *Seward;* wrought me — *F1.*

---

  71. *I ... wait*] I am not accustomed to waiting.
  75. *set*] fixed, settled, resolute.
  76. *temper*] appease.
  81. *wronged*] F1 and F2 read 'wrought'. Seward acknowledges that 'wrought me' might mean 'wrought me into this passion', but his emendation to 'wronged' seems to make better sense and is justified by Caesar's answer, 'I wronged you, fair?'
  83. *But that*] were it not that.
  87. *vexed*] upset.
  88. *patience*] pronounced 'patience'.

      That will with honour suffer me. Know I hate ye:
      Let that begin the story. Now I'll tell ye.            90
*Caesar.* But do it milder. In a noble lady,
      Softness of spirit and a sober nature
      That moves like summer winds, cool, and blows sweetness
      Shows blessèd like herself.
*Cleopatra.*               And that great blessedness
      You first reaped of me till you taught my nature     95
      Like a rude storm to talk aloud and thunder.
      Sleep was not gentler than my soul, and stiller.
      You had the spring of my affections,
      And my fair fruits I gave you leave to taste of:
      You must expect the winter of mine anger.        100
      You flung me off, before the court disgraced me
      When in the pride I appeared of all my beauty —
      Appeared your mistress — took into your eyes
      The common-strumpet love of hated lucre,
      Courted with covetous heart, the slave of nature,    105
      Gave all your thoughts to gold, that men of glory
      And minds adorned with noble love would kick at.
      Soldiers of royal mark scorn such base purchase:
      Beauty and honour are the marks they shoot at.
      I spake to ye then, I courted ye and wooed ye,     110
      Called ye 'dear Caesar', hung about ye tenderly,
      Was proud to appear your friend —
*Caesar.*                     You have mistaken me.
*Cleopatra.* But neither eye nor favour, not a smile
      Was I blessed back withal, but shook off rudely,

---

97. than] *F2;* to *F1.* 112. friend —] *Colman;* friend. *F1.* 114. withal] *Seward;* with *F2;* not in *F1.*

---

  89. *suffer me*] allow me to do it.
  91. *milder*] more mildly.
  98. *affections*] pronounced 'affectìons'.
 101. *flung me off*] disowned me.
 108. *purchase*] gain, spoil.
 109. *marks*] targets.
 111. *hung about*] hugged.
 114. *withal*] with.
    *shook*] shaken.

|  |  |
|---|---|
| | And, as ye had been sold to sordid infamy, 115 |
| | You fell before the images of treasure |
| | And in your soul you worshipped. I stood slighted, |
| | Forgotten and contemned; my soft embraces |
| | And those sweet kisses you called Elysium, |
| | As letters writ in sand, no more remembered; 120 |
| | The name and glory of your Cleopatra |
| | Laughed at and made a story to your captains. |
| | Shall I endure? |
| *Caesar.* | You are deceived in all this, |
| | Upon my life you are: 'tis your much tenderness. |
| *Cleopatra.* | No, no, I love not that way. You are cozened. 125 |
| | I love with as much ambition as a conqueror |
| | And, where I love, will triumph. |
| *Caesar.* | So you shall. |
| | My heart shall be the chariot that shall bear ye; |
| | All I have won shall wait upon ye. [*Aside*] By the gods, |
| | The bravery of this woman's mind has fired me. — 130 |
| | Dear mistress, shall I but this night — |
| *Cleopatra.* | How, Caesar? |
| | Have I let slip a second vanity |
| | That gives thee hope? |
| *Caesar.* | You shall be absolute |
| | And reign alone as queen. You shall be anything. |
| *Cleopatra.* | Make me a maid again, and then I'll hear thee. 135 |
| | Examine all thy art of war to do that, |
| | And, if thou findst it possible, I'll love thee. |
| | Till when, farewell, unthankful. |
| *Caesar.* | Stay. |
| *Cleopatra.* | I will not. |

---

118. *contemned*] scorned, despised.
119. *Elysium*] a place of ideal happiness. In Greek mythology, it was the state or abode of the blessed after death.
120. *writ*] written.
124. *tenderness*] youthfulness.
125. *cozened*] deceived.
129. *wait upon*] accompany.
132. *vanity*] instance of foolishness.
135. *maid*] virgin.

*Caesar.* I command.
*Cleopatra.*        Command and go without, sir.
   I do command thee be my slave forever                    140
   And vex while I laugh at thee.
*Caesar.*              Thus low, beauty —
                                         [*He kneels.*]
*Cleopatra.* It is too late. When I have found thee absolute,
   The man that fame reports thee, and to me,
   Maybe I shall think better. Farewell, conqueror.
      *Exit* [*with* ARSINOE, EROS *and* APOLLODORUS].
*Caesar.* She mocks me too. [*Rising*] I will enjoy her beauty,   145
   I will not be denied. I'll force my longing:
   Love is best pleased when roundly we compel him,
   And as he is imperious, so will I be.
   Stay, fool, and be advised: that dulls the appetite,
   Takes off the strength and sweetness of delight.          150
   By heaven, she is a miracle I must use
   A handsome way to win —

      *Enter* SCAEVA, ANTONY [*and*] DOLABELLA.

                        How now? What fear
   Dwells in your faces? You look all distracted.
*Scaeva.* If it be fear, 'tis fear of your undoing,
   Not of ourselves, fear of your poor declining.            155
   Our lives and deaths are equal benefits,
   And we make louder prayers to die nobly

---

141. beauty —] *Colman;* beauty. *F2;* beauty? *F1.*   144.1. SD] *Weber; Exit. F1.*   150. off] *F2;* of *F1.*   152. SD] *Weber; placed at line 153.1 in F1.*

---

   139. *without*] out.
   141. *vex*] suffer.
   142. *absolute*] determined, but also unaffected by anything outside yourself. Probably in response to Caesar's promise to make Cleopatra an 'absolute' (133) ruler above.
   145–52. *I ... win*] Caesar is arguing with himself. He first determines to take Cleopatra by force but then considers that this 'dulls the appetite'; hence, he concludes he must use a 'handsome way' to win her back.
   152. *handsome*] courteous, gracious (*OED* adj. 2a).
   153. *distracted*] greatly troubled.

                Than to live high and wantonly. Whilst you are secure
                    here
                And offer hecatombs of lazy kisses
                To the lewd god of love and cowardice,                    160
                And most lasciviously die in delights,
                You are begirt with the fierce Alexandrians.
*Dolabella.* The spawn of Egypt flow about your palace,
            Armed all and ready to assault.
*Antony.*                             Led on
            By the false and base Pothinus and his ministers.            165
            No stirring out, no peeping through a loophole,
            But straight saluted with an armèd dart.
*Scaeva.* No parley: they are deaf to all but danger.
            They swear they will flay us and then dry our quarters:
            A rasher of a salt lover is such a shoeing-horn.             170
            Can you kiss away this conspiracy and set us free?
            Or will the giant god of love fight for ye?
            Will his fierce warlike bow kill a cock sparrow?
            Bring out the lady: she can quell this mutiny
            And with her powerful looks strike awe into them.            175

---

158.] See 3.2.28–31.
*high*] richly.
*wantonly*] lasciviously.
*secure*] overconfident.
159. *hecatombs*] a great public sacrifice (originally of a hundred oxen), but also used more loosely, as here, to mean 'a very great number'.
161. *die in delights*] playing on the familiar idea of orgasm as a 'little death'.
162. *begirt with*] surrounded by.
163. *your palace*] that is, the palace in which you waste your time with Cleopatra.
169. *flay us*] strip our skin off.
170–1.] See 3.2.28–31.
170. *rasher*] slice, portion.
*salt*] in heat, lecherous, but also playing on the literal meaning as part of the food metaphor that informs the entire line.
*shoeing-horn*] appetizer for food or drink; also 'a pretext or incitement' (Farmer and Henley, 6.185).
173.] There seems to be a play here on the nursery rhyme 'Who killed Cock Robin? / I, said the Sparrow, / With my bow and arrow'.
*cock*] male.

         She can destroy and build again the city:
         Your goddesses have mighty gifts. Show 'em her fair
             breasts,
         The impregnable bulwarks of proud love, and let 'em
         Begin their battery there; she will laugh at 'em:
         They are not above a hundred thousand, sir.                180
         A mist, a mist that when her eyes break out —
         Her powerful radiant eyes — and shake their flashes,
         Will fly before her heats.
*Caesar.*                        Begirt with villains?
*Scaeva.* They come to play you and your love a hunt's-up.
         You were told what this same whoreson wenching long
             ago would come to.                                     185
         You are taken napping now. Has not a soldier
         A time to kiss his friend and a time to consider,
         But he must lie still digging, like a pioneer,
         Making of mines and burying of his honour there?
         'Twere good you would think —
*Dolabella.*                     And time too, or you will find else   190
         A harder task than courting a coy beauty.
*Antony.* Look out, and then believe.
*Scaeva.*                        No, no, hang danger.


185. to] *F2;* too *F1.*

---

   178. *bulwarks*] ramparts.
   179. *battery*] attack, assault.
   181. *break out*] spring out, emerge.
   184. *hunt's-up*] a daybreak song to wake huntsmen. The word is a favourite of Fletcher's. Cf. *Bond* 2.4.85–8: 'Ye shall have wine or anything. Go file; / I'll see ye have your share. Drag out your dormice / And stow 'em somewhere where they may sleep handsomely: / They'll hear a hunt's-up shortly'; *Monsieur* 3.1.405–6: 'My spiteful dame, I'll pipe ye such a hunt's-up / Shall make ye dance a-tiptoe'; *Tamer* 3.2.74–5: 'I would to her chambermaid, and in her hearing / Begin her such a hunt's-up.'
   185.] See 3.2.28–31.
   *whoreson wenching*] execrable association with women of loose morals.
   188. *still*] always.
   *pioneer*] soldiers employed in digging roads, trenches, fortifications, and mines (*OED* n. 1a). They were dirty, ill-paid, and considered the lowest kind of soldiery.
   190. *else*] otherwise.

sc 2]                    THE FALSE ONE                    163

    Take me provoking broth, and then go to her,
    Go to your love and let her feel your valour.
    Charge her whole body: when the sword's in your
        throat, sir,                                              195
    You may cry 'Caesar!' and see if that will help ye.
Caesar. I'll be myself again and meet their furies,
    Meet and consume their mischiefs. Make some shift,
        Scaeva,
    To recover the fleet and bring me up two legions,
    And you shall see me, how I'll break like thunder         200
    Amongst these beds of slimy eels and scatter 'em.
Scaeva. Now ye speak sense. I'll put my life to the hazard.
    Before I go: no more of this warm lady,
    She will spoil your sword-hand.
Caesar.                              Go.        [*Exit* SCAEVA.]
                                Come, let's to counsel
    How to prevent and then to execute.       [*Exeunt.*]      205

193. me] *F1*; ye *conj* Dutton.   204. SD] Dyce; not in *F1*.   205. SD] *1711*;
not in *F1*.

193. *Take me*] I consider 'me' to function as an ethic dative (see also 5.3.52), in the sense of 'Come on, do it for me', though sarcastically so. This is a relatively common construction in early modern English, implying that an individual other than the subject or object of the sentence has an indirect interest in the situation that has been described. Dutton (pers. comm.) conjectures that the actual reading may be 'Take ye', as he believes that a typo looks like an easier explanation. I have not accepted Dutton's conjecture, but I have recorded it in the collation.
    *provoking broth*] stimulating broth, perhaps with an obscene pun on broth as female sexual fluid (Williams, 1.155).
    196.] In addition to a possible pun on 'Caesar/seize her', Scaeva here seems to be mocking Caesar's habit of referring to himself in the third person by implying that such a practice is useless in the absence of the appropriate martial behaviour. See also 2.2.28 and 5.4.4.
    198–9. *Make ... legions*] Caesar's order serves as an implicit admission that things have drastically changed since he first arrived in Egypt and explicitly turned down Antony's suggestion of bringing troops ashore (cf. 2.3.5–8), preferring to let the mystique associated with his name do its magic instead.
    198. *Make ... shift*] try all means.
    200–1. *I'll ... 'em*] This was a common early modern zoological belief; cf. *Per* 4.2.134–6: 'I warrant you, mistress, thunder shall not so awake the beds of eels as my giving out her beauty stirs up the lewdly-inclined.' It may have been proverbial: see Dent (?T276): 'Thunder looses beds of eels.'
    205. *to prevent ... execute*] to forestall them and then put it into action.

[ACT 4] SCENE 3

*Enter [the three lame] Soldiers.*

*1 Soldier.* Did ye see this penitence?
*2 Soldier.*                              Yes, I saw and heard it.
*3 Soldier.* And I, too, looked upon him and observed it.
  He's the strangest Septimius now —
*1 Soldier.*                         I heard he was altered
  And had given away his gold to honest uses,
  Cried monstrously.
*2 Soldier.*           He cries abundantly:                    5
  He is blind almost with weeping.
*3 Soldier.*                        'Tis most wonderful
  That a hard-hearted man and an old soldier
  Should have so much kind moisture. When his mother died,
  He laughed aloud and made the wickedest ballads —
*1 Soldier.* 'Tis like enough: he never loved his parents.    10
  Nor can I blame him, for they ne'er loved him:
  His mother dreamed before she was delivered
  That she was brought abed with a buzzard, and ever after

---

0.1. SD] *Dyce (subst); Enter the Three Soldiers. Weber; Enter Souldiers. F1.*

4.3.0.] Weber adds the setting: '*A Street*'.
6–8. '*Tis ... moisture*] According to the theory of humours, the early moderns assumed that the human body contained four fluids: blood, yellow bile, black bile, and phlegm. These humours were believed to correspond to the four elements – air, fire, earth, and water – and to the qualities of hot, cold, wet, and dry. These fluids were thought to be mixed in different amounts in each individual, thus determining their personality, but they were also related to sex: men were said to have a propensity to be hot and dry; women were assumed to have a tendency to be cold and moist.
  8. *kind*] gentle.
  13. *brought ... with*] delivered of.
  *buzzard*] The buzzard was considered an inferior kind of hawk, a scavenger rather than a raptor. Because it did not train readily, it also became a synonym for a stupid person.

SC 3]                THE FALSE ONE                    165

        She whistled him off to th' world. His brave clothes too
        He has flung away and goes like one of us now,              15
        Walks with his hands in's pockets, poor and sorrowful,
        And gives the best instructions —
    2 Soldier.                         And tells stories
        Of honest and good people that were honoured,
        And how they were remembered, and runs mad
        If he but hear of any ungrateful person,                    20
        A bloody or betraying man —
    3 Soldier.                         If it be possible
        That an arch-villain may ever be recovered,
        This penitent rascal will put hard. 'Twere worth our
           labour
        To see him once again.

        *Enter* SEPTIMIUS [*all in black, with a book in his hand*].

    1 Soldier.                         He spares us that labour,
        For here he comes.
    Septimius.              Bless ye, my honest friends,            25
        Bless ye from base unworthy men. Come not near me,
        For I am yet too taking for your company.


14. off] *Turner;* up *F1*.  24. SD] *Dyce (subst); Enter* Septimius [*mourning*]. *Turner; Enter* SEPTIMIUS *in black Clothes, with a Book in his Hand. Weber; Enter Septinius. F1.*  25. Bless ye] *Colman;* Heaven bless ye *Weber;* — Blesse ye *F1*.

---

   14. *whistled him off*] dismissed him by whistling. As Turner explains, 'Because Septimius' mother dreamed she bore a buzzard, the Soldier ironically employs a hawking term.' Cf. *Bond* 4.3.62–3: 'he that basely / Whistled his honour off to th' wind'.
   16. *in's*] in his.
   22. *recovered*] rescued, redeemed.
   23. *put*] try.
   25. *Bless ye*] As Turner illustrates (quoting Howard-Hill, 'Introduction', vii), 'Editors have taken the dash preceding this word to represent an omission, but the line as it stands is a complete, although shared, pentameter. The dash may be instead the compositor's interpretation of the pen-stroke Crane sometimes inserted in the left margin "possibly to draw attention to entrances in the right margin" (Septimius' in this case).'
   27. *taking*] pernicious, infectious.

*1 Soldier.* [*To* Soldiers] Did I not tell ye?
*2 Soldier.* What book's that?
*1 Soldier.* No doubt
    Some excellent salve for a sore heart. — Are you
    Septimius, that base knave that betrayed Pompey?    30
*Septimius.* I was and am. Unless your honest thoughts
    Will look upon my penitence and save me,
    I must be ever villain. O good soldiers,
    You, that have Roman hearts, take heed of falsehood,
    Take heed of blood, take heed of foul ingratitude:    35
    The gods have scarce a mercy for those mischiefs.
    Take heed of pride: 'twas that that brought me to it.
*2 Soldier.* [*Aside to* Soldiers] This fellow would make a rare
    speech at the gallows.
*3 Soldier.* [*Aside to* Soldiers] 'Tis very fit he were hanged to
    edify us.
*Septimius.* Let all your thoughts be humble and obedient,    40
    Love your commanders, honour them that feed ye,
    Pray that ye may be strong in honesty
    As in the use of arms. Labour, and diligently,
    To keep your hearts from ease and her base issues,
    Pride and ambitious wantonness: those spoiled me.    45
    Rather lose all your limbs than the least honesty:
    You are never lame indeed till loss of credit
    Benumb ye through. Scars and those maims of honour
    Are memorable crutches that shall bear,
    When you are dead, your noble names to eternity.    50

---

29. *salve*] remedy.
   *salve ... heart*] Such titles to books were far from uncommon in the seventeenth century. See, for example, Theodore Herring, *Panacea Christiana, or A Christian's Sovereign Salve for Every Sore* (1624); Phillip Skippon, *A Salve for Every Sore* (1643); Thomas Powell, *A Salve for Soul-Sores* (1679).
33. *ever*] forever.
34. *take heed*] be careful.
38. *rare*] extraordinary.
44. *issues*] children.
45. *wantonness*] 'insolence in triumph or prosperity; haughty disregard for others; arrogance' (*OED* n. 5).
48. *Benumb*] stupefy, deaden.

SC 3]                THE FALSE ONE                      167

*1 Soldier.* [*To* Soldiers] I cry.
*2 Soldier.*                    And so do I.
*3 Soldier.*                              An excellent villain.
*1 Soldier.* A more sweet pious knave I never heard yet.
*2 Soldier.* He was happy he was rascal, to come to this.

                    *Enter* ACOREUS.

   Who's this? A priest?
*Septimius.*           [*To* ACOREUS] Oh, stay, most holy sir,
   And, by the gods of Egypt — I conjure ye,              55
   Isis and great Osiris — pity me,
   Pity a loaden man and tell me truly
   With what most humble sacrifice I may
   Wash off my sin and appease the powers that hate me.
   Take from my heart those thousand thousand furies      60
   That restless gnaw upon my life, and save me.
   Orestes' bloody hands fell on his mother,
   Yet at the holy altar he was pardoned.
*Acoreus.* Orestes out of madness did his murder,
   And therefore he found grace; thou, worst of all men,  65
   Out of cold blood and hope of gain, base lucre,
   Slewst thine own feeder. Come not near the altar,
   Nor with thy reeking hands pollute the sacrifice.
   Thou art marked for shame eternal.             *Exit.*
*Septimius.*                           Look all on me
   And let me be a story left to time                     70
   Of blood and infamy: how base and ugly
   Ingratitude appears with all her profits,
   How monstrous my hoped grace at court. Good
      soldiers,
   Let neither flattery nor the witching sound

---

57. *loaden*] burdened, afflicted.
62-3. *Orestes ... pardoned*] Orestes avenged the murder of his father Agamemnon, the King of Mycenae, by his mother Clytemnestra and her lover Aegisthus. In the version of the myth dramatized in Aeschylus' *Eumenides*, Orestes went mad after the matricide and was pursued by the Erinyes. He faced a trial in Athens, at which he was acquitted through Athena's intervention.
68. *reeking*] both stinking and soaked with blood.
72. *with*] despite.
74. *witching*] bewitching, enchanting.

168 THE FALSE ONE [ACT 4

  Of high and soft preferment touch your goodness. 75
  To be valiant, old and honest: oh, what blessedness —
*1 Soldier.* Dost thou want anything?
*Septimius.*       Nothing but your prayers.
*2 Soldier.* Be thus, and let the blind priest do his worst.
  We have gods as well as they, and they will hear us.
*3 Soldier.* Come, cry no more. Thou hast wept out twenty
  Pompeys. 80

   *Enter* POTHINUS [*and*] ACHILLAS.

*Pothinus.* [*To* ACHILLAS] So penitent?
*Achillas.*       It seems so.
*Pothinus.*        Yet, for all this,
  We must employ him.
*1 Soldier.* [*Aside to* Soldiers] These are the armed soldier
  leaders.
  Away, and let's to th' fort: we shall be snapped else.
           *Exeunt* [Soldiers].
*Pothinus.* [*To* SEPTIMIUS] How now? Why thus? What
  cause of this dejection?
*Achillas.* Why dost thou weep?
*Septimius.*    Pray, leave me. You have ruined me, 85
  You have made me a famous villain.
*Pothinus.*    [*Aside to* ACHILLAS] Does that touch thee?
*Achillas.* [*Aside to* POTHINUS] He will be hard to win: he
  feels his lewdness.
*Pothinus.* [*Aside to* ACHILLAS] He must be won, or we shall
  want our right hand.
  This fellow dares and knows, and must be heartened.
  [*To* SEPTIMIUS] Art thou so poor to blench at what
  thou hast done? 90
  Is conscience a comrade for an old soldier?

---

83.1. SD] *Dyce; Exeunt. F2; Exit. F1.*

---

 78. *blind*] lacking in discernment.
 81. *for*] despite.
 83. *snapped*] captured.
  *else*] otherwise.
 87. *lewdness*] wickedness.
 90. *blench*] shrink, shudder.
 91. *comrade*] probably stressed on the second syllable: 'comràde'.

*Achillas.* [*To* POTHINUS] It is not that. It may be some
    disgrace
  That he takes heavily, and would be cherished.
  Septimius ever scorned to show such weakness.
*Septimius.* Let me alone. I am not for your purpose:      95
  I am now a new man.
*Pothinus.*              We have new affairs for thee,
  Those that would raise thy head.
*Septimius.*                     I would 'twere off,
  And in your bellies, for the love you bear me.
  I'll be no more knave: I have stings enough
  Already in my breast.
*Pothinus.*          Thou shalt be noble,            100
  And who dares think, then, that thou art not honest?
*Achillas.* Thou shalt command in chief all our strong forces,
  And, if thou serv'st a use, must not all justify it?
*Septimius.* I am rogue enough.
*Pothinus.*              Thou wilt be more and baser.
  A poor rogue is all rogues, open to all shames,      105
  Nothing to shadow him. Dost thou think crying
  Can keep thee from the censure of the multitude
  Or to be kneeling at the altar save thee?
  'Tis poor and servile. Wert thou thine own sacrifice,
  'Twould seem so low people would spit the fire out.   110
*Achillas.* Keep thyself glorious still, though ne'er so stained,
  And that will lessen it, if not work it out.
  To go complaining thus and thus repenting
  Like a poor girl that had betrayed her maidenhead —
*Septimius.* I'll stop mine ears.
*Achillas.*                Will show so in a soldier,   115

---

109.] *Seward; F1 lines* 'Tis ... servile: / Wert ... Sacrifice *F1.*

105. *A ... rogues*] Seward interprets 'a poor rogue is all rogues in one', but Pothinus may also mean that 'a poor rogue is just an ordinary rogue and not a powerful one'.

107. *censure*] reproach.

110. *spit ... out*] put out the fire by spitting on it (*OED* v. 5, first recorded usage dated 1681).

111. *glorious*] haughty, proud.

112. *work it out*] remove it.

So simply and so ridiculously, so tamely —
*Pothinus.* If people would believe thee, 'twere some honesty,
And for thy penitence would not laugh at thee
(As sure they will) and beat thee for thy poverty.
If they would allow thy foolery, there were some hope. 120
*Septimius.* My foolery?
*Pothinus.*             Nay, more than that, thy misery,
Thy monstrous misery.
*Achillas.*       [*Aside to* POTHINUS] He begins to hearken.
[*To* SEPTIMIUS] Thy misery so great, men will not
    bury thee.
*Septimius.* That this were true!
*Pothinus.*               Why does this conquering Caesar
Labour through the world's deep seas of toils and
    troubles, 125
Dangers and desperate hopes? To repent afterwards?
Why does he slaughter thousands in a battle
And whip his country with the sword? To cry for't?
Thou killedst great Pompey; he'll kill all his kindred
And justify it; nay, raise up trophies to it. 130
When thou hearst him repent — he's held most holy
    too —
And cry for doing daily bloody murders,
Take thou example and go ask forgiveness,
Call up the thing thou nam'st thy conscience
And let it work: then 'twill seem well, Septimius. 135
*Septimius.* He does all this.
*Achillas.*             Yes, and is honoured for it;
Nay, called the honoured Caesar. So mayst thou be:
Thou wert born as near a crown as he.
*Septimius.*                           He was poor.
*Pothinus.* And desperate bloody tricks got him this credit.

---

    134. *conscience*] pronounced 'conscience'.
    138–9.] Caesar came from an ancient and renowned patrician family, the *gens* Iulia. Although the family was not particularly rich or influential by the standards of Roman nobility, it was not exactly 'poor' either. There may be a reference here to the fact that Caesar had to contract heavy debts to finance his political career, though it is more likely that Achillas' and Pothinus' words are intended by the playwrights to expose their argument as specious.

*Septimius.* I am afraid you will once more —
*Pothinus.*                              Help to raise thee.          140
  Off with thy pining black — it dulls a soldier —
  And put on resolution like a man.
  A noble fate waits on thee.
*Septimius.*              I now feel
  Myself returning rascal speedily.
  Oh, that I had the power —
*Achillas.*              Thou shalt have all          145
  And do all through thy power. Men shall admire thee,
  And the vices of Septimius shall turn virtues.
*Septimius.* Off! Off! Thou must off! Off, my cowardice!
  Puling repentance, off!
*Pothinus.*            Now thou speakst nobly.
*Septimius.* Off, my dejected looks, and welcome, impudence!          150
  My daring shall be deity, to save me.
  Give me instructions and put action on me,
  A glorious cause upon my sword's point, gentlemen,
  And let my wit and valour work. You will raise me
  And make me outdare all my miseries?          155
*Pothinus.* All this and all thy wishes.
*Septimius.*                              Use me, then.
  Womanish fear, farewell. I'll never melt more.
  Lead on to some great thing to wake my spirit.
  I cut the cedar Pompey and I'll fell
  This huge oak Caesar too.
*Pothinus.*              Now thou singst sweetly,          160
  And Ptolemy shall crown thee for thy service.

---

158. wake] *F2;* weale *F1.*

148–9. *Off ... off*] Cf. Bosola in Webster, *Duchess* 4.2.325: 'Off, my painted honour!' Martin Wiggins suggested this parallel during a Zoom reading of the play on 11 December 2020.
149. *Puling*] whining.
150. *impudence*] 'freedom from shamefastness; cool confidence' (*OED* n. 3).
155. *outdare*] defy.
157. *melt*] soften into tears.
159–60. *I ... too*] Cf. *Sej* 5.2.241–6: 'I, that did help / To fell the lofty cedar of the world, / Germanicus; that, at one stroke, cut down / Drusus, that upright elm; withered his vine; / Laid Silius and Sabinus, two strong oaks, / Flat on the earth.'

172 THE FALSE ONE [ACT 5

*Achillas.* [*Aside to* POTHINUS] He's well wrought: put him
    on apace for cooling. *Exeunt.*

### ACT 5 SCENE 1

*Enter* CAESAR, ANTONY [*and*] DOLABELLA.

*Antony.* The tumult still increases.
*Caesar.*                     Oh, my fortune!
    My lustful folly, rather! But 'tis well,
    And worthily I am made a bondman's prey,
    That after all my glorious victories,
    In which I passed so many seas of dangers     5
    When all the elements conspired against me,
    Would yield up the dominion of this head
    To any mortal power, so blind and stupid
    To trust these base Egyptians, that proclaimed
    Their perjuries in noble Pompey's death —     10
    And yet that could not warn me.
*Dolabella.*                   Be still Caesar,
    Who ever loved to exercise his fate
    Where danger looked most dreadful.
*Antony.*                     If you fall,
    Fall not alone. Let the King and his sister
    Be buried in your ruins. On my life,     15
    They both are guilty. Reason may assure you
    Pothinus nor Achillas durst attempt you
    Or shake one dart or sword aimed at your safety
    Without their warrant.
*Caesar.*                 For the young King, I know not

---

11. still Caesar] *F2*; still, Caesar *F1*.

  162. *wrought*] worked up.
  *for*] to prevent it from.

  5.1.0.] Weber adds the setting: 'Caesar's *Apartments in the Palace*'.
  3. *worthily*] deservedly.
  *bondman*] slave.
  8. *blind*] lacking in discernment.
  9. *proclaimed*] made evident.
  12. *exercise his fate*] 'apply his genius, and dare destiny' (Luce).
  19. *warrant*] authorization, sanction.
  *For*] as for. Also in the next line.

SC I] THE FALSE ONE 173

> How he may be misled; but for his sister, 20
> Unequalled Cleopatra, 'twere a kind
> Of blasphemy to doubt her. Ugly treason
> Durst never dwell in such a glorious building,
> Nor can so clear and great a spirit as hers is
> Admit of falsehood.

*Antony.* Let us seize on him, then, 25
> And leave her to her fortune.

*Dolabella.* If he have power,
> Use it to your security, and let
> His honesty acquit him. If he be false,
> It is too great an honour he should die
> By your victorious hand.

*Enter* PTOLEMY, ACOREUS [*and*] APOLLODORUS.

*Caesar.* He comes, and I 30
> Shall do as I find cause.

*Ptolemy.* Let not great Caesar
> Impute the breach of hospitality
> To you, my guest, to me. I am contemned,
> And my rebellious subjects lift their hands
> Against my head; and would they aimed no farther, 35
> Provided that I fell a sacrifice
> To gain you safety. That this is not feigned
> The boldness of my innocence may confirm you.
> Had I been privy to their bloody plot,
> I now had led them on and given fair gloss 40
> To their bad cause by being present with them.
> But I, that yet taste of the punishment
> In being false to Pompey, will not make
> A second fault to Caesar uncompelled.
> With such as have not yet shook off obedience 45

---

30. SD] *this edn; placed at line 31 in F1.*

---

22–3. *Ugly ... building*] Cf. *Temp* 1.2.457: 'There's nothing ill can dwell in such a temple.'
25. *Admit*] allow for the presence of.
33. *contemned*] scorned, despised.
35. *would ... aimed*] I wish they would aim.
40. *had*] would have.
*gloss*] semblance.
45. *shook*] shaken.

        I yield myself to you and will take part
        In all your dangers.
*Caesar.*                 This pleads your excuse,
        And I receive it.
*Acoreus.*              If they have any touch
        Of justice or religion, I will use
        The authority of our gods to call them back       50
        From their bad purpose.
*Apollodorus.*               This part of the palace
        Is yet defensible. We may make it good
        Till your powers rescue us.
*Caesar.*                   Caesar besieged?
        Oh, stain to my great actions! 'Twas my custom,
        An army routed — as my feet had wings —       55
        To be first in the chase: nor walls nor bulwarks
        Could guard those that escaped the battle's fury
        From this strong arm. And I to be enclosed?
        My heart! My heart! But 'tis necessity,
        To which the gods must yield and I obey       60
        Till I redeem it by some glorious way.       *Exeunt.*

---

  52. *good*] secure against attack.
  53. *powers*] forces.
  53–61. *Caesar ... way*] Cf. Lucan, 10.439–44, 449–54: 'Caesar, on his part, distrusted the city walls and defended himself by closing the gates of the palace, thus submitting to an unworthy hiding-place. Hemmed in as he was, the whole palace was not at his disposal: he had gathered his forces in one corner of it. His pride was touched by rage and fear – fear of attack, and wrath at his own fear ... Not long ago, beneath the height of Mount Haemus in Thessaly, Caesar had boldly defied all the magnates of Rome, and the Senate in battle array under the leadership of Pompey; and, though the badness of his cause was adverse to his hopes, yet he was sanguine of undeserved success. But now he dreaded the wickedness of slaves, and crouched within walls while missiles rained upon him.'
  55. *routed*] defeated resoundingly and compelled to retreat in disorder and haste.
  56. *chase*] pursuit of the enemies.
  *bulwarks*] ramparts.
  61. *redeem*] make up for, counterbalance.

[ACT 5] SCENE 2

*Enter* POTHINUS, ACHILLAS, SEPTIMIUS [*and*] Soldiers.

*Pothinus.* There's no retiring now: we are broke in,
    The deed past hope of pardon. If we prosper,
    'Twill be styled lawful, and we shall give laws
    To those that now command us. Stop not at
    Or loyalty or duty. Bold ambition                5
    To dare and power to do gave the first difference
    Between the king and subject. Caesar's motto,
    *Aut Caesar aut nihil*, each of us must claim
    And use it as our own.
*Achillas.*                    The deed is bloody
    If we conclude in Ptolemy's death.
*Pothinus.*                              The better.    10
    The glebe of empire must be so manured.

---

3. 'Twill] *F2;* A will *F1.* 11. glebe] *Dyce;* globe *F1.* manured] *F2;* manur *F1.*

---

5.2.0.] Weber adds the setting: '*Before the Palace*'. Dyce sets the scene in '*An inner court of the Palace*'. It could be either. It is true that the Egyptians are besieging the Romans, but the Romans are defending only one part of the palace, not all of it. Thus, the meeting might indeed take place inside the palace.

1. *broke in*] past the point of no return.
3. *styled*] called, known as.
5. *Or*] either.
8. Aut ... nihil] Either a Caesar or nothing. This sentence, denoting an absolute aspiration to become the supreme political commander and nothing else, was the motto of Ladislao d'Angiò-Durazzo (1376–1414) and of Cesare Borgia (1475–1507). It was believed to have originated from Julius Caesar himself. The spirit of the sentence comes from an anecdote told in Plutarch's 'Caesar', 768C–D: 'In his journey it is reported that, passing over the mountains of the Alps, they came through a little poor village that had not many households and yet poor cottages. There, his friends that did accompany him asked him merrily if there were any contending for offices in that town and whether there were any strife there amongst the noble men for honour. Caesar, speaking in good earnest, answered: "I cannot tell that," said he, "but, for my part, I had rather be the chiefest man here than the second person in Rome."' This is the second instance of Pothinus' attempt speciously to appropriate Caesarean maxims. Cf. 1.1.371.

11. *glebe*] soil, land.

*Septimius.* Rome, that from Romulus first took her name,
    Had her walls watered with a crimson shower
    Drained from a brother's heart; nor was she raised
    To this prodigious height that overlooks           15
    Three full parts of the earth that pay her tribute
    But by enlarging of her narrow bounds
    By the sack of neighbour cities, ne'er made hers
    Till they were cemented with the blood of those
    That did possess 'em. Caesar, Ptolemy,              20
    Now I am steeled, to me are empty names,
    Esteemed as Pompey's was.
*Pothinus.*                   Well said, Septimius,
    Thou now art right again.
*Achillas.*                   But what course take we
    For the princess Cleopatra?
*Pothinus.*                  Let her live
    A while to make us sport. She shall authorize       25
    Our undertakings to the ignorant people
    As if what we do were by her command.
    But, our triumvirate government once confirmed,
    She bears her brother company. That's my province:
    Leave me to work her.
*Achillas.*                 I will undertake             30
    For Ptolemy.
*Septimius.*           Caesar shall be my task,
    And, as in Pompey I began a name,
    I'll perfect it in Caesar.

---

18. ne'er] *Dyce;* not *F2;* were *F1.*

    12–14. *Rome … heart*] The reference is to Romulus' murder of his twin brother Remus, which paved the way for the foundation of Rome in 753 BCE.
    16. *Three … earth*] Europe, Africa, and Asia.
    18. *By*] by means of.
    25. *sport*] amuse ourselves.
    28. *triumvirate government*] Pothinus, Achillas, and Septimius here ironically plan to form what sounds like a grotesque parody of the First Triumvirate of Rome (Caesar, Pompey, and Crassus).
    29. *province*] sphere of action.

*Enter (above)* CAESAR, PTOLEMY, ACOREUS,
APOLLODORUS, ANTONY [*and*] DOLABELLA.

*Pothinus.*                    'Tis resolved then.
   We'll force our passage.
*Achillas.*                    See: they do appear
   As they desired a parley.
*Pothinus.*                    I am proud yet                    35
   I have brought them to capitulate.
*Ptolemy.*                     Now, Pothinus?
*Pothinus.* Now, Ptolemy?
*Ptolemy.*                     No addition?
*Pothinus.*                    We are equal,
   Though Caesar's name were put into the scale
   In which our worth is weighed.
*Caesar.*                      Presumptuous villain,
   Upon what grounds hast thou presumed to raise    40
   Thy servile hand against the King or me,
   That have a greater name?
*Pothinus.*                    On those by which
   Thou didst presume to pass the Rubicon
   Against the laws of Rome and at the name
   Of traitor smile, as thou didst when Marcellus,  45
   The Consul, with the Senate's full consent,
   Pronounced thee for an enemy to thy country.
   Yet thou wentst on, and thy rebellious cause
   Was crowned with fair success. Why should we fear
      then?
   Think on that, Caesar.
*Caesar.*                      Oh, the gods! Be braved thus?    50
   And be compelled to bear this from a slave,

---

37. *No addition*] 'Have you forgotten to address me by my royal title?'
(Luce).
  41. *servile*] slavish.
  42–9. *On ... success*] See 2.3.35.
  43. *Thou*] See 2.1.92.
  45. *Marcellus*] See 1.1.235–6.
  50. *braved*] defied.

That would not brook great Pompey his superior?
*Achillas.* Thy glories now have touched the highest point
    And must descend.
*Pothinus.*                Despair, and think we stand
    The champions of Rome to wreak her wrongs         55
    Upon whose liberty thou hast set thy foot.
*Septimius.* And that the ghosts of all those noble Romans
    That by thy sword fell in this civil war
    Expect revenge.
*Antony.*            Dar'st thou speak, and remember
    There was a Pompey?
*Pothinus.*                There is no hope to 'scape us.    60
    If that, against the odds we have upon you,
    You dare come forth and fight, receive the honour
    To die like Romans. If ye faint, resolve
    To starve like wretches. I disdain to change
    Another syllable with you.
            [*Exeunt* POTHINUS, ACHILLAS, SEPTIMIUS
                                *and* Soldiers.]
*Antony.*                Let us die nobly            65
    And rather fall upon each other's sword
    Than come into these villains' hands.
*Caesar.*                        That fortune

---

65. SD] *Weber; Exeunt* [*those below*]. *Turner; Exeunt Pho. Achil. Sept. (and placed after* nobly) *Colman; Exeunt.* F2; *Exit.* F1 *(and placed at line 64).*

---

52. *That*] I, one who.
    *brook ... superior*] Cf. Florus, 396: 'Pompey now was jealous of Caesar's greatness, and Caesar badly endured Pompey's supereminence. The one brooked no equal, the other no superior' (*Iam Pompeio suspectae Caesaris opes et Caesari Pompeiana dignitas gravis. Nec ille ferebat parem, nec hic superiorem*, 2.13.14). But cf. also Lucan, 1.125–6: 'Caesar could no longer endure a superior, nor Pompey an equal' (*nec quemquam iam ferre potest, Caesarve priorem, / Pompeiusve parem*). See Introduction, 29.
    53–4. *Thy ... descend*] as being on the wheel of fortune, by the turning of which victory sooner or later becomes defeat.
    55. *wreak*] avenge.
    60. *'scape*] escape.
    61. *If that*] if.
    62. *forth*] out.
    63. *faint*] are afraid.
    64. *change*] exchange.
    67–76. *That ... all*] For Caesar as *fortunatus*, see 2.1.194.

Which to this hour hath been a friend to Caesar,
Though for a while she clothe her brow with frowns,
Will smile again upon me. Who will pay her          70
Or sacrifice or vows if she forsake
Her best of works in me? Or suffer him
Whom, with a strong hand, she hath led triumphant
Through the whole western world, and Rome
    acknowledged
Her sovereign lord, to end ingloriously             75
A life admired by all? The threatened danger
Must by a way more horrid be avoided,
And I will run the hazard: fire the palace
And the rich magazines that neighbour it,
In which the wealth of Egypt is contained.          80
Start not. It shall be so. That while the people
Labour in quenching the ensuing flames,
Like Caesar, with this handful of my friends,
Through fire and swords I force a passage to
My conquering legions. — King, if thou dar'st follow  85
Where Caesar leads, or live or die a freeman;
If not, stay here a bondman to thy slave
And, dead, be thought unworthy of a grave.    *Exeunt.*

---

71. *Or*] either.
78–80. *fire ... contained*] The play here deviates from the sources, none of which say that Caesar set the palace on fire. The closest account is that of Florus, 416–17: 'When Caesar's pleasure therefore was that she should be restored to her kingdom ... he, being forthwith beset in the palace royal by the same instruments who murdered Pompey, with wondrous valour and a slender company did bear the brunt of a mighty army. For, by firing the next tenements and the arsenal, he dislodged the enemy, who plied him from thence with shot' (*Quam ubi Caesar restitui iussit in regnum, statim ab isdem percussoribus Pompei obsessus in regia quamvis exigua manu ingentis exercitus molem mira virtute sustinuit. Ac primum proximorum aedificiorum atque navalium incendio infestorum hostium tela summovit*, 2.13.58–9). Cf. also Lucan, 10.491–2: 'He ordered brands steeped in resin to be hurled at the sails of the crowded ships.' See Introduction, 29.
81. *Start not*] Do not flinch. This may be addressed to all the characters on stage, and not only to the Egyptians, given the exceptionality of the solution devised by Caesar and its potentially destructive consequences.
86. *or ... or*] either ... or.
87. *bondman*] slave.

## [ACT 5] SCENE 3

*Enter* SEPTIMIUS.

*Septimius.* I feel my resolution melts again
  And that I am not knave alone but fool
  In all my purposes. This devil Pothinus
  Employs me as a property and, grown useless,
  Will shake me off again. He told me so        5
  When I killed Pompey, nor can I hope better
  When Caesar is dispatched. Services done
  For such as only study their own ends,
  Too great to be rewarded, are returned
  With deadly hate. I learned this principle    10
  In his own school, yet still he fools me — well.
  And yet he trusts me. Since I in my nature
  Was fashioned to be false, wherefore should I,
  That killed my general — and a Roman, one
  To whom I owed all nourishments of life —     15
  Be true to an Egyptian? To save Caesar
  And turn Pothinus' plots on his own head,
  As it is in my power, redeem my credit

---

9. are] *F2*; or *F1*.   15. owed] *F2*; owe *F1*.

---

5.3.0.] Weber adds the setting: '*An open Place in the City*'.
  1. *melts*] weakens.
  4. *property*] a means to an end, an instrument, but also with the theatrical sense of a stage accessory.
  *grown*] when I become.
  7. *dispatched*] made away with.
  7–10. *Services ... hate*] From Tacitus, 95: 'for good turns are no longer well taken than they may be recompensed; when they grow greater than hope of requital, instead of thankfulness they breed hatred and ill will' (*Nam beneficia eo usque laeta sunt, dum videntur exsolvi posse; ubi multum antevenere, pro gratia odium redditur,* 4.18.3). This passage is also probably imitated in *Volp* 4.5.44–7: 'For these, not knowing how to owe a gift / Of that dear grace but with their shame, being placed / So above all powers of their gratitude, / Began to hate the benefit.'
  12–13. *I ... false*] an eloquent admission on Septimius' part, which strongly suggests that he is the 'false one' of the play's title.
  18. *redeem*] regain.

SC 3]  THE FALSE ONE  181

    And live to lie and swear again in fashion,
    Oh, 'twere a masterpiece!

    *Enter* CAESAR, PTOLEMY, ANTONY, DOLABELLA,
    ACOREUS, APOLLODORUS [*and*] Soldiers.

                    Ha? Damn me! Caesar? 20
How's he got off?
*Caesar.*          The fire has took
    And shows the city like a second Troy.
    The navy too is scorched, the people greedy
    To save their wealth and houses, while their soldiers
    Make spoil of all. Only Achillas' troops 25
    Make good their guard: break through them, we are
      safe.
    I'll lead you like a thunderbolt.
*Septimius.*             Stay, Caesar.
*Caesar.* Who's this? The dog Septimius?
*Antony.*                 Cut his throat.
*Dolabella.* You barked but now, fawn you so soon?
*Septimius.*             Oh, hear me,
    What I'll deliver is for Caesar's safety, 30
    For all your good.
*Antony.*      Good from a mouth like thine
    That never belched but blasphemy and treason
    On festival days?
*Septimius.*        I am an altered man,
    Altered indeed, and I will give you cause

---

20. SD] *this edn; placed at line 21 in F1.*  20. Damn] *Turner;* blast *Dyce;* Curse *Colman;* — *F1.*  31. mouth] *F2;* moneth *F1.*  32–5. That ... thee.] *Colman; F1 lines* That ... dayes / I ... indeed, / And ... thee.

---

21.] This is an incomplete line of pentameter, being made up of only eight syllables, which may depend on the need to allow some additional time for the characters' entry.
    *took*] taken.
22. *Troy*] a city in the north-west of Asia Minor (modern Turkey) and the setting of the Trojan War as narrated in the *Iliad*. It was burned to the ground by the Greeks as narrated in Virgil's *Aeneid*, Book 2.
23. *greedy*] eager.
26. *Make ... guard*] Resist successfully.
32. *belched*] vomited.

|  | To say I am a Roman. |  |
| --- | --- | --- |
| *Dolabella.* | Rogue, I grant thee. | 35 |

*Septimius.* Trust me, I'll make the passage smooth and easy
   For your escape.
*Antony.*              I'll trust the devil sooner
   And make a safer bargain.
*Septimius.*             I am trusted
   With all Pothinus' secrets.
*Antony.*              There's no doubt, then,
   Thou wilt be false.
*Septimius.*        Still to be true to you.          40
*Dolabella.* And very likely.
*Caesar.*      [*To* SEPTIMIUS] Be brief, the means?
*Septimius.*                Thus, Caesar:
   To me alone, but bound by terrible oaths
   Not to discover it, he hath revealed
   A dismal vault, whose dreadful mouth does open
   A mile beyond the city. In this cave         45
   Lie but two hours concealed.
*Antony.*           [*To* CAESAR] If you believe him,
   He'll bury us alive.
*Dolabella.*        I'll fly in the air first.
*Septimius.* Then, in the dead of night, I'll bring you back
   Into a private room, where you shall find
   Pothinus and Achillas, and the rest          50
   Of their commanders, close at counsel.
*Caesar.*                 Good.
   What follows?
*Septimius.*      Fall me fairly on their throats.

---

51–2. Of ... Good. / What ... throats.] Colman; *F1 lines* Of ... Counsell. / Good ... followes? / Fall ... throates,.

---

  41. *likely*] used ironically to express disbelief in response to Septimius' promised truthfulness.
  44. *dismal*] terrible, dire.
  49. *private*] secret.
  52. *Fall ... throats*] Attack them unexpectedly and cautiously. 'Me' acts as an ethic dative with the approximate meaning of 'to my joy'. See 4.2.193.

|  |  |
|---|---|
| | Their heads cut off and shorn, the multitude |
| | Will easily disperse. |
| *Caesar.* | O devil! [*To* Soldiers] Away with him. — |
| | Nor true to friend nor enemy? Caesar scorns 55 |
| | To find his safety or revenge his wrongs |
| | So base a way or owe the means of life |
| | To such a leprous traitor. I have tow'red |
| | For victory like a falcon in the clouds, |
| | Not digged for't like a mole. Our swords and cause 60 |
| | Make way for us, and, that it may appear |
| | We took a noble course and hate base treason, |
| | Some soldiers that would merit Caesar's favour |
| | Hang him on yonder turret and then follow |
| | The lane this sword makes for you. |

[*Exeunt all but* SEPTIMIUS *and two* Soldiers, *who have seized upon him.*]

*1 Soldier.*              Here's a belt.                65
  Though I die for it, I'll use it.
*2 Soldier.*              'Tis too good
  To truss a cur in.
*Septimius.*     Save me. Here's gold.
                                 [*He offers them gold.*]
*1 Soldier.*              If Rome
  Were offered for thy ransom, it could not help thee.
*2 Soldier.* [*To* 1 Soldier] Hang not an arse.
*1 Soldier.*          Goad him on with thy sword.
  [*To* SEPTIMIUS] Thou dost deserve a worser end, and
    may                                                 70
  All such conclude so, that their friends betray.  *Exeunt.*

---

65. SD] *Weber (subst); Exit. F1.*

---

55. *Nor*] neither.
63. *would merit*] wish to deserve.
69. *Hang ... arse*] Hurry, do not waste time (*OED* 'hang', v. 4c).
*Goad*] 'to prick or spur ... with a brief, forceful action, typically using the end of a goad or other pointed implement' (*OED* v. 2).
71. *conclude so*] suffer the same fate.

## [ACT 5] SCENE 4

*Enter (severally)* ARSINOE, EROS [*and*] CLEOPATRA.

*Arsinoe.* We are lost.
*Eros.*           Undone.
*Arsinoe.*                Confusion, fire and swords,
  And fury in the soldier's face, more horrid,
  Circle us round.
*Eros.*               The King's command they laugh at
  And jeer at Caesar's threats.
*Arsinoe.*                My brother seized on
  By the Roman, as thought guilty of the tumult,         5
  And forced to bear him company, as marked out
  For his protection or revenge.
*Eros.*                    They have broke
  Into my cabinet: my trunks are ransacked.
*Arsinoe.* I have lost my jewels too, but that's the least.
  The barbarous rascals, against all humanity              10
  Or sense of pity, have killed my little dog
  And broke my monkey's chain.
*Eros.*                     They ruffled me,
  But that I could endure, and tire 'em too,
  Would they proceed no further.
*Arsinoe.*                 Oh, my sister!
*Eros.* My Queen, my mistress!
*Arsinoe.*               Can you stand unmoved     15

---

2. soldier's] *Seward;* souldiers *F1*.   12. ruffled] *F1;* rifled *F2*.

---

5.4.0.] Weber adds the setting: '*Another Part of the City*'.
0.1. SD severally] from different doors.
2. *soldier*] soldiery.
4–7. *My ... revenge*] Cf. Lucan, 10.461–4: 'Yet he has the king for companion and takes him everywhere with him: he means to get satisfaction from Ptolemy and consolation, if he himself must die; and, if missiles and firebrands are lacking, he will hurl against the slaves the head of their king.' Arsinoe is clearly unaware of Ptolemy's recent decision to side with Caesar.
4. *seized*] potentially another instance of the 'Caesar/seizer' pun. See 2.2.28 and 4.2.196.
5. *the Roman*] that is, Caesar.
7. *broke*] broken.
8. *cabinet*] private apartment.
12. *ruffled*] handled with rude familiarity, also with sexual implications (Williams, 3.1179–80)

sc 4]    THE FALSE ONE    185

 When an earthquake of rebellion shakes the city
 And the court trembles?
*Cleopatra.*     Yes, Arsinoe,
 And with a masculine constancy deride
 Fortune's worst malice as a servant to
 My virtues, not a mistress. Then we forsake   20
 The strong fort of ourselves, when we once yield
 Or shrink at her assaults. I am still myself
 And, though disrobed of sovereignty and ravished
 Of ceremonious duty, that attends it,
 Nay, grant they had slaved my body, my free mind, 25
 Like to the palm tree walling fruitful Nile,
 Shall grow up straighter and enlarge itself
 Spite of the envious weight that loads it with.

---

17–18. Arsinoe, / And with] *F1;* Turner *lines* Arsino, *and* / With.

---

 17.] Turner's emendation for the metre appears unnecessary. This would seem to be an incomplete line of pentameter, being made up of nine syllables. Yet the play exhibits several instances of shared lines that are not perfect pentameters. In addition, l. 18 is fine as it stands if 'masculine' is pronounced as disyllabic, and it scans better than if one moves 'And' to the end of l. 17. Moreover, it is possible that the name Arsinoe may have been intended in this case as made up of four syllables (Arsinoë), which would make l. 17 a perfect pentameter.
 18. *masculine constancy*] Other women displaying 'masculine constancy' in the Fletcher canon are the Queen in *Corinth* 5.4.129, and Zenocia in *CustCount* 2.2.51. As this phrase always occurs in plays to which Massinger contributed, it is possible to concur with Hoy, 'Massinger', 67, in viewing this as 'Massinger's highest tribute to the kind of fortitude great ladies are capable of displaying in adversity'.
 19. *malice*] wickedness, malicious act.
 22. *I ... myself*] Cf. Webster, *Duchess* 4.2.137: 'I am Duchess of Malfi still.' I am grateful to Lisa Hopkins (pers. comm.) for suggesting this parallel.
 23. *disrobed*] divested.
 *ravished*] deprived, though this verb, the previous 'disrobed', and the reference to the potential enslavement of Cleopatra's 'body' together suggest that she implicitly likens the loss of female royal power to rape.
 25. *grant*] let us concede that.
 *slaved*] enslaved.
 26. *walling*] enclosing.
 28. *Spite*] in spite.
 *envious weight*] spiteful burden.
 *that*] 'the calamity in question' (Dyce).

> Think of thy birth, Arsinoe. Common burdens
> Fit common shoulders. Teach the multitude 30
> By suffering nobly what they fear to touch at.
> The greatness of thy mind does soar a pitch
> Their dim eyes, darkened by their narrow souls,
> Cannot arrive at.

*Arsinoe.*               I am new created
> And owe this second being to you, best sister, 35
> For now I feel you have infused into me
> Part of your fortitude.

*Eros.*                 I still am fearful;
> I dare not tell a lie. You that were born
> Daughters and sisters unto kings may nourish
> Great thoughts, which I, that am your humble
>    handmaid, 40
> Must not presume to rival.

*Cleopatra.*            Yet, my Eros,
> Though thou hast profited nothing by observing
> The whole course of my life, learn in my death,
> Though not to equal, yet to imitate
> Thy fearless mistress.

*Enter* POTHINUS [*with his sword drawn*].

*Eros.*              Oh, a man in arms? 45
> His weapon drawn too?

*Cleopatra.*           Though upon the point
> Death sat, I'll meet it and outdare the danger.

*Pothinus.* [*To those within*] Keep the watch strong and guard
>    the passage sure
> That leads unto the sea.

*Cleopatra.*           What sea of rudeness
> Breaks in upon us? Or what subject's breath 50
> Dare raise a storm when we command a calm?
> Are duty and obedience fled to heaven,

---

45. SD] *this edn; Enter* PHOTINUS, *with Soldiers Weber; Enter Photinus.* F1.

29. *birth*] lineage.
34. *new*] anew.
51. *calm*] absence of wind.

And in their room ambition and pride
Sent into Egypt? That face speaks thee, Pothinus,
A thing thy mother brought into the world                55
My brother's and my slave, but thy behaviour,
Opposed to that, an insolent intruder
Upon that sovereignty thou shouldst bow to.
If in the gulf of base ingratitude
All loyalty to Ptolemy the King                           60
Be swallowed up, remember who I am,
Whose daughter and whose sister. Or, suppose
That is forgot too, let the name of Caesar,
Which nations quake at, stop thy desperate madness
From running headlong on to thy confusion.                65
Throw from thee quickly those rebellious arms
And let me read submission in thine eyes:
Thy wrongs to us we will not only pardon
But be a ready advocate to plead for thee
To Caesar and my brother.
*Pothinus.*                    Plead my pardon?           70
To you I bow but scorn as much to stoop thus
To Ptolemy, to Caesar, nay, the gods,
As to put off the figure of a man
And change my essence with a sensual beast.
All my designs, my counsels and dark ends                 75
Were aimed to purchase you.
*Cleopatra.*                   How durst thou, being
The scorn of baseness, nourish such a thought?
*Pothinus.* They that have power are royal, and those base
That live at the devotion of another.

---

54. thee,] *F2*; thee *F1*.   64. thy] *Seward*; the *F1*.

53. *ambition*] pronounced 'ambitíon'.
54. *speaks*] manifests, shows.
63. *forgot*] forgotten.
65. *confusion*] overthrow, ruin.
68. *us*] the royal 'we'.
73. *put off*] cast off, remove.
74. *sensual*] 'endowed with the faculty of sensation but lacking the power of reason' (*OED* adj. 4).
76. *purchase*] obtain.
79. *devotion*] disposal (*OED* n. 6a).

What birth gave Ptolemy or fortune Caesar,        80
By engines fashioned on this protean anvil,
I have made mine, and only stoop at you,
Whom I would still preserve free to command me.
For Caesar's frowns, they are below my thoughts,
And, but in these fair eyes I still have read     85
The story of a supreme monarchy
To which all hearts with mine gladly pay tribute,
Pothinus' name had long since been as great
As Ptolemy's e'er was, or Caesar's is.
This made me, as a weaker tie, to unloose         90
The knot of loyalty that chained my freedom
And slight the fear that Caesar's threats might cause,
That I and they might see no sun appear
But Cleopatra in th'Egyptian sphere.
*Cleopatra.* O giant-like ambition, married to    95
Cimmerian darkness! Inconsiderate fool,
Though flattered with self-love, couldst thou believe —
Were all crowns on the earth made into one,
And that by kings set on thy head, all sceptres
Within thy grasp and laid down at my feet —      100
I would vouchsafe a kiss to a no-man,
A gelded eunuch?
*Pothinus.*          Fairest, that makes for me
And shows it is no sensual appetite,
But true love to the greatness of thy spirit
That, when that you are mine, shall yield me pleasures   105

---

81. on] *Dyce;* in *F1.*

81. *protean anvil*] shape-changing anvil, that is, his sword.
82. *stoop at*] lower myself before, with the secondary meaning of fall upon (as a hawk on its prey).
84. *For*] as for.
85. *but*] were it not that.
*still*] always.
88. *had*] would have.
96. *Cimmerian darkness*] perpetual darkness. Homer, *Odyssey*, 11.14–15, identifies the Cimmerians as a people inhabiting a land beyond the ocean, where the sun never shines.
101. *vouchsafe*] grant.
102. *gelded*] castrated.
*makes for me*] operates in my favour.
105. *when that*] when.

|  | Hymen, though blessing a new married pair, |  |
|---|---|---|
|  | Shall blush to think on and our certain issue, |  |
|  | The glorious splendour of dread majesty, |  |
|  | Whose beams shall dazzle Rome and awe the world. |  |
|  | My wants in that kind others shall supply, | 110 |
|  | And I give way to it. |  |

*Cleopatra.*            Baser than thy birth.
  Can there be gods and hear this, and no thunder
  Ram thee into the earth?
*Pothinus.*                  They are asleep
  And cannot hear thee; or, with open eyes
  Did Jove look on us, I would laugh and swear                115
  That his artillery is cloyed by me;
  Or, if that they have power to hurt, his bolts
  Are in my hand.
*Cleopatra.*         Most impious!
*Pothinus.*                         They are dreams
  Religious fools shake at. Yet, to assure thee,
  If Nemesis, that scourges pride and scorn,                  120
  Be anything but a name, she lives in me,
  For by myself — an oath to me more dreadful
  Than Styx is to your gods — weak Ptolemy dead

---

114.] *Seward; F1 lines* And ... thee: / Or ... eyes,.

106. *Hymen*] the classical god of marriage.
107. *issue*] offspring.
108. *dread*] greatly feared.
110. *wants*] deficiencies.
   *kind*] natural activity (i.e., sexual intercourse).
112–13. *Can ... earth*] Cf. *Phaedra* 671–4: 'Great ruler of the gods, dost thou so calmly hear crimes, so calmly look upon them? And when wilt thou send forth thy thunderbolt with angry hand, if now 'tis cloudless?' (*Magne regnator deum, / tam lentus audis scelera? tam lentus vides? / et quando saeva fulmen emittes manu, / si nunc serenum est?*).
115. *Jove*] Jupiter, the ruler of the Roman gods, who wielded thunderbolts to exert his authority.
116. *cloyed*] obstructed, blocked.
117. *if that*] if.
120. *Nemesis*] the ancient Greek goddess of divine retribution and revenge, who would show her wrath to any human being who would succumb to hubris (i.e., arrogance before the gods).
123. *Styx*] river boundary of the classical underworld.

        And Caesar (both being in my toil) removed,
        The poorest rascals that are in my camp        125
        Shall in my presence quench their lustful heat
        In thee and young Arsinoe while I laugh
        To hear you howl in vain. I deride those gods
        That you think can protect you.
*Cleopatra.*                     To prevent thee
        In that, I am the mistress of my fate,          130
        So hope I of my sister; to confirm it,
        I spit at thee and scorn thee.      [*She spits at him.*]
*Pothinus.*              I will tame
        That haughty courage and make it stoop too.
*Cleopatra.*                          Never.
        I was born to command, and I will die so.

*Enter* ACHILLAS *and* Soldiers, *with the body of* PTOLEMY.

*Pothinus.* The King dead? This is a fair entrance to        135
        Our future happiness.     [ACHILLAS *whispers in his ear.*]
*Arsinoe.*              O my dear brother!
*Cleopatra.* Weep not, Arsinoe: common women do so.
        Nor lose a tear for him — it cannot help him —
        But study to die nobly.
*Pothinus.*              [*To* ACHILLAS] Caesar fled?
        'Tis deadly aconite to my cold heart.          140
        It chokes my vital spirits. Where was your care?

---

128.] Seward; *F1 lines* To ... vaine: / I ... Gods,.   129–30. thee / In that,] *conj* Heath; thee, / In that *F1*.   133. it] *F1;* thee *F2*.

---

   124. *toil*] snare, net.
   140. *aconite*] 'any of various poisonous Eurasian plants constituting the genus Aconitum ... having spikes of hooded flowers, formerly (and sometimes still) used as a poison or for medicinal purposes' (*OED* n. 1a).
   141. *chokes*] clogs, blocks the flow of.
   *vital spirits*] subtle or rarefied substances believed to permeate the blood and to be responsible for giving life to all parts of the body. Walkington, sigs H2v–H3r, explains that 'A spirit is a most subtle, airy and lightsome substance, generated of the purest part of blood, whereby the soul can easily perform her functions in the natural body. They have their original and offspring from the heart, not from the brain as some hold. For they, being so pure and elaborate into the nature of air, cannot be generated in the brain, being by nature cold, where nothing is product but that which is very vaporous ... the spirits, in special, they be of three sorts, vital, natural and animal: vital in the heart, natural in the liver, animal in the brain. Vital, because they

|||Did the guards sleep?
*Achillas.*          He roused them with his sword —
We talk of Mars, but I am sure his courage
Admits of no comparison but itself —
And, as inspired by him, his following friends,               145
With such a confidence as young eaglets prey
Under the large wing of their fiercer dam,
Brake through our troops and scattered 'em. He went on,
But still pursued by us, when on the sudden
He turned his head, and from his eyes flew terror,            150
Which struck in us no less fear and amazement
Than if we had encountered with the lightning
Hurled from Jove's cloudy brow.
*Cleopatra.*               'Twas like my Caesar.
*Achillas.* We fall'n back, he made on, and, as our fear
Had parted from us with his dreadful looks,                   155
Again we followed, but, got near the sea,
On which his navy anchored, in one hand
Holding a scroll he had above the waves
And in the other grasping fast his sword
As it had been a trident forged by Vulcan                     160
To calm the raging ocean, he made a way
As if he had been Neptune. His friends, like
So many Tritons, followed their bold shouts,
Yielding a cheerful music. We showered darts
Upon them, but in vain: they reached their ships,             165

---

146. young] *F2*; you *F1*.   161. a way] *conj Colman*; away *F1*.

---

give power of motion and pulsion unto the arteries, which motion any living creature hath so long as it hath a being, and, that being extinct, the life is also extinct.'

143. *Mars*] the Roman god of war.

146. *as*] as that with which.

146–7. *as ... dam*] a favourite simile of Massinger's. Cf. *Pict* 2.2.285–6: 'like young eaglets preying under / The wings of their fierce dam'; *UnnComb* 2.1.173–4: 'As the young eaglet, covered with the wings / Of her fierce dam'.

157–62. *in ... Neptune*] See Introduction, 26.

160. *Vulcan*] the Roman deity of fire and metalworking and the forge, husband to Venus.

162. *Neptune*] the Roman god of freshwater and the sea.

163. *Tritons*] inferior sea deities, or imaginary sea monsters, of semi-human form.

                    And in their safety we are sunk, for Caesar
                    Prepares for war.
*Pothinus.*               How fell the King?
*Achillas.*                            Unable
                    To follow Caesar, he was trod to death
                    By the pursuers, and with him the priest
                    Of Isis, good Acoreus.
*Arsinoe.*                       May the earth                                170
                    Lie gently on their ashes.
*Pothinus.*                       I feel now
                    That there are powers above us and that 'tis not
                    Within the searching policies of man
                    To alter their decrees.
*Cleopatra.*                      I laugh at thee.
                    Where are thy threats now, fool, thy scoffs and scorns   175
                    Against the gods? I see calamity
                    Is the best mistress of religion
                    And can convert an atheist.           *Shout within.*
*Pothinus.*                       Oh, they come.
                    Mountains fall on me! Oh, for him to die
                    That placed his heaven on earth is an assurance          180
                    Of his descent to hell. Where shall I hide me?
                    The greatest daring to a man dishonest
                    Is but a bastard courage, ever fainting.
                              *Exit [with* ACHILLAS *and* Soldiers].

            *Enter* CAESAR, SCAEVA, ANTONY [*and*] DOLABELLA.

---

178. SD] *F2; centred in F1.*   183.1. SD] *Turner; Dyce inserts an additional Exit* ACHILLAS *with* Soldiers. *at line 171; Exit. F1.*   183.2. SD] *F1; Enter Caesar, Sceva, Antony, Dollabella [and Souldiers]. Turner.*

---

   173. *searching*] inquisitive, penetrating.
   177. *mistress*] teacher.
   *religion*] pronounced 'religìon'.
   179–81. *Mountains ... hell*] Cf. Rev. 6.16: 'And said to the mountains and rocks, Fall on us, and hide us from the presence of him that sitteth on the throne, and from the wrath of the Lamb'; Marlowe, *Dr Faustus*, A.5.2.84–5: 'Mountains and hills, come, come and fall on me / And hide me from the heavy wrath of God!'
   181. *me*] myself.
   183. *ever fainting*] always growing weak.

sc 4]                    THE FALSE ONE                    193

*Caesar.* [*To* CLEOPATRA] Look on your Caesar. Banish fear,
   my fairest,
      You now are safe.
*Scaeva.*                By Venus, not a kiss                185
   Till our work be done. The traitors once dispatched,
   To it, and we'll cry 'Aim!'
*Caesar.*                [*To* CLEOPATRA] I will be speedy.
      *Exeunt* [CAESAR, SCAEVA, ANTONY *and* DOLABELLA].
*Cleopatra.* Farewell again. — Arsinoe? — How now, Eros,
   Ever faint-hearted?
*Eros.*              But that I am assured
   Your excellency can command the general,              190
   I fear the soldiers, for they look as if
   They would be nibbling too.
*Cleopatra.*                  He is all honour,
   Nor do I now repent me of my favours,
   Nor can I think nature e'er made a woman
   That in her prime deserved him.

      *Enter* CAESAR, SCAEVA, ANTONY, DOLABELLA
      [*again, and*] Soldiers, *with the heads* [*of* POTHINUS
                     *and* ACHILLAS].

*Arsinoe.*                    He's come back.              195
*Caesar.* [*To those within*] Pursue no farther, curb the
   soldiers' fury.

---

187.1. SD] *Dyce (subst); Exeunt* [*Romans*]. *Turner; Exeunt Caesar and train. Colman; Exeunt. F1.* 195. SD] *Dyce (subst); Enter Caesar, Sceva, Antony, Dollabella, Souldiers, With the heads. F1.* 196. SP *Caesar*] *Seward; F2 assigns the speech to Caesar from line 197; not in F1, which assigns the speech to Arsinoe.*

---

185. *Venus*] the Roman goddess of love.
186. *dispatched*] got rid of.
187. *we'll ... 'Aim!'*] "'Aim!" ... was always addressed to the person about to shoot [in the sport of archery:] it was an hortatory exclamation of the by-standers ... intended for his encouragement' (Weber). The sport of archery is here a metaphor for sex.
   *I ... speedy*] Caesar was particularly celebrated for his *celeritas* in his military expeditions (see Grillo, 14–36; Lovano, 258), though his celerity is here referenced ironically.
189. *Ever*] still.
   *But that*] even though.
190. *general*] the common people.
192. *nibbling*] taking a small bite, with the secondary meaning of engaging in sexual intercourse.

[*To* CLEOPATRA] See, beauteous mistress, their
　　　　accursed heads
　　That did conspire against us.
*Scaeva.*　　　　　　　　　　Furies plague 'em.
　　They had too fair an end to die like soldiers.
　　Pompey fell by the sword; the cross or halter          200
　　Should have dispatched them.
*Caesar.*　　　　　　　All is but death, good Scaeva,
　　Be therefore satisfied. [*To* CLEOPATRA] And now, my
　　　dearest,
　　Look upon Caesar as he still appeared,
　　A conqueror, and, [*Pointing to the body of* PTOLEMY]
　　　this unfortunate King
　　Entombed with honour, we'll for Rome, where Caesar    205
　　Will show he can give kingdoms, for the Senate,
　　Thy brother dead, shall willingly decree
　　The crown of Egypt, that was his, to thee.
　　　　　　　　　　　　　　　　　*Exeunt omnes.*

203. upon] *F2*; up on *F1*.

---

197–8. their ... That] the accursed heads of those who.
198. *Furies*] See 1.1.15.
199–201. *They ... them*] Cf. Lucan, 10.515–19: 'he postponed no longer the punishment of death which Pothinus had so richly earned. But Caesar's wrath did not destroy him by fitting means – the gallows, or the stake, or the teeth of wild beasts: he died the death of Magnus.'
200. *cross*] 'a stake, generally with a transverse bar, on which they put to a cruel and ignominious death certain criminals, who were nailed or otherwise fastened to it by their extremities' (*OED* n. 1).
201. *dispatched*] killed.
*All ... death*] Cf. Plutarch, 'Pompey', 718c: 'Achillas and Pothinus he put to death.'

# The Epilogue

I now should wish another had my place,
But that I hope to come off, and with grace.
And, but express some sign that you are pleased,
We of our doubts, they of their fears are eased.
I would beg further, gentlemen, and much say   5
In the favour of ourselves, them and the play,
Did I not rest assured the most I see
Hate impudence and cherish modesty.

---

 2. *But*] were it not.
*come off*] acquit myself well.
 3. *but*] just.
 4. *We*] that is, the players.
*they*] that is, the playwrights.
 7. *the most*] the most people.

# APPENDIX 1
# Latin transcription of passages from Lucan's *Pharsalia* cited in the Commentary

*False One*, 1.1.71–8; Lucan, 6.108–17
*Sed patitur saevam, veluti circumdatus arta / Obsidione, famem. nondum turgentibus altam / In segetem culmis, cernit miserabile vulgus / In pecudum cecidisse cibos, et carpere dumos / Et morsu spoliare nemus, letumque minantis / Vellere ab ignotis dubias radicibus herbas: / Quae mollire queunt flamma, quae frangere morsu, / Quaeque per abrasas utero demittere fauces, / Plurimaque humanis antehac incognita mensis / Diripiens miles, saturum tamen obsidet hostem.*

*False One*, 1.1.78–9; Lucan, 7.259–60
*Haec, fato quae teste probet, quis iustius arma / Sumpserit.*

*False One*, 1.1.223–8; Lucan, 7.574–8
*Ipse manu subicit gladius, ac tela ministrat / Adversosque iubet ferro confundere vultus. / Promovet ipse acies: impellit terga suorum: / Verbere conversae cessantes excitat hastae. / In plebem vetat ire manus, monstratque Senatum.*

*False One*, 1.1.231–7; Lucan, 7.579–85
*Scit cruor imperii qui sit, quae viscera legum / Unde petat Romam, libertas ultima mundi / Quo steterit ferienda loco. permixta secundo / Ordine nobilitas venerandaque corpora ferro / Urgentur: caedunt Lepidos, caeduntque Metellos, / Corvinosque simul, Torquataque nomina legum, / Saepe duces, summosque hominum te, Magne, remoto.*

*False One*, 1.1.239–40; Lucan, 7.635–7
*sanguis ibi fluxit Achaeus, / Ponticus, Assyrius: cunctos haerere cruores / Romanus campisque vetat consistere torrens.*

*False One*, 1.1.240–9; Lucan, 7.647–51, 654–5, 666–9
*iam Magnus transisse Deos, Romanaque fata / Senserat infelix, tota vix clade coactus / Fortunam damnare suam, stetit aggere campi, / Eminus*

197

*unde omnis sparsas per Thessala rura / Aspiceret clades, quae bello obstante latebant. / ... / Nec, sicut mos est miseris, trahere omnia secum / Mersa iuvat, gentesque suae miscere ruinae: / ... / ... et arma, / Signaque, et afflictas omni iam parte catervas / Circuit, et revocat matura in fata ruentes / Seque negat tanti.*

*False One*, 1.1.270; Lucan, 8.448–9
*Sceptra puer Ptolemaeus habet tibi debita, Magne, / Tutelae commissa tuae.*

*False One*, 1.1.285–94; Lucan, 8.474–6, 480–1
*Consilii vix tempus erat: tamen omnia monstra / Pellaeae coiere domus: quos inter Achoreus / Iam placidus senior, fractisque modestior annis / ... / Consilii vox prima fuit, meritumque, fidemque / Sacraque defuncti iactavit pignora patris.*

*False One*, 1.1.295–312; Lucan, 8.482–95
*Sed melior suadere malis, et nosse tyrannos, / Ausus Pompeium leto damnare Pothinus; / Ius, et fas multos faciunt, Ptolemaee, nocentes. / Dat poenas laudata fides, cum sustinet, inquit, / Quos fortuna premit. fatis accede, Deisque, / Et cole felices, miseros fuge. sidera terra / Ut distant, et flamma mari, sic utile recto. Sceptrorum vis tota perit, si pendere iusta / Incipit: evertitque arces respectus honesti. / Libertas scelerum est, quae regna invisa tuetur, / Sublatusque modus gladiis, facere omnia saeve / Non inpune licet, nisi dum facis. exeat aula / Qui volet esse pius. virtus, et summa potestas / Non coeunt: semper metuet, quem saeva pudebunt.*

*False One*, 1.1.314–43; Lucan, 8.496–519
*Non inpune tuos Magnus contempserit annos; / Qui te nec victos arcere a litore nostro / Posse putat. neu te sceptris privaverit hospes, / Pignora sunt propiora tibi: Nilumque, Pharonque, / Si regnare piget, damnatae redde sorori. / Aegyptem certe Latiis tueamur ab armis. / Quidquid non fuerit Magni dum bella geruntur, / Nec victoris erit. toto iam pulsus ab orbe, / Postquam nulla manet rerum fiducia, quaerit / Cum qua gente cadat: rapitur civilibus umbris. / Nec soceri tantum arma fugit: fugit ora Senatus, / Cuius Thessalicas saturat pars magna volucres. / Et metuit gentes, quas uno in sanguine mixtas / Deseruit, regesque timet, quorum omnia mersit: / Thessaliaeque reus, nulla tellure receptus, / Sollicitat nostrum, quem nondum perdidit, orbem. / Iustior in Magnum nobis, Ptolemaee, querelae / Causa data est. quid sepositam, semperque quietam*

/ Crimine bellorum maculas Pharon, arvaque nostra / Victori suspecta facis? cur sola cadenti / Haec placuit tellus, in quam Pharsalica fata / Conferres poenasque tuas? iam crimen habemus / Purgandum gladio, quod nobis sceptra Senatus / Te suadente dedit, votis tua fovimus arma.

False One, 1.1.347–62; Lucan, 8.520–2, 526–35
Hoc ferrum, quod fata iubent proferre, paravi / Non tibi, sed victo, feriam tua viscera, Magne: / Malueram soceri: rapimur, quo cuncta feruntur. / … / Arvaque vix refugo fodientem mollia Nilo? / Metiri sua regna decet, viresque fateri. / Tu Ptolemaee potes Magni fulcire ruinam, / Sub qua Roma iacet? bustum, cineresque movere / Thessalicos audes, bellumque in regna vocare? / Ante aciem Emathiam nullis accessimus armis: / Pompei nunc castra placent, quae deserit orbis? / Nunc victoris opes, et cognita fata lacessis? / Adversis non deesse decet, sed laeta secutos. / Nulla fides umquam miseros elegit amicos.

False One, 2.1.49–50; Lucan, 8.674–5
At postquam trunco cervix abscisa recessit, / Vindicat hoc Pharius dextra gestare satelles.

False One, 2.1.73; Lucan, 8.665–7
Nihil ultima mortis / Ex habitu, vultuque viri mutasse, fatentur / Qui lacerum videre caput.

False One, 2.1.89–125; Lucan, 9.1014–33
Terrarum domitor, Romanae maxime gentis; / Et, quod adhuc nescis, genero secure perempto; / Rex tibi Pellaeus belli pelagique labores / Donat, et, Emathiis quod solum defuit armis, / Exhibet: absenti bellum civile peractum est. / Thessalicas Magnus quaerens reparare ruinas, / Ense iacet nostro: tanto te pignore Caesar / Emimus: hoc tecum percussum est sanguine foedus. / Accipe regna Phari nullo quaesita cruore: / Accipe Niliaci ius gurgitis: accipe quidquid / Pro Magni cervice dares; dignumque clientem / Castris crede tuis, cui tantum fata licere / In generum volvere tuum. nec vile putaris / Hoc meritum, facili nobis quod caede peractum est. / Hospes avitus erat: depulso sceptra parenti / Reddiderat. quid plura feram? tu nomina tanto / Invenies operi, vel famam consule mundi. / Si scelus est, plus te nobis debere fateris, / Quod scelus hoc non ipse facis. sic fatus, opertum / Detexit, tenuitque caput.

False One, 2.1.145–6; Lucan, 9.1066–8
unica belli / Praemia civilis, victis donare salutem, / Perdidimus.

*False One*, 2.1.172–3; Lucan, 9.1087–9
*sed parcimus annis / Donamusque nefas. sciat hac pro caede tyrannus / Nil venia plus posse dari.*

*False One*, 2.1.178–82; Lucan, 9.1068–71
*quod si Phario germana tyranno / Non invisa foret, potuissem reddere regi, / Quod meruit; fratrique tuum pro munere tali / Misissem Cleopatra caput.*

*False One*, 2.1.191–7; Lucan, 9.1071–2, 1081–4
*secreta quid arma / Movit, et inseruit nostro sua tela labori? / ... / ... nec fallere vos me / Credite victorem: nobis quoque tale paratum / Litoris hospitium: ne sic mea colla gerantur / Thessaliae fortuna facit.*

*False One*, 2.1.207–12; Lucan, 9.1089–93
*vos condite busto / Tanti colla ducis: sed non ut crimina tantum / Vestra tegat tellus. iusto date tura sepulcro / Et placate caput, cineresque in litore fusos / Colligite, atque unam sparsis date manibus urnam.*

*False One*, 2.3.61.1. SD; Lucan, 10.56–8
*cum se parva Cleopatra bireme, / Corrupto custode Phari laxare catenas, / Intulit Emathiis ignaro Caesare tectis.*

*False One*, 2.3.133–8, 139–55; Lucan, 10.82–99, 104–6
*Quem formae confisa suae Cleopatra sine ullis / Tristis adit lacrimis, simulatum compta dolorem, / Quem decuit, veluti laceros dispersa capillos, / Et sic orsa loqui: si qua est o maxime Caesar / Nobilitas, Pharii proles clarissima Lagi, / Exul in aeternum sceptris depulsa paternis, / Si tua restituat veteri me dextera fato, / Complector regina pedes. tu gentibus aequum / Sidus ades nostris. non urbes prima tenebo / Femina Niliacas: nullo discrimine sexus / Reginam scit ferre Pharos. lege summa perempti / Verba patris, qui iura mihi communia regni / ... puer ipse sororem, / Sit modo liber, amet: sed habet sub iure Pothini / Affectus, ensesque suos. nil ipsa paterni / Iuris habere peto: culpa, tantoque pudore / Solve domum: remove funesta satellitis arma / Et regem regnare iube. ... / ... / Nequiquam duras temptasset Caesaris aures: / Vultus adest precibus, faciesque incesta perorate. / Exigit infandam corrupto iudice noctem.*

*False One*, 2.3.170–1; Lucan, 10.65
*Caesare captivo Pharios ductura triumphos.*

# APPENDIX I

*False One*, 3.3.15–17; Lucan, 10.146–9
*pro caecus et amens / Ambitione furor, civilia bella gerenti / Divitias aperire suas, incendere mentem / Hospitis armati.*

*False One*, 3.4.77–80; Lucan, 10.169–71
*Discit opes Caesar spoliati perdere mundi, / Et gessisse pudet genero cum paupere bellum, / Et causas Martis Phariis cum gentibus optat.*

*False One*, 5.1.53–61; Lucan, 10.439–44, 449–54
*at Caesar moenibus urbis / Diffisus, foribus clausae se protegit aulae, / Degeneres passus latebras. nec tota vacabat / Regia compresso: minima collegerat arma / Parte domus: tangunt animos iraeque metusque: / Et timet incursus, indignaturque timere. / ... / Audax Thessalici qui nuper rupe sub Aemi, / Hesperiae cunctos proceres, aciemque Senatus, / Pompeiumque ducem, causa sperare vetante / Non timuit, fatumque sibi promisit iniquum, / Expavit servile nefas, intraque penates / Obruitur telis.*

*False One*, 5.2.78–80; Lucan, 10.491–2
*piceo iubet unguine tinctas / Lampadas immitti iunctis in bella carinis.*

*False One*, 5.4.4–7; Lucan, 10.461–4
*Non sine rege tamen; quem ducit in omnia secum, / Sumpturus poenas et grata piacula morti; / Missurusque tuum, si non sint tela, nec ignes, / In famulos Ptolemaee caput.*

*False One*, 5.4.199–201; Lucan, 10.515–19
*Nec poenas inde Pothini / Distulit ulterius: sed non qua debuit ira, / Non cruce, non flammis, rabido non dente ferarum: / Heu facinus, cervix gladio male caesa pependit: / Magni morte perit.*

# APPENDIX 2
## 'Look out, bright eyes, and bless the air'

*The False One* features five songs: four are sung during the masque of Act 3, scene 4 (33–42, 43–64, 65–76, 81–99) and one (1.2.35–44) is 'A cheering serenade arranged for the captive Cleopatra by her faithful servant and guardian Apollodorus; it develops an impressive first entrance for her, and her response to it has characterizing value', as William R. Bowden points out.[1] Only for this last song does a musical setting survive in manuscript form in Bodleian MS Mus.b.1 (fol. 40). A transcription in modern notation with my modernized text is included below.[2] As is the case with the songs of the masque, it seems likely that the lyrics to the Boy's song were separated from the manuscript text of the play.[3]

The song was composed by John Wilson (1595–1674), lutenist, composer, and Professor of Music at the University of Oxford from 1656 to 1661. As Ian Spink argues, 'he was probably the "Iohn Wilson" who was apprenticed on 18 February 1611, for eight years, to the actor John Heminges'.[4] By early 1614 Wilson was composing regularly for the King's Men (alongside Robert Johnson), and he would continue to do so for roughly fifteen years. His career from playhouse apprentice to Professor of Music at Oxford is an interesting object lesson in what was possible at the time. Plays that contain Wilson's extant songs include Richard Brome's *The Northern Lass*, John Ford's *The Lovers' Melancholy*, Thomas Middleton's *The Witch*, and several other plays in the Fletcher canon: *The Beggars' Bush*, *Rollo*, *Love's Cure*, *The Loyal Subject*, *The Mad Lover*, *The Pilgrim*, *The Queen of Corinth*, *Valentinian*, *The Wild-Goose Chase*, and *Women Pleased*.[5]

While the music survives only in Bodleian MS Mus.b.1 (fol. 40), the lyrics can also be found in Folger MS V.b.43 (fols 7v–8) and Yale University Library Osborne MS Chest II no. 21 (fol. 6). In these manuscripts, the following variants from F1 occur:

35. bless] cleere *Bodleian*
37. shut-up] caged *Bodleian*
40. soft] lost *Osborne*
a] be *Folger*

## Look out, bright eyes, and bless the air

John Wilson

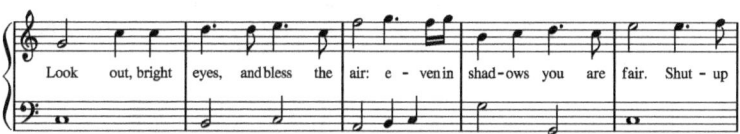

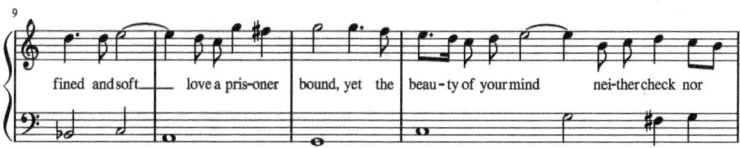

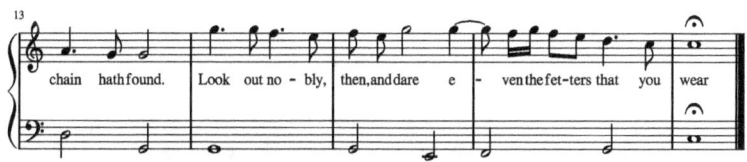

42. chain hath] change has *Osborne*
44. fetters that] fetters [for 'shadows', cancelled] wch *Osborne*.

As Turner illustrates, leaving aside the 'indifferent variant in line 44', it seems that 'Osborne's readings are ... corruptions of F1, and Folger's "be" (line 40) may have been carried down from line 39. Bodleian's readings are superficially attractive, but they too are probably wrong', given that the air into which the bright eyes are invited to look out from the shadows of captivity is probably not gloomy, so that the eyes are supposed to bless the air 'rather than clear it'. In addition, '"Bless" ... alliterates with "bright", "beauty", and so on, whereas "cleere" may be an anticipation of "clearer" in line 38'. Finally, 'the image of the fire breaking out is that of the explosion intensified by compression, to which "shut-up", implying lack of oxygen as well as confinement, contributes more than "caged"'.

The lyrics of this song were frequently reprinted and anthologized in the seventeenth century and then again from the nineteenth to the twentieth century. In the seventeenth century the words were reprinted with corruptions in:

> *Poems by Francis Beaumont* (London, 1653), sig. [I5v], from F1, with 'Shut up, beauty' instead of 'Shut-up beauty' (37) and 'lost' instead of 'soft' (40)
> *The Marrow of Compliments* (London, 1654), sig. [G8v], from F1, with 'soft lost' instead of 'soft' (40) and the omission of the last two lines (43–4)
> *The New Academy of Compliments* (London, 1669), sig. L4v, from F1, with 'sought' instead of 'soft' (40)
> Edward Phillips, *The Mysteries of Love and Eloquence* (London, 1685), 77, from Bodleian, with 'the body' instead of 'your body' (39)
> Edward Phillips, *The Beau's Academy* (London, 1699), 77, from Bodleian, with 'the body' instead of 'your body' (39)

### ENDNOTES

1 Bowden, 140.
2 I would like to thank Jennifer Moss Waghorn for checking my transcription. The song was also transcribed and briefly discussed in Cutts, 88, 174.
3 See Introduction, 53; Commentary, 3.4.32. On the regular early modern practice of removing songs from playscripts, see Stern, 134–73.
4 Spink, n.p.
5 Spink, n.p.

# Index

abuse 2.1.75, 2.3.92, 3.1.22
Achillas Characters in the Play 11
aconite 5.4.140
Acoreus Characters in the Play 10
admit 5.1.25
Aeschylus: *Eumenides* 4.3.62–3
affront 2.3.54
Afranius, Lucius 2.3.48
Alexander, William: *Julius Caesar* 2.3.29–61
Alexandrian War p. 18
amain 3.4.54
American Shakespeare Center pp. 48–9
Antony, Mark Characters in the Play 2
Apicius, Marcus Gavius 1.1.60
Apollodorus Characters in the Play 18
Appian: *Civil Wars* pp. 20, 35, 2.1.160–5
Appleton, William W. pp. 39, 57
Aristotle: *Nicomachean Ethics* p. 27
Armitage, David pp. 47, 58
Arsinoe p. 18, Characters in the Play 16
Astley, Sir John p. 1
attend 1.1.219
Augustine, Saint: *The City of God* p. 27
Ayres, Harry Morgan pp. 36, 57

babies 2.3.172
Bacon, Sir Francis p. 47
Baldwin, Thomas Whitfield Characters in the Play 1–22
ban 2.3.124
bane 2.3.186
basilisk 4.2.52
battery 4.2.179
Bawcutt, Nigel W. p. 54

Beaumont, Francis pp. 11, 51, 54
Beaumont, Francis, and John Fletcher
  *A King and No King* p. 25
  *The Maid's Tragedy* p. 25
belch 5.3.32
Benfield, Robert p. 1, Characters in the Play 1–22
Birch, George p. 1, Characters in the Play 1–22
Blackfriars Playhouse (VA) p. 48
Blackfriars Theatre pp. 5–8, 10–11, 55
blench 4.3.90
bless off 2.3.83
blind 2.1.134, 4.3.78, 5.1.8
blush 2.3.207
Bohemia p. 42
Bolton, Edmund pp. 2, 16, 28–9
bondman 1.2.59, 2.3.152, 5.1.3, 5.2.87
bone lace 3.2.30
Borgia, Cesare 5.2.8
botch 3.2.63
Bowden, William R. p. 202
Brant, Sebastian p. 47
brave 3.2.51, 5.2.50
Breitenberg, Mark p. 56
broker 4.2.70
brook p. 29, 5.2.52
Browne, Thomas Characters in the Play 21
Buc, Sir George p. 13
Buchanan, George p. 47
bulwark 3.2.6, 4.2.178, 5.1.56
Burbage, Richard p. 1
Burrow, Colin p. 17
Burstein, Stanley Mayer Characters in the Play 2
Bushnell, Rebecca W. pp. 25, 56, 2.3.179–80
buzzard 4.3.13

205

cabinet 1.1.142, 1.2.32, 5.4.8
Caesar, Julius pp. 18, 20–1,
    Characters in the Play 1,
    4.3.138–9, 5.2.8
  *celeritas* 5.4.187
  *Commentarii de bello civili* p. 20,
    Characters in the Play 4,
    2.3.32–3
Caesar/seizer, pun on 2.2.28,
    4.2.196, 5.4.4
*Caesar's Revenge* Characters in the
    Play 2, 3, Prologue 8,
    2.3.29–61, 3.2.6–9
calm 5.4.51
Canfora, Luciano 2.1.160–5,
    2.3.29–61
Cantor, Paul A. pp. 13, 55
Capitol Prologue 9
Cary, Elizabeth: *The Tragedy of
    Mariam* p. 9, 2.1.160–5
* case 3.2.11
catching 3.2.8
Cato, Marcus Porcius p. 13, 2.3.53,
    3.2.47
Chapman, George: *Caesar and
    Pompey* pp. 20, 48, 57,
    2.3.29–61, 2.3.53
Charles V, Holy Roman Emperor
    p. 47
Cicero pp. 45, 56
Cimmerian darkness 5.4.96
circuit 1.2.20
Clark, Ira pp. 28, 56
Cleopatra p. 18, Characters in the
    Play 15
climate 1.1.27
cloy 1.1.329, 4.2.32, 5.4.116
Coeffeteau, Nicolas p. 57
colonialism pp. 45–8
commit 1.1.8
confess 1.1.13, 1.1.64
confound 1.1.88
confusion 5.4.65
contain 2.3.15
contemn 2.3.133, 3.2.210, 4.1.7,
    4.2.118, 5.1.33
Corneille, Pierre: *La Mort de
    Pompée* p. 48
Cornelia Metella 1.1.251
cow-calf 3.2.44

cozen 2.3.13, 4.2.125
Crane, Ralph pp. 53–4, 59, 1.1.102,
    4.3.25
Crassus, Marcus Licinius 1.1.253
* crest 1.1.124
cross 5.4.200
Curran, John E. Jr pp. 21, 27, 56
Cutts, John P. p. 294

d'Angiò-Durazzo, Ladislao 5.2.8
Daniel, Samuel: *Cleopatra*
    Characters in the Play 17
Dante: *Monarchia* p. 47
dare 1.2.43
decline 2.1.204
defeature 1.1.253
Dekker, Thomas, and Philip
    Massinger: *VM* pp. 2–3, 11–12
Dessen, Alan 2.1.0.1. SD
Dessen, Alan, and Leslie Thomson
    2.3.61.1. SD
devotion 1.1.264, 1.2.26, 5.4.79
Dimitrova, Myriana Characters in
    the Play 4
Dio, Cassius pp. 26, 56, 2.1.160–5
dismal 5.3.44
dispatch 1.1.368, 2.3.89, 5.3.7,
    5.4.186, 5.4.201
Dolabella, Publius Cornelius
    Characters in the Play 3
Donaldson, Ian p. 56
Dustagheer, Sarah pp. 5–7, 55
Dutton, Richard p. 58
Dyce, Alexander pp. 39, 54, 57

Elizabeth I p. 42
Elysium 4.2.119
emasculation pp. 23–5
entertainment 1.1.268
Erasmus p. 47
ethic dative 4.2.193, 5.3.52
Ethiop 1.2.50
Eunoë p. 9, 1.2.93

fair 1.1.26
fall off 1.1.183
'The False Friend' p. 1
fame 1.1.187
fantastical 2.3.110
Farnaby, Thomas pp. 2, 16–17

# INDEX

Ferdinand II pp. 6, 42
*fiddle 3.2.27
*fiddler 1.1.116
Finkelpearl, Philip J. p. 58
Fisher, Jasper: *Fuimus Troes* 2.3.31
Fitzmaurice, Andrew pp. 44, 58
fleshed 1.1.69
Fletcher, John pp. 1, 3–5, 8, 10, 13–18, 20–1, 25–38, 40–1, 45–6, 48–9, 55–6
  *Bond* pp. 11–12, 44, 2.1.0.1. SD, 4.2.184, 4.3.14
  *The Chances* p. 51
  *The Coxcomb* p. 51
  First Folio pp. 51–4, 58–9
  *The Island Princess* pp. 9, 44
  *Loyal* 2.1.92
  *Monsieur* 4.2.184
  *NW* 2.1.92
  *Tamer* pp. 30, 39, 1.2.50, 4.2.184
  *Val* pp. 11–12, 25, 2.1.92
  *Wife* p. 25, 2.1.92
  *The Woman's Prize* see *Tamer*
  *Women Pleased* p. 2
Fletcher, John, and Philip Massinger
  *Corinth* 5.4.18
  *Cure* 1.2.50
  *CustCount* p. 50, 1.2.50
  *The Double Marriage* 2.1.0.1. SD
  *The Elder Brother* pp. 3, 50
  *Lawyer* p. 2, 1.2.50
  *Prophetess, The* pp. 11–12
  *Rollo* pp. 11, 39, 55, 2.1.0.1. SD
  *The Sea Voyage* p. 44
  *SJVOB* pp. 2, 11, 13, 42, 2.1.0.1. SD
  *Thierry and Theodoret* p. 11
  *Woman* 3.2.133–5
fling off 4.2.101
Florus: *Epitome* pp. 2, 16, 20, 28–9, 57, 1.1.152–3, 1.1.251, 2.1.21–2, 2.1.160–5, 5.2.52, 5.2.78–80
*Fortuna* 3.2.41
Foucault, Michel p. 56
Frederick V, Elector Palatine p. 42
furlong 3.2.43

gamester 1.1.107, 2.3.114
Gayley, Charles Mills 3.2.28–31
geld 5.4.102
general 5.4.190
Gentillet, Innocent: *A Discourse upon the Means of Well Governing* pp. 36–7, 57, 2.1.88–90
gilded 2.3.186, 3.2.63, 3.2.192
give up 3.2.171
Globe Theatre pp. 5, 7–8, 10
glorious 4.1.9, 4.3.111
glow-worm 4.2.18
Graves, Robert pp. 7, 55
Griffin, Julia pp. 27, 56
Grillo, Luca 5.4.187
Grotius, Hugo p. 17
grow 2.3.142
Gurr, Andrew, and Mariko Ichikawa 2.1.0.1. SD

Hall, Kim F. p. 8, 1.2.50
handsome 4.2.152
Hastings, Henry, Earl of Huntingdon p. 40
Hatchuel, Sarah pp. 24, 32, 35, 38, 56–7
Hazlitt, William pp. 39, 57
heads Characters in the Play 21, 2.1.0.1. SD, 2.3.58
heave at 2.1.21
Hecuba p. 31
hem 1.1.67
Hensman, Bertha pp. 18, 36, 54–7
Herbert, Philip, Earl of Montgomery p. 41
Herbert, Sir Henry pp. 1, 12, 54
Herbert, William, Earl of Pembroke p. 41
Hila, Marina pp. 42–3, 58
Hirrel, Michael J. 2.1.0.1. SD
Holmberg, Eva Johanna p. 8, 55
Holy Roman Empire pp. 42, 47
Homer: *Odyssey* 5.4.96
Hopkins, Lisa 2.2.28, 5.4.22
Howard-Hill, Trevor p. 59, 1.1.102, 4.3.25
Hoy, Cyrus pp. 3, 55, 59
humours, theory of 4.3.6–8
hunt's-up 4.2.184

## INDEX

impotence 3.3.16
inured 1.1.70
invade 1.1.233, 2.1.184
Isis Characters in the Play 20
Iyengar, Sujata p. 55

James I pp. 41–3, 56
Jenner, Simon pp. 50, 58
Jensen, Freyja Cox pp. 25, 27, 29, 56–7, 2.1.160–5, 2.3.179–80
Jonson, Ben pp. 16–18, 45
   *Beauty* 1.2.50
   *Blackness* 1.2.50
   *Epigr* 2.1.55
   *Sej* p. 48, 4.3.159–60
   *The Staple of News* p. 46
   *Volp* 5.3.7–10
Jowett, John p. 58
Jowitt, Claire p. 55
Juba I 2.3.55, 3.2.47
Juvenal p. 45

Karim-Cooper, Farah pp. 9–10, 55
Kewes, Paulina pp. 18, 42, 56–8
Kyd, Thomas: *Cornelia* pp. 47, 58

Labienus, Titus Characters in the Play 5
Leviathan 2.2.14
Lewis, Edward Danby 3.2.28–31
light 1.1.156
Lin, Erika p. 10
litter 2.3.113
Livy p. 45
*Locrine* 3.2.29
Loomba, Ania pp. 8, 55
*Lost Plays Database* p. 57
Lovano, Michael 5.4.187
Lovascio, Domenico pp. 54–5, 57–8, 2.3.29–61
Lowin, John p. 1, Characters in the Play 1–22
Lucan: *Pharsalia* pp. 2, 14–18, 20–1, 23–4, 27, 29, 35, 43, 57, 197–201, Characters in the Play 4, 1.1.71–8, 1.1.78–9, 1.1.223–8, 1.1.231–7, 1.1.235–6, 1.1.239–40, 1.1.240–9, 1.1.269, 1.1.285–94, 1.1.295–312, 1.1.314–43, 1.1.347–62, 2.1.21–2, 2.1.49–50, 2.1.73, 89–125, 2.1.145–6, 2.1.160–5, 2.1.172–3, 2.1.178–82, 2.1.191–7, 2.1.207–12, 2.3.61.1. SD, 2.3.133–8, 139–55, 2.3.170–1, 3.3.15–17, 3.4.0, 3.4.77–80, 5.1.53–61, 5.2.52, 5.2.78–80, 5.4.4–7
Luce, Morton p. 54
Lucullus, Lucius Licinius 1.1.60

maintainer 1.1.134
mangily 2.3.105
Marcellus, Gaius Claudius p. 14
Marlowe, Christopher: *Dr Faustus* 5.4.179–81
Mason, John Monck pp. 37, 57
Mason, John: *The Turk* 2.1.92
Massinger, Philip pp. 1–3, 5, 8–18, 20–1, 25–41, 44–6, 48–50, 54–8
   *Believe As You List* pp. 11–12
   *Bondman* p. 12, 1.2.50
   *Duke* p. 12, 1.1.215–16
   *The Emperor of the East* p. 12
   *MH* 1.1.215–6
   *Parl* 1.2.50, 2.3.107
   *Pict* 1.1.215–6, 5.4.146–7
   *RA* pp. 11–12, 25, 44, 1.1.60
   *UnnComb* 5.4.146–7
Maxwell, Baldwin pp. 31, 41–2, 57–8
May, Thomas p. 17
McDermott, James p. 56
MacDonald, Joyce Green pp. 8, 37, 55, 57
McInnis, David 2.1.0.1. SD
McKeithan, Daniel Morley p. 57
McManus, Clare p. 56
milliner 3.2.76
Milo of Croton 3.2.43
mistress 5.4.177
Montaigne, Michel de p. 47
Morell, Jason pp. 48, 50
Moseley, Humphrey p. 51
Munro, Lucy pp. 10, 55

Neill, Michael p. 57
nibble 5.4.192

Nicoll, Allardyce p. 55
Nile Characters in the Play 21, 2.3.58
Nine Worthies 2.1.212

observer 1.1.151
Oliphant, E. H. C. pp. 39, 57
Orodes II 1.1.252, 1.1.253
Osiris 1.1.82
Owens, Margaret E. pp. 13, 15, 55–6

Paleit, Edward pp. 14, 16, 21, 43–4, 56, 58
part 2.3.116
peevish 3.2.102
Petrarch: *Triumphi* p. 24, 2.3.170–1
Petreius, Marcus 2.3.48
phoenix 2.1.209–11
pile 1.1.212
pioneer 4.2.188
pledge 1.1.318
Plutarch
   'Antony' Characters in the Play 9, 1.1.251
   'Caesar' pp. 16, 23, 26, 32, 56, Characters in the Play 4, 12, 18, 1.1.61–4, 1.1.195–8, 2.2.27–9, 2.3.61.1. SD, 2.3.120, 5.2.8
   'Pompey' pp. 16, 20, 57, Characters in the Play 12, 1.1.61–4, 1.1.251, 1.1.252, 2.1.21–2, 2.1.160–5, 5.4.201
Poitevin, Kimberly Woosley pp. 9, 55
politic 2.3.25
Pompey the Great 1.1.39, 3.2.46
Pompey, Gnaeus 2.3.56
Pompey, Sextus 2.3.56
* posture 3.2.35
Pothinus Characters in the Play 9
power 1.1.171, 1.1.257, 5.1.53
* precipice 3.3.13
Priam Prologue 6
private 2.3.129, 4.2.61, 5.3.49
proclaim 2.3.126, 5.1.9
prop 1.1.353
* provoking broth 4.2.193
* ptolemy 1.1.126
Ptolemy IX 2.1.111
Ptolemy XII 1.1.37–41
Ptolemy XIII p. 18, Characters in the Play 8
Ptolemy XIV p. 18
purchase 3.2.146, 4.2.108, 5.4.76

Quintilian p. 45
quit 3.2.176

raked 2.1.151
Ralegh, Sir Walter pp. 41–2
rare 3.1.54, 3.2.7, 4.3.38
rasher 4.2.170
rate Prologue 14
ravish 1.1.271, 5.4.23
Read Not Dead pp. 48, 50
redeem 1.1.342, 5.1.61, 5.3.18
Rice, John p. 1, Characters in the Play 1–22
Richards, Nathanael: *Messalina* p. 48
Robinson, Humphrey p. 51
Roche, Paul 1.1.235–6
Roman Empire pp. 12–15
Rome
   First Triumvirate of 5.2.28
   foundation of 5.2.12–14
Romulus p. 46
Ronan, Clifford J. pp. 57–8, Characters in the Play 2
routed 1.2.69, 5.1.55
Rubicon 2.3.35
* ruffle 5.4.12

Sabaean bed 2.1.209
Salic Law p. 36
Sallust p. 45
salve 4.3.29
Sam Wanamaker Playhouse pp. 6, 10
Scaeva, Marcus Cassius p. 20, Characters in the Play 4
Sebastian, King of Portugal p. 12
Seneca p. 45
   *Phaedra* 5.4.112–13
sensible 2.1.28, 3.1.36, 4.1.66
sensual 5.4.74
Septimius, Lucius p. 20, Characters in the Play 12

sequester 1.1.299
* service 4.2.56
set down 1.1.123
Seward, Thomas pp. 16, 39, 54, 56–7
Shakespeare's Globe p. 48
Shakespeare, William pp. 2, 5, 9–10, 13, 15, 20, 29, 32, 38, 46, 48, 54, 57
  *3H6* 1.1.174
  *A&C* pp. 9, 23, 33, Characters in the Play 9, Prologue 8, 12, 15, 16, 1.1.73, 1.2.10–13, 1.2.66–8, 2.3.61.1. SD, 2.3.79–82, 3.2.1, 3.2.17, 3.2.34–40, 3.3.4
  *Coriolanus* p. 30
  First Folio pp. 31, 45
  *JC* pp. 26, 28, 58, 2.1.129–31, 2.3.6–7, 2.3.8, 2.3.177, 4.2.32
  *KL* 1.1.104–45
  *LLL* 2.1.212
  *Mac* 1.1.194–5, 3.2.71–4
  *MAdo* 2.3.107
  *Othello* p. 55
  *Per* 4.2.200–1
  *The Taming of the Shrew* pp. 30, 39
  *Temp* p. 30, 5.1.22–3
Shakespeare, William, and John Fletcher
  *All Is True, or Henry VIII* p. 11
  *The Two Noble Kinsmen* p. 39
sharp 1.1.330
Sharpe, Richard p. 1, Characters in the Play 1–22
Shepard, Alexandra 2.3.179–80
shift 4.2.198
* shoeing-horn 4.2.170
short 3.2.139
Sidney, Mary: *Antonius* Characters in the Play 17
skill 1.2.106
skulking 1.1.126
slubbered 2.3.50
snuff 2.1.55
Soellner, Ralph 2.1.194
Spear, Gary p. 24, 56
Spink, Ian p. 202
* spit out 4.3.110

Stanhope, Lady Katherine p. 41
Stationers' Register pp. 2, 51
Stern, Tiffany p. 204
stirring 1.2.1
Stukeley, Sir Lewis p. 41
success 1.1.49
Suetonius: *Lives of the Caesars* pp. 16, 26, 56, 1.1.61–4, 1.2.91, 1.2.93
suitor 3.2.167
Sweet Wag Shakespeare p. 48

Tacitus pp. 16, 45, 5.3.7–10
take 1.1.94
taking 4.3.27
tall 3.2.3
Tappan, Elizabeth 2.1.194
target 2.3.120
Tarlinskaja, Marina 3.2.28–31
task 2.1.144
Taylor, Joseph p. 1, Characters in the Play 1–22
tempt 1.1.355
thou/you 1.1.353, 2.1.92, 2.1.129, 2.3.77, 2.3.136, 2.3.183, 3.2.192
* tilt 2.3.172
toil 5.4.124
Tooley, Nicholas p. 1, Characters in the Play 1–22
toothache 2.3.107
touch 1.1.118
trade 4.1.5
trapping 3.2.54
* trim 2.3.88
trusty 2.1.192
Turner, Robert K. pp. 36, 51, 53–4, 57–9, 203–4

Ulrich, Otto pp. 28, 57
Underwood, John p. 1, Characters in the Play 1–22
usage 4.2.5
use 2.1.221

vanity 4.2.132
vapour 3.2.200
Vaught, Jennifer C. pp. 27, 56
vermin 2.3.18
villain 3.2.128

Virgil: *Aeneid* Prologue 6, 5.3.2
vital spirits 5.4.141
vouchsafe 5.4.101

Waghorn, Jennifer Moss p. 204
Waith, Eugene M. pp. 15, 20, 24,
    26, 39–40, 56, 58, 2.3.61.1. SD
Wallace, Lia pp. 48–9
wanting 1.2.30
wanton 1.1.141, 2.3.186, 3.2.49,
    3.2.145, 3.4.51, 3.4.93
wantonness 4.3.45
warrant Prologue 1, 5.1.19
Weber, Henry pp. 3, 39
Webster, John
    *Duchess* pp. 6, 41–2, 4.3.148–9,
        5.4.22
    *The White Devil* pp. 41–2

Weir, Robert pp. 17, 56
whistle off 4.3.14
White, Martin p. 7
Wiggins, Martin pp. 1, 11, 37, 41,
    54–8, Characters in the Play
    1–22, 4.3.148–9
Williamson, Matthew p. 50
Wilson, John p. 202
Wilson, William pp. 51, 53
witching 4.3.74
Woolf, Daniel R. pp. 29, 57
Wray, Ramona pp. 9, 55
wreak 5.2.55

EU authorised representative for GPSR:
Easy Access System Europe, Mustamäe tee 50,
10621 Tallinn, Estonia
gpsr.requests@easproject.com

www.ingramcontent.com/pod-product-compliance
Lightning Source LLC
Chambersburg PA
CBHW051611230426
43668CB00013B/2062